Tim Isted
Tom Harrington

Core Data for iOS

Developing Data-Driven Applications for the iPad®, iPhone®, and iPod touch®

✦Addison-Wesley

Upper Saddle River, NJ · Boston · Indianapolis · San Francisco

New York · Toronto · Montreal · London · Munich · Paris · Madrid

Cape Town · Sydney · Tokyo · Singapore · Mexico City

The publisher offers excellent discounts on this book when ordered in quantity for bulk purchases or special sales, which may include electronic versions and/or custom covers and content particular to your business, training goals, marketing focus, and branding interests. For more information, please contact:

U.S. Corporate and Government Sales

(800) 382-3419

corpsales@pearsontechgroup.com

For sales outside the United States please contact:

International Sales

international@pearson.com

Visit us on the Web: informit.com/aw

Library of Congress Cataloging-in-Publication Data is on file.

Copyright © 2011 Pearson Education, Inc.

ISBN-13: 978-0-321-67042-7

ISBN-10: 0-321-67042-6

Text printed in the United States on recycled paper at R.R. Donnelley in Crawfordsville, Indiana

Second printing June 2011

Editor-in-Chief
Mark Taub

Senior Acquisitions Editor
Chuck Toporek

Development Editor
Chuck Toporek

Managing Editor
Kristy Hart

Project Editor
Andy Beaster

Indexer
Larry Sweazy

Proofreader
Jennifer Gallant

Technical Reviewers
Jim Correia
Robert McGovern
Mike Swan

Publishing Coordinator
Olivia Basegio

Interior Designer
Gary Adair

Cover Designer
Chuti Prasertsith

Compositor
Gloria Schurick

Table of Contents

Preface

We live in a data-driven world. We consume social data, like email, Twitter, and Facebook, business data, like share prices, financial forecasts, and bank accounts, and occasionally we might have a little fun with the more recreational side to life, like brainteasers, or games involving squawking birds and mock air traffic control, where we expect to be able to track our progress and rejoice when we beat our previous high scores.

As mobile devices increase in performance, capacity, and capability, we place ever-increasing demands on our phones or tablet devices to consume, save, fetch, search and display our data. Consumers buy iPhones, iPod touches and iPads with storage capacities unheard of in handheld or even desktop devices only a few years ago, and they expect to fill those capacities either with media, or with applications and data.

It's increasingly difficult to imagine an application with any non-trivial functionality that doesn't maintain at least some kind of data store. Even if a Twitter client maintains only a temporary store of downloaded tweets, it will at least need to keep permanent track of one or more Twitter account usernames for timeline refresh; calculator applications have persistent memories for calculated values, or store a history of previous calculations; and, in order for us to feel a sense of achievement, games store a history of high scores, as well as a state of play so that we can return immediately to our gun-slinging 3D shoot-'em-up just as soon as we finish our FaceTime chat.

For us mobile app developers, the demands are high. Not only do users expect our apps to store data as efficiently as possible, they expect their applications to run quickly, smoothly, and without crashing. Given the relatively limited runtime memory capacities of these mobile devices, dealing with persistent data can quickly become a nightmare. Mobile devices also introduce the issue of power management, which is rarely a concern when writing software for desktop computers. An app that eats batteries will not please its users.

When the iPhone SDK first launched, developers were left to fend for themselves when it came to data access. Data persistence was possible only via basic file storage, or through direct access to a SQLite database. SQLite can certainly help out with the limited runtime memory problems, but generally requires developers to fashion their own persistence layer to interact with model objects and generate the underlying SQL commands necessary to save and restore plain data.

Core Data changes all that. From version 3.0 of the iPhone SDK (renamed to iOS as of version 4.0) onwards, Apple provides us with a ready-made data persistence layer. We define a schema for the model objects we want to store, then leave Core Data to figure out what to do to persist our model data to disk. We don't have to worry about low-level SQL commands, or the memory meltdowns involved when loading 1GB of data from a single file. Instead we work with a "data store," a term that is intentionally vague since details of managing data files are abstracted away. Developers are free to work with their objects and leave the file management to the framework.

If Core Animation is the sexy framework for views, we now have an equally sexy (though possibly less visually glamorous) framework to help us with our model. By taking away much of the drudgery of data persistence, we're left with more time to work on the features and functionality unique to our applications.

Core Data can be the perfect answer to many data-related prayers, but it comes with a steep initial learning curve. Because of its ability to work easily with a SQLite database for its storage, it's often mistaken for a database itself and, although this is inaccurate, it certainly helps to have a basic understanding of general database terms and techniques.

Although the number of Core Data classes is relatively small, it's necessary to make use of most of them before you can do anything at all with the framework. It's hard to understand terms like "managed object context" before you understand "managed object," or "persistent store," but in order to make use of a managed object, you need a managed object context, and a persistent store. Getting over the initial leap of faith in a basic Core Data stack can seem a sizeable obstacle in making use of the framework.

This book teaches Core Data from the ground up. You'll learn about these primary classes in the framework, seeing how they interact to provide amazing functionality with very little configuration and tweaking. You'll find out how to store and fetch data, look at best practices for providing data to the staple view of many data-driven apps, UITableView, and discover how easy it can be to perform data validation to ensure data integrity. Finally, you'll look at ways to troubleshoot your Core Data applications, or enhance data-related performance bottlenecks.

By the end of the book, you'll have a thorough understanding of the framework and its classes, and probably be left wondering how you ever managed without it.

Audience for This Book

Aimed at intermediate to advanced iOS developers, the book assumes that you have a reasonable working knowledge of programming iOS applications. In particular, you should be comfortable working with Apple's basic developer tools (Xcode), the Objective-C language, and the Cocoa Touch framework.

It is not assumed that you have already worked with Core Data on the desktop, although the vast majority of the information included in this book applies to Core Data in general, both on iOS devices, and under Mac OS X (10.4 or later). Once you've mastered Core Data on iOS, you'll be able to use the same tools (Xcode's data modeler) and much of the same code (with the exception of NSFetchedResultsController, which is iOS-only) to build Core Data applications on the desktop.

Who Should Read this Book

If you write iOS applications, you'll probably have data persistence needs. If you need to work with anything other than the most trivial data storage, you'll likely find it easier to work with Core Data than to create your own file-based or low-level SQLite-based persistence layer. If you need to work with Core Data, you should read this book.

If you've never used Core Data before, this book will teach you what you need to know to get started. Once you've mastered the fundamentals of the framework, including the iOS-specific NSFetchedResultsController, and walked through the construction of a complete Core Data-based application, you'll find performance tips and troubleshooting information.

If you've already been using Core Data for a while, and keep wondering why your app crashes when you work with large numbers of model objects, or can't figure out why you're suffering a performance hit in certain situations, this book will help clear up any mysteries with the fundamentals of the framework, and help you use Apple's developer tools to isolate the sources of those problems.

Who Shouldn't Read This Book

Core Data is definitely not the easiest to understand of the Cocoa Touch frameworks. If you've never created an iOS application before, or struggle to remember the difference between a UIView and a UIViewController, you'll have problems working through this book.

Although the first few chapters aim to flatten the learning curve as much as possible, it's assumed that you have a solid understanding of both the Objective-C language, and the Cocoa Touch framework. If you don't, you'd be better looking at a suitable introductory iOS programming book.

It's also worth noting that Core Data is commonly mistaken for a database. Although Core Data can use SQLite, it's not by any means a SQLite wrapper nor is it designed for typical database usage. If what you really need is a database, Core Data may not be the right solution and this book might not be appropriate.

Finally, if you're looking for creative visual interface inspiration, or suggestions for stunning data representations, you might prefer to look elsewhere. The sample applications in this book are specifically designed with interfaces that are as simple as possible to help you learn the Core Data framework with minimal distractions. For this reason, all the sample projects are for iPhones or iPod touches, and don't include iPad-specific resources. Equally, if you're looking for tips to beautify table views or design jaw-dropping custom views, you'll likely be disappointed.

Do bear in mind, however, that just because many of the sample projects in this book make use of the more traditional data display controls (i.e., table views), you can use Core Data in any situation where you need easy and efficient access to data. Need to store a list of high scores to draw in an OpenGL view for a game? Core Data makes that easy (well, the storage part anyway). Need to store enough information to draw icons that represent the weather for the next 24 hours? Core Data can help with that too.

What You Need to Know

The book also assumes that you're familiar and comfortable with Xcode and programming in Objective-C. You won't find any primers on how to define a method, or how to install and launch Xcode; there are plenty of entry-level books for newbies and converts from other platforms and programming environments, and if you're messing around with data models and such, we can assume that you've already got that grounding.

As with any iOS development, you'll need at least a free Apple developer account. To test your applications on real devices, or sell on the App Store, you'll need a paid iOS developer account ($99 per year at the time of writing). Go to **developer.apple.com/devcenter/ios** to register for access to all of the relevant updates for iOS, as well as Xcode, developer documentation, sample code, and even the session videos from Apple's annual World Wide Developer Conference. Without a paid account it's still possible to develop iOS code, but you'll only be able to run this code on the iPhone Simulator. While the Simulator is extremely useful, it's no substitute for getting your code on a real iOS device.

Core Data can support a number of different persistent store types, the inner workings of which it mostly hides from the developer. By far the most common type on iOS devices is the SQLite store, which saves persistent data into a SQLite database. You don't need to know anything about SQLite to read this book, but if you're already a database super-user, you'll probably know that there is some controversy about the pronunciation of SQLite. D. Richard Hipp, the creator of SQLite, pronounces it "like a mineral", pronouncing Ess-Queue-Ell-Ite as one might pronounce "pyrite" or "kryptonite".[1] Hipp does not insist on this pronunciation though, and in practice the vast majority of Mac and iOS developers we've encountered pronounce it Sequel-ite. For this reason we've chosen the latter pronunciation, so you'll find we talk about "a SQLite store" rather than "an SQLite store."

How This Book is Organized

The book offers a comprehensive discussion of Apple's Core Data framework as it applies on iOS devices, building a firm grounding in the subject before covering more advanced and real-world examples of its use. Many of the chapters in the book are divided into two parts—you start by learning the relevant information, and then cement your understanding by putting the knowledge into practice with a sample project.

Chapter 10 walks you through the complete construction of a Core Data-based note taking application, from start to finish. If you want to jump straight in and find out what's possible with Core Data, you might like to begin with Chapter 10 to whet your appetite, then return to the beginning of the book to find out how it all works.

---

[1] *Hipp discussed "SQLite" pronunciation at the C4[2] conference in September 2008. His presentation can be viewed at* **http://www.viddler.com/explore/rentzsch/videos/25/**

▶ **Part I: Introduction**

Apple's Core Data framework presents a unified and powerful solution to storing an application's data. This book offers a comprehensive reference for the framework and its use in versions of iOS from iPhone SDK 3.0 onwards. As well as covering Core Data basics, this section discusses more general topics like object modeling and data persistence, and demonstrates how to build an object model using Xcode's data modeling tool.

▶ **Chapter 1: An Overview of Core Data on iOS Devices**

This first chapter introduces Core Data as a framework to fit into the MVC-pattern for development of applications for iOS. It gives a brief outline of its history as the Enterprise Objects Framework for web development, before discussing when, how and why Core Data is useful. It explains how there is little difference between working with Core Data on the desktop and on iOS, with the notable exception of the lack of support for Bindings on iOS. The overview finishes by showcasing a few real-world examples of Core Data use in publicly-available iOS applications, including MoneyWell for iPhone, Calcuccino and the Associated Press news application.

▶ **Chapter 2: A Core Data Primer**

Having given a high-level overview in Chapter 1, this chapter delves deeper and introduces the key features in Core Data, covering the interaction between Managed Object Contexts, Managed Objects and the underlying Persistent Stores. It also introduces the framework classes behind these and explains how impressive functionality can be achieved with very little code, often without the need to subclass the basic framework classes. The chapter continues by explaining the process of writing applications that use Core Data. It concludes by taking a look at what is happening behind-the-scenes in Apple's Xcode template projects for Core Data iOS applications.

▶ **Chapter 3: Modeling Your Data**

This chapter introduces general ideas behind data modeling. Having expressed clearly that Core Data is not in itself a database, the chapter does discuss basic relational database techniques and relevant best practices (for example, data normalization that applies to object model design). This chapter also explains how data stored in a relational database can be mapped into a relational object model for use in object-oriented programming languages and concludes with a demonstration of how an object model is defined for Core Data using the Data Model editor in Xcode.

▶ **Part II: Working with Core Data**

The second part of the book focuses on a discussion of topics that apply to most applications wanting to make use of Core Data on iOS. Each facet of the framework or its related technologies is given a separate chapter so it is possible either to read this part of the book in order, building knowledge in incremental steps, or to pick out the chapters that are of particular interest. Each of these chapters is divided into two sections: the first introduces the particular feature or functionality, discusses why and when it might be useful, then walks through the relevant classes and methods; the second section is written in a tutorial format that starts by adding a basic feature to a simple application, before building on more advanced functionality. The aim of these tutorial sections is to enable you to learn by doing, but in such a way that you relate the same techniques to your own applications.

▶ **Chapter 4: Basic Storing and Fetching**

This chapter guides you through the process of building a simple iPhone application that uses a `UITableView` to display managed objects. It includes more information about managed object contexts, and how they relate to the underlying data—a good understanding of managed object contexts is absolutely fundamental to using Core Data effectively. This chapter explains what contexts are, how to use them, where a context 'comes from' and how they interact with each other and the data store. The project for this chapter features a simple Add button to add objects that are fetched and displayed in a table view; to keep it simple for now, each object is pre-populated with randomly-generated information.

▶ **Chapter 5: Using NSFetchedResultsController**

This chapter demonstrates how to make use of the Fetched Results Controller, an object unique to iOS, to handle much of the functionality necessary to fetch and display objects in a table view. It explains why memory usage is so important on iOS, and how a fetched results controller works to keep to a minimum the number of objects held in memory at any one time.

▶ **Chapter 6: Working with Managed Objects**

This chapter introduces the functionality provided by `NSManagedObject`, such as basic data validation. Although it frequently isn't necessary to subclass `NSManagedObject`, this chapter explains why, when and how to do so. You'll learn about the lifecycle of managed objects, and look at different types of modeled properties. The chapter covers features offered by Objective-C 2.0 to simplify accessor method code and finishes by looking at custom validation logic.

▶ **Chapter 7: Working with Predicates**

This chapter begins with the basics of creating an NSPredicate, discussing simple predicate format strings. You'll learn how to use predicates to match against scalar values like numbers or dates, and also how to match objects, particularly across relationships, such as when fetching employees who work in a specific department. There's a whole section dedicated to working with strings, including information on case sensitivity, and you'll see how to examine the raw SQL that Core Data generates to query a SQLite store.

▶ **Chapter 8: Migration and Versioning**

This chapter looks at how to use the provided versioning and migration functionality to maintain compatibility between old and new versions of an application's data model. By default, an application built around a newer model version won't be able to open an older version's model; through using automatic migration, the user can continue to work with their old data even after an application upgrade has occurred. You'll learn about both simple migration, where the Core Data framework itself works out how one data model version relates to another, as well as custom migration using mapping models and entity migration policies.

▶ **Chapter 9: Working with Multiple View Controllers and Undo**

To keep the examples as simple as possible, and to minimize distractions, the previous projects up to this point have made use of only a single view controller. In this chapter, you'll see how to keep track of managed object contexts across multiple view controllers, and how to use editing view controllers to change values on existing managed objects. You'll learn how to work with multiple managed object contexts, and find out how to refer to managed objects across these multiple contexts, before finding out how simple it is to make use of the automatic Undo functionality provided by Core Data.

▶ **Part III: Building a Simple Core Data Application**

The third part of the book takes the reader through building a complete application using Core Data.

▶ **Chapter 10: Sample Application: Note Collector**

This chapter puts your Core Data knowledge into context by walking through the creation of a more substantial application than you've worked with so far. You'll see how to work with abstract entities, entity inheritance and multiple view controllers to create a fully functional note-taking application that stores notes and organizes them in collections.

You'll learn how to examine a raw SQLite file to peek at what Core Data is doing, and find out how to include a pre-populated data store so that users of the application see some sample data when they launch the application for the first time. You'll also look at one way to persist application state across launches, seeing how to archive the managed object information necessary to recreate a navigation-based stack of view controllers.

▶ **Part IV: Optimizing and Troubleshooting**

The final part of the book looks at performance issues, optimization for the restricted memory requirements of iOS devices, and at debugging tools to aid in developing with Core Data on iOS.

▶ **Chapter 11: Optimizing for iOS Performance and Memory Requirements**

This chapter is all about performance, optimization, and speed. You'll learn some simple tricks to help your application run faster and be more responsive for the user without consuming all available memory or running down the battery. This chapter assumes you already understand about retain counts and when objects are deallocated, which affects your memory usage but which are not directly related to Core Data.

▶ **Chapter 12: Troubleshooting Core Data**

When things go amiss with Core Data the symptoms and error messages can seem obscure, even if you've been using it for a while. You can't very well fix your code if you don't understand what's wrong. In this chapter, you'll look at ways to help you diagnose and fix some of the most common Core Data problems. Keep in mind that Core Data can be affected by problems that are not specific to Core Data; for example, memory management errors can affect any Cocoa object, and managed objects are no exception. This chapter focuses on problems specifically related to Core Data.

Although the book is designed to be read in order, each chapter is mostly self-contained, so feel free to skip around to learn about specific topics. Some of the example projects in each chapter require code from a previous chapter as a starting point; if you need to grab a ready-made project from an earlier chapter, the sample code for the book is available online.

About the Sample Code and Coding Style

All of the source code necessary to run the examples in this book is provided inline within chapters; in order to fit within the confines of a page, the code may have rather more newline characters than you might expect.

Because of the nature of the subject, the code includes a large number of accessor methods. As this book is likely to be read both by developers who prefer using full accessor methods and lots of nested square brackets, as well as those who have embraced Objective-C 2.0 dot syntax, we felt it important to include examples demonstrating both styles. The included code therefore uses a mixture of both traditional method calls and dot notation throughout the example listings. Feel free to substitute according to your own coding preferences.

The complete source code for the projects in this book is available as a downloadable disk image (.dmg), which you can get by clicking on the Resources tab on the book's catalog page:

http://www.informit.com/title/9780321670427

The disk image contains a README file along with folders containing the projects for each chapter.

Apple shipped Xcode 4 (with substantial changes over Xcode 3) just before this book went to press. The screenshots in the book are taken from Xcode 4, but if you're still using Xcode 3, it should be relatively straightforward to work out any differences. We've added Xcode 3-specific instructions in the text anywhere that there might be confusion over major differences.

Although Mac OS X Lion had been announced, it hadn't yet shipped publicly when this book was published, so the screenshots are taken from Mac OS X Snow Leopard, which is the current required environment for iOS (i.e., iPhone, iPad, and iPod touch) development. For Core Data development for iOS, you don't need anything else: all the libraries, headers, and documentation are included with the Xcode tools and the iOS SDK.

Acknowledgments from Tim Isted

Although writing a book notoriously takes longer than expected, I've certainly pushed the boundaries on this one. I have a vivid memory of the moment the words "Core Data" appeared on a slide at Apple's announcement of iPhone SDK 3.0. Half an hour later, Chuck and I were discussing the outline for a book dedicated to Core Data on iPhone. That was back in June 2009.

Since then, the iPhone OS has become iOS, the iPad was released, iPhone 4 appeared, multitasking was introduced, Xcode 4 went public, and the goal posts kept moving. It's hard to pick a time to publish a book on something that changes so frequently, but putting overall iOS changes aside, the Core Data framework (and certainly its API) has remained fairly stable, probably due to its earlier existence on the Mac. This book would never have made it were it not for the wonderfully patient and encouraging editorial guidance Chuck Toporek has given me, not to mention his personal friendship. Together we hope we've ensured it should remain useful across the inevitable series of major iOS version releases that will occur the moment the book hits the shelves.

After a few lengthy pauses for me to deal with various nasty bouts of illness among my close family, Tom Harrington agreed to come on board to help get the book out before iOS became obsolete. His work specifically on the two performance chapters, together with his contributions across the whole book, has taken it up so many notches.

The four anonymous (for the most part) technical reviewers have been fantastic. It's all too easy to become blinkered as an Indie developer and I thank the reviewers for saving me from too many of those "I've always done it like this" moments.

Finally, I can never thank enough the friends I have throughout the Mac/iOS developer community. It's a wonderful team to be a part of.

Acknowledgments from Tom Harrington

I'd like to thank my wife Carey for encouraging me to embark on a career that appealed to me but seemed too risky to jump into. After the dot-com boom in 2001, Carey was the one who suggested there might be more interesting things to do than look for another day job. I never expected to run my own business and would not have done so without Carey's help. I've been independent ever since and have never looked back.

I'd also like to thank Tim Isted and Chuck Toporek for giving me the opportunity to work on this book, and to Marcus Zarra for introducing me to Tim in the first place. Also, this book would not have been possible without the technical reviewers who help make Tim and I look good.

About the Authors

Tim Isted

Tim Isted has been writing software for Macintosh computers since 1995. He also builds web applications using Rails, PHP, and .NET and has been known to develop for Windows machines too. Also a professional musician and singing teacher, he tries to divide his time fairly equally between conducting, accompanying, teaching, and writing software. Previous musings on Core Data for desktop development can be found on his blog at **www.timisted.net**, and he is also co-organizer of NSConference, a new Mac developer conference taking place in both Europe and the USA.

Tom Harrington

Tom Harrington switched from writing software for embedded systems and Linux to Mac OS X in 2002 when he started Atomic Bird, LLC. After six years of developing highly regarded Mac software he moved to iPhone in 2008. He develops iOS software on a contract basis for a variety of clients. Tom also organizes iOS developer events in Colorado. When not writing software he can often be found on his mountain bike. His website is **www.atomicbird.com**.

PART I

Introduction

Apple's Core Data framework presents a unified and powerful solution to storing an application's data. This book
offers a comprehensive reference for the framework and its
use in versions of iOS greater than iPhone SDK 3.0. As well
as covering Core Data basics, this section discusses more
general topics like object modeling and data persistence,
and demonstrates how to build an object model using
Xcode's data modeling tool.

CHAPTER 1

An Overview of Core Data on iOS Devices

Mac OS X 10.4 Tiger introduced Core Data to provide a unified framework for storing and fetching an application's model data. Further enhanced under Mac OS X 10.5 Leopard, Apple subsequently made it available for use on iOS devices from iPhone OS 3.0 onward. The Core Data framework certainly alleviates most of the hassle of working with model data, but it can also seem to have a pretty steep learning curve.

This overview begins with a brief history of Core Data's development, before looking at a high-level overview of the framework itself. The final section of this chapter looks at some real-world examples of how iOS developers have leveraged the power of Core Data to simplify the model handling in their applications.

A Little History

A large portion of what is now Core Data previously existed as the Enterprise Objects Framework (EOF). Created by NeXT, as part of WebObjects, EOF is used for accessing data held in relational database systems. To save developers from having to write lots of low-level database-access code, EOF provides a mechanism for accessing the data as an object-oriented class structure, using object-relational mapping.

Instead of having to write code to talk to a database and ask it for rows of database tables and columns, object-relational mapping "maps" those tables into classes, the columns into class attributes, and the rows into class instances. This makes it possible to change the underlying database or storage mechanism beneath the classes without worrying about changing any code that accesses those classes, since EOF handles everything behind the scenes.

The Birth of Core Data

Much of the functionality behind Core Data later "grew" out of EOF, but it is important to emphasize that Core Data is neither a database in itself, nor a database-access framework. Instead, Core Data is a complete data model solution allowing visual design of an *object graph*, code to *create* and *query* objects in that graph, and code to *persist* the objects to disk.

Although it is certainly common to use Core Data to store objects in an SQL database (SQLite to be precise), it's equally possible to use non-database storage such as XML files, binary files, or even completely custom *persistent stores* created by developers to suit their specific needs. On the desktop, Apple provides SQLite, XML, and binary storage options. Under iOS, there's no XML store, and most iOS applications end up using SQLite stores.

It's also important to emphasize that a Core Data-backed model can be used to store all kinds of data. It doesn't necessarily have to be data that would traditionally be thought of as database-style data, like patient records for a doctor's surgery, or invoices and financial information for a company accounts application.

It's just as easy to use Core Data to store vector graphics information for an iOS drawing application, account information and search terms for a social networking app, or high scores and persistent state information for a game.

Why Use Core Data on iOS?

The Core Data framework provides a tried and tested, very fast means of accessing model data. It doesn't need to cost much in terms of memory or processor usage, and it bundles up a great deal of very useful functionality that we get *for free*.

Relationship Management

Because of its heritage as an aid to working with relational database systems, one of Core Data's main selling points is its ability to manage *relationships* between the objects it maintains, such as patients belonging to a doctor in a surgery. Using the visual data modeler, you define the links between objects using terms like *one-to-one*, *one-to-many*, and *many-to-many*. The framework is designed to use inverse relationships wherever possible, so it is extremely easy to maintain "referential integrity" among your data.

The relationships you define can even be given rules, such as requiring that a particular relationship is always defined (for example a financial transaction must be linked to a bank account), or specifying that a company must have at least one director. When it comes time to save, or *persist*, new objects into the underlying store, the framework refuses to accept objects that don't obey the required rules, thereby maintaining the *integrity* of the object graph.

Similarly, if you change one side of a relationship, Core Data automatically handles the relevant changes on the other side. If you transferred a patient from one doctor to another, for example, each doctor's relevant patient list would automatically be updated accordingly. Likewise, if you deleted a bank account from a financial application, all the relevant transactions would automatically be deleted as well, provided the relationship rules were set up correctly in the data model.

Managed Objects and Data Validation

When you work with objects backed by a Core Data store, you work with what are called *managed objects*. The standard managed object functionality encompasses some of the relationship handling mentioned earlier, but it also allows for *data validation*.

Validation of objects happens on the attributes, or *properties*, of those objects. You can either set per-property rules in the model itself, such as:

▶ a person's salary can't be less than zero

or use custom validation rules to enforce rules between multiple properties, such as:

▶ a patient couldn't have any children if they were younger than a certain age.

As noted earlier, if you try to update an object with values that don't pass the validation tests, Core Data will complain and prevent you from saving incorrect data.

Undo and State Management

Core Data will also automatically maintain an undo stack, if required, which means that changes to objects can be undone even after they've been saved to the persistent store. Again, this is handled automatically for you so you don't have to worry about writing undo management code yourself.

So, the case for using Core Data is extremely strong. And, because it's exactly the same underlying framework code on both platforms, once you've learned how it works under iOS, you already know a great deal about how it works on the desktop! Having said this, there are a few differences in practice between working with Core Data on iOS as opposed to the Mac desktop.

Core Data iOS and Desktop Differences

One major difference between desktop and iOS Core Data support is that there is currently no support for *Bindings* on iOS. On the desktop, Bindings use Key-Value-Observing (KVO) and Key-Value-Coding (KVC) to maintain links between user interface items and model objects or attributes. With Bindings, it's possible to build an impressive Core Data application on the desktop without writing any code at all—you simply use Xcode 4's Interface Editor (the separate Interface Builder application under Xcode 3) to Bind interface items like table views and text fields to groups of managed objects fetched automatically from the Core Data store by object and array controllers.

On iOS, this instant gratification style of Core-Data-with-Bindings development is not possible; instead you need to work directly with various parts of the Core Data framework to supply the relevant information to your user interface.

The Fetched Results Controller

To aid in this process, Apple offers a class new to Core Data and unique to iOS, called NSFetchedResultsController. As its name implies, NSFetchedResultsController (which has an entire chapter devoted to its coverage, Chapter 5) is used as a controller-layer class to help in the interaction between a view and the data fetched from the persistent store. It is designed primarily to function as a data source for a UITableView, governing how many rows and sections the view should display, and providing the contents for each row.

The fetched results controller works in the most efficient way possible to eliminate the need to load all the fetched objects into memory at once, and automatically disposes of objects not currently being accessed. This makes working with large numbers of objects much easier.

If you use a fetched results controller to display a collection of several thousand objects in a table view, for example, only a handful of those objects will ever be loaded into memory at any given time.

Core Data Case Studies

MoneyWell for iPhone

MoneyWell is a personal finance application designed to make the process of tracking expenses and managing cash flow obvious. It uses the envelope-budgeting method in the form of onscreen buckets to hold transactions, which allow the user to manage available cash proactively by seeing exactly what is available in any income or expense category.

When MoneyWell was being designed, Mac OS X Tiger and Core Data were brand new. The data relationships in MoneyWell are fairly complex, but Core Data simplified both schema design and the development process. When Apple announced an SDK for the iPhone, it was obvious that MoneyWell would be a perfect app to have in your pocket. The problem was that Core Data was not available to developers in that first release. We actually delayed development of MoneyWell for iPhone, assuming Apple would migrate Core Data to their device platform. That turned out to be a smart decision because Apple did include Core Data in the 3.0 SDK.

This solved so many development problems. Creating the model layer in MoneyWell for iPhone was a simple matter of copying the Xcode data model into the new project. Additionally, both the Mac and iOS versions of MoneyWell share the same data files allowing us to use all our existing test documents. We also benefited from Core Data being a first class framework that has been retooled extensively for performance on the iOS platform. Things like data access, data persistence, and object graph manipulation were trivial throughout the development process, allowing us to concentrate on solving more important problems like creating a good user experience. One particularly big win for us was the use of Core Data in conjunction with UITableView. As one might imagine, a typical user can have years' worth of financial data that could easily cripple the memory space on a mobile device. Without Core Data, we would have been forced to write complex paging algorithms or extensive SQLite queries, but instead we are able to query for a set of transactions and rely on Core Data's ability to page data intelligently in and out of memory as needed.

Using Core Data easily saved us five or more months of development time.

—*Kevin Hoctor and Michael Fey, No Thirst Software LLC*

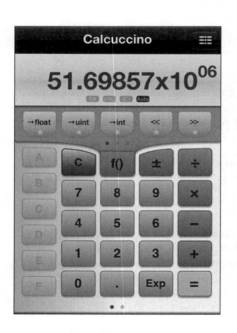

Calcuccino

Calcuccino is a programmers' calculator that uses the iPhone's menus and swipe gestures to improve on the conventional calculator. The result is a powerful calculator for programming, engineering, and scientific use, with big buttons for fast and reliable entry.

The decision to use Core Data for Calcuccino was not an obvious one. Calcuccino does not have any large data handling needs, but it does need to store a reasonable history of the user's calculations so they can view them later, or reuse a previous result. Calcuccino also needs to keep state information for the current calculation so it can be restored should the user switch from the app and return sometime later. Before Core Data, both of these requirements would have been done using XML files to persist the information, but this can lead to large portions of code being written just to handle the XML itself.

Core Data offers a data model designer in Xcode, so this was used to map out the data structure—primarily a store of HistoryStep entities for the history steps, and OpStep entities for the state of the current calculation. For the calculation engine itself we define a

CalcValue class—this is the basic number type used throughout Calcuccino (analogous to Cocoa's NSNumber class, but with additions for integer size and format). All CalcValue instances are stored in the Core Data store using instances of a GeneralValue entity.

The data model for Calcuccino is clean and maps nicely to the requirements of the app. There is a CalcStore class that handles the interface between the Objective-C classes of the app and calls to Core Data. It disappoints me that there is still mapping code to map between Objective-C classes and entities, but this is no different than the code needed to pack and unpack classes to and from XML. I suspect that we will move further away from raw NSManagedObjects and more toward custom classes to reduce this mapping code. There is also a change of thinking needed to shift between Cocoa's regular container classes (NSArray, NSDictionary) and accessing entities with predicates and fetch requests.

Given our experience of using Core Data now, the question would be "would we use Core Data again?"

The answer is *yes*, which confirms that we believe we have made the right decision. Interfacing between UITableViews and Core Data with NSFetchedResultsController is a joy, especially using attributes to group calculations automatically by day in the history view. Once we get a few more versions of Calcuccino under our belt and we have had to version control the database using Core Data's versioning capabilities, we hope that we will continue to believe that we made the right decision!

—*Andy Dean, Cambridge Coders Ltd*

Associated Press

When I first started on the Associated Press mobile application, I knew that it was going to need to be a Core Data application. The amount of data we were working with was simply too voluminous to attempt to use any other type of persistence layer. In addition, based on our requirements of asynchronous data transfers, Core Data was an easy choice.

Being able to set up data parsers that feed directly into the Core Data model, and that could be saved on a background thread, was extremely helpful in making the application perform well for its users.

When we started designing the application, we knew that the interface to the server was going to be used for more than one application, so we designed it as a separate library. By designing the library to "merely" add data to the Core Data persistent store, we were able to provide a common, easily understood interface to any application that was built upon it. Each application only had to watch for changes in Core Data to know that the underlying data had changed. By doing so, we were able to keep the interface code between the application and the library to a bare minimum.

We have now been using this library design for over a year with virtually no issues. The library has been used in dozens of applications at this point and is performing very well. Had we used another persistence engine I suspect we would still be battling with performance issues and memory issues.

—*Marcus S. Zarra, Zarra Studios LLC*

CHAPTER 2

A Core Data Primer

In order to get the most out of Core Data, it's extremely important to have a firm understanding of its fundamental operations. Over the course of this chapter, you'll learn the key terms and features of the different parts of a Core Data-based application.

Before looking at the Core Data terms, though, take a moment to think about how you might work with persisted data in an application *without* using Core Data.

Persisting Objects to Disk

When you're working with data to be saved in an application, you typically have collections of objects, maybe held in arrays, sets or dictionaries, which need to be archived to disk. When it comes time to save the data, you might encode or serialize those objects ready to be saved into a binary file or, for small datasets, store them in a `.plist` file.

As an alternative to working with binary files, and before Core Data came to iOS, developers could also make direct use of SQLite, a simple and very lightweight database, available on iOS devices since the early versions of iPhone OS. When writing an application that made use of large collections of objects, it would make sense to store those items in a database, offering huge increases in speed when saving and fetching objects.

SQLite, as its name implies, is based around the *Structured Query Language*, or SQL. You talk to an SQL database by issuing commands to, for example, *insert* or *select* (fetch) data. If you only need a specific object from the database, you can issue a command to fetch just that object; you don't need to worry about the efficiency and performance issues with loading an entire binary file from disk just to get hold of a particular object.

In order to work with SQLite, however, you need to make heavy use of procedural C APIs, writing lengthy portions of code to handle data access. To save an object into a SQLite database, for example, you would need to write out a string containing an SQL INSERT statement, populate that string with the values held by the object's instance variables, convert the string to a C-string, before finally passing it to a C function.

The Core Data Approach

Core Data, on the other hand, combines all the speed and efficiency of database storage with the object-oriented goodness of object serialization.

Entities and Managed Objects

When you create your model objects, instead of starting out by writing the .h @interface for the class, you typically begin by modeling your *entities*, using the Xcode Data Modeler. An entity corresponds to one *type* of object, such as a Patient or Doctor object, and sets out the *attributes* for that entity, such as firstName and lastName. You use the data modeler to set which attributes will be persisted to disk, along with various other features such as the type of data that an attribute will hold, data validation requirements, or whether an attribute is optional or required.

When you work with actual instances of model objects, such as a specific Patient object, you're dealing with an instance of a *managed* object. These objects will either be instances of the NSManagedObject class, or a custom subclass of NSManagedObject. If you don't specify a custom subclass in the modeler, you would typically access the attributes of the object through *Key Value Coding* (KVC), using code like that in Listing 2.1.

LISTING 2.1   Accessing the attributes of a managed object

```
NSManagedObject *aPatientObject; // Assuming this has already been fetched

NSString *firstName = [aPatientObject valueForKey:@"firstName"];
NSString *lastName = [aPatientObject valueForKey:@"lastName"];

[aPatientObject setValue:@"Pain killers" forKey:@"currentMedication"];
[aPatientObject setValue:@"Headache" forKey:@"currentIllness"];
```

If you choose to do so, you can also provide your own subclass of NSManagedObject, to expose *accessor methods* and/or *properties* for your managed object, so you could use the code shown in Listing 2.2. You'll look at this in more detail in Chapter 6, "Working with Managed Objects."

LISTING 2.2   Using a custom subclass of NSManagedObject

```
Patient *aPatientObject; // Assuming this has already been fetched

NSString *firstName = [aPatientObject firstName];
NSString *lastName = aPatientObject.lastName;

[aPatientObject setCurrentMedication:@"Pain killers"];
aPatientObject.currentIllness = @"Headache";
```

You could also still access the values of the object using valueForKey:, etc., if you wish.

Relationships

The Data Modeler is also the place where you define the *relationships* between your entities. As an example, a Patient object would have a relationship to a Doctor, and the Doctor would have a relationship to the Patient, as shown in Figure 2.1.

FIGURE 2.1   A Patient-Doctor relationship

When modeling relationships, you typically think in relational database terms, such as *one-to-one*, *one-to-many*, and *many-to-many*. In the example shown in Figure 2.1, a patient has only *one* doctor, but a doctor has *many* patients, so the doctor-patient relationship is one-to-many.

If the doctor-patient relationship is one-to-many, the *inverse* relationship (patient-doctor) is obviously *many-to-one*. When you model these relationships in the Data Modeler, you need to model them *both*, explicitly, and set one as the inverse of the other. By setting the inverse relationship explicitly, Core Data ensures the integrity of your data is automatically maintained; if you set a patient to have a particular doctor, the patient will also be added to the doctor's list of patients without you having to do it yourself.

You specify a *name* for each relationship, so that they are exposed in a similar way to an entity's attributes. Again, you can either work with KVC methods, or provide your own accessors and property declarations in a custom subclass, using code like that in Listing 2.3.

LISTING 2.3   Working with relationships

```
Patient *aPatientObject; // Assuming this has already been fetched
Doctor *aDoctorObject = [aPatientObject valueForKey:@"doctor"];

Patient *anotherPatientObject; // also already fetched
anotherPatientObject.doctor = aDoctorObject;
    // The inverse relationship is automatically set too

NSLog(@"Doctor's patients = %@", [aDoctorObject patients]);
/* Outputs:
    Doctor's patients = (
                        aPatientObject,
                        anotherPatientObject,
                        etc...

                    )
*/
```

It's important to note that Core Data doesn't maintain any *order* in collections of objects, including to-many relationships. You'll see later in the book how objects probably won't be returned to you in the order in which you input them. If order is important, you'll need to keep track of it yourself, perhaps using an ascending numerical index property for each object.

If you're used to working with databases such as MySQL, PostgreSQL, or MS SQL Server (maybe with web-based applications in Ruby/Rails, PHP, ASP.NET, etc.), you're probably used to every *record* in the database having a unique id of some sort. When you work with Core Data, you don't need to model any kind of unique identifier, nor do you have to deal with join tables between related records. Core Data handles this in the background; all you have to do is to define the relationships between objects, and the framework will decide how best to generate the underlying mechanisms, behind the scenes.

Managed Object Contexts

So far, the code in this chapter has assumed that you've fetched an object "from somewhere." When you're working with managed objects and Core Data, you're working within a certain *context*, known as the *Managed Object Context*. This context keeps track of the persistent storage of your data on disk (which on iOS is probably a SQLite store) and acts as a kind of container for the objects that you work with.

Conceptually, it's a bit like working with a document object in a desktop application—the document represents the data stored on disk. It loads the data from disk when a document is opened, perhaps allowing you to display the contents in a window on screen. It keeps track of changes to the document, likely holding them in memory, and is then responsible for writing those changes to disk when it's time to save the data.

The Managed Object Context (MOC) works in a similar way. It is responsible for fetching the data from the store when needed, keeping track of the changes made to objects in memory, and then writing those changes back to disk when told to save. Unless you specifically tell the MOC to save, any changes you make to any managed objects in that context will be temporary, and won't affect the underlying data on disk.

Unlike a normal document object, however, you are able to work with more than one managed object context at a time, even though they all relate to the same underlying data. You might, for example, load the same patient object into two different contexts, and make changes to the patient in one of the contexts (as shown in Figure 2.2). The object in the other context would be unaffected by these changes, unless you chose to save the first context. At that point, a notification would be sent to inform you that another context had changed the data, and you could reload the second context if you wanted to.

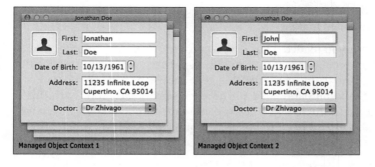

FIGURE 2.2   Managed Object Contexts and their Managed Objects

Although it's less common to work with multiple contexts on iOS than it is on the desktop, you typically use a separate context if you're working with objects in the background, such as pulling information from an online source and saving it into your local app's data. If you choose to use the automatic Undo handling offered by managed object contexts, you might set up a second context to work with an individual object, handling undo for any changes to individual attributes as separate actions. When it was time to save that object back into your primary context, the act of saving all those changes would count as one undo action in the primary context, allowing the user to undo all the changes in one go if they wanted to. You'll see examples of this in later chapters.

Fetching Objects

The managed object context is also the medium through which you fetch objects from disk, using NSFetchRequest objects. A fetch request has at minimum the name of an entity; if you wanted to fetch all the patient records from the persistent store, you would create a fetch request object, specify the Patient entity to be retrieved, and tell the MOC to execute that fetch request. The MOC returns the results back to you as an array. Again, it's important to note that the order in that array probably won't be the same as the order in which you stored the objects, or the same as the next time you execute the fetch request, unless you request the results to be sorted in a particular order.

To fetch specific objects, or objects that match certain criteria, you can specify a *fetch predicate*; to sort the results in a certain order, you can provide an array of *sort descriptors*. You might choose to fetch all the patient records for a particular doctor, sorting them by last name. Or, if you had previously stored a numerical index on each patient as they were stored, you could ask for the results to be sorted by that index so that they would be returned to you in the same order each time.

Faulting and Uniquing

Core Data also works hard to optimize performance and keep memory usage to a minimum, using a technique called *faulting*.

Consider what could happen if you loaded a Patient record into memory; in order that you have access to that patient's Doctor object, it might seem that you'd want to have the Doctor object loaded as well. And, since you might need to access the other patients related to that doctor, you should probably load all those Patient objects too. With this behavior, what you thought was a single-object fetch could turn into a fetch of thousands of objects—every related object would need to be fetched, possibly resulting in fetching your entire dataset.

To solve this problem, Core Data *doesn't* fetch all the relationships on an object. It simply returns you the managed object that you asked for, with the relationships set to *faults*. If you try and access one of those relationships, such as asking for the name of the patient's doctor, the "fault will fire" and Core Data will fetch the requested object for you. And, as before, the relationships on a newly fetched doctor object will also be set to faults, ready to fire when you need to access any of the related objects. All of this happens automatically, without you needing to worry about it.

A managed object context will also ensure that if an object has already been loaded, it will always return the existing instance in any subsequent fetches. Consider the code in Listing 2.4.

LISTING 2.4   Fetching unique objects

```
Patient *firstPatient; // From one fetch request
Doctor *firstPatientsDoctor = firstPatient.doctor;
```

```
Patient *secondPatient; // From a second fetch request
Doctor *secondPatientsDoctor = secondPatient.doctor;

/* If the two patients share the same doctor, then the doctor instance
   returned after each fault fires will be the same instance: */

if( firstPatientsDoctor == secondPatientsDoctor )
{
    NSLog(@"Patients share a doctor!");
}
```

This is known as *uniquing*—you will only ever be given one object instance in any managed object context for, say, a particular `Patient`.

Persistent Stores and Persistent Store Coordinators

The underlying data is held on disk in a *persistent store*. On an iOS device, this is usually a SQLite store. You can also choose to use a binary store or even your own custom atomic store type, but these require the entire object graph to be loaded into memory, which can quickly become a problem on a device with limited resources.

You never need to communicate directly with a persistent store, or worry about how it is storing data. Instead, you rely on the relationship between the managed object context and a *persistent store coordinator*.

The persistent store coordinator acts as a mediator to the managed object contexts; it's also possible to have a coordinator talk to multiple persistent stores on disk, meaning that the coordinator would expose the union of those stores to be accessed by the managed object contexts.

You won't typically need to worry too much about persistent stores and coordinators unless you want to work with multiple stores or define your own store type. In the next section, you'll see the code from the Xcode template project that sets up the persistent store for you. Once this is dealt with, you'll spend most of your time concentrating on the managed objects, held within managed object contexts.

Examining the Xcode Core Data Templates

Now that you have a better idea of Core Data terminology, let's take a look inside a standard Core Data template project for an iOS application to see how all of this works in practice.

The Navigation-Based Project Template

The Xcode project templates for the Navigation-based, Split View-based, Utility and Window-based applications all offer the option to *Use Core Data*, as shown in Figure 2.3.

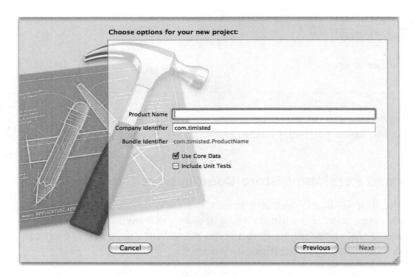

FIGURE 2.3   The New Project Window

To follow the rest of this chapter, launch Xcode and choose File > New > New Project (Shift-⌘-N), then select the Navigation-based Application template. Call the project TemplateProject, and tick the Use Core Data checkbox.

When the project window appears, you'll see that there are some extra items compared to a standard project. First, the project links to the CoreData.framework. Second, there is an item called TemplateProject.xcdatamodeld. This defines the structure of your data model, which you build visually using the Xcode Data Modeler. Click on the file to open it.

There are two ways to view a data model in Xcode 4—as a Table or a Graph, as shown in Figure 2.4.

> **NOTE**
>
> Xcode 3 has only one editor mode, which combines the Table and Graph into a single view.

The Data Modeler

At the top-left of the editor, you'll see a list of *Entities*. In the template file, there is a single entity, called Event. If you select this entity for display using the Table editor style, you'll see a list of the entity's *attributes*, *relationships* and *fetched properties*.

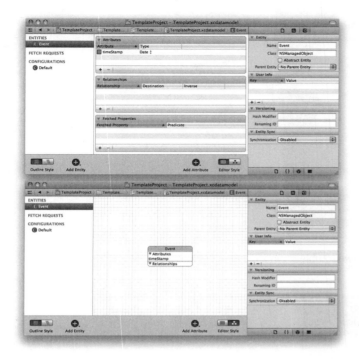

FIGURE 2.4   The two Editor Styles in the Xcode 4 Data Modeler

The Event entity has a single attribute listed, called timeStamp. If you click this attribute to select it, and look in Xcode 4's Data Model Inspector (Option-⌘-3), you'll see that its *Type* is set to Date.

This inspector offers a number of other options relating to that attribute. For example, this is where you can choose to validate the data that is stored, or mark an attribute as being optional; these options are covered in Chapter 3, "Modeling Your Data."

Xcode 4's Graph editor style offers a visual representation of the entities in your object model. At present, there is only a single entity in the model, but if there were more than one, you would see the relationships between the entities represented by lines and arrows connecting the two, as in Figure 2.5.

Setting up the Core Data Stack

When working with data held in a persistent store, you will need to have built up a *stack* of objects; at the bottom is the actual persistent store on disk, then comes a persistent store controller to liaise between the store and the next level, the managed object context, as shown in Figure 2.6.

It's also possible to have more than one persistent store under the one coordinator, as well as multiple managed object contexts (as discussed earlier in the chapter).

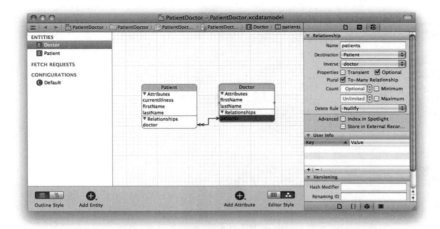

FIGURE 2.5   Relationships between objects in the Object Graph

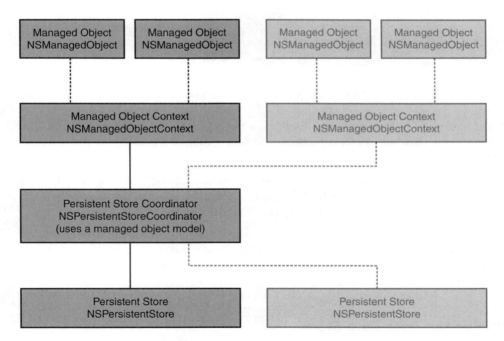

FIGURE 2.6   The Core Data Stack

Let's examine the template code provided to set up this Core Data stack. Open the
TemplateProjectAppDelegate.h interface file, and you'll find that there are a number of
property declarations defined for the app delegate, as shown in Listing 2.5 (the Xcode 4
templates make use of the modern runtime feature of synthesizing the corresponding
instance variables).

LISTING 2.5   The app delegate interface

```
@interface TemplateProjectAppDelegate : NSObject <UIApplicationDelegate> {

}

@property (nonatomic, retain) IBOutlet UIWindow *window;

@property (nonatomic, retain, readonly) NSManagedObjectContext
                                                  *managedObjectContext;
@property (nonatomic, retain, readonly) NSManagedObjectModel *managedObjectModel;
@property (nonatomic, retain, readonly) NSPersistentStoreCoordinator
                                                  *persistentStoreCoordinator;

- (void)saveContext;
- (NSURL *)applicationDocumentsDirectory;

@property (nonatomic, retain) IBOutlet UINavigationController *navigationController;

@end
```

The app delegate keeps track of the managed object model, which is the information contained within the `TemplateProject.xcdatamodeld` file. It also has a reference to a persistent store coordinator, along with a managed object context. The `applicationDocumentsDirectory` is used to determine where the data will be held on disk.

Switch to the `TemplateProjectAppDelegate.m` interface file and scroll through the various methods that are provided. Near the bottom, you'll find the `applicationDocumentsDirectory` method. As the name implies, it simply returns the path to the application's documents directory.

Next find the `persistentStoreCoordinator` method. This method sets up a persistent store coordinator, to access a SQLite store file called `TemplateProject.sqlite`, located in the application's documents directory. The persistent store is initialized using the model provided by the `managedObjectModel` method, so jump to this method next.

The `managedObjectModel` method returns an `NSManagedObjectModel` object created from a file called `TemplateProject.momd`. When you compile the project, the `TemplateProject.xcdatamodeld` data model is compiled into this `.momd` resource and stored in the application's bundle.

It's also possible to create an `NSManagedObjectModel` by merging all the available model files using the class method `mergedModelFromBundles:`, or by merging selected models using `modelByMergingModels:`. Although there is only a single model file (it's actually a model bundle) in this template application, it is possible to split your model into multiple `.xcdatamodeld` files, if you wish.

At the top of the stack, you'll find the `managedObjectContext` method. This method sets up the context using the persistent store coordinator. If you look in the `awakeFromNib` method, towards the top of the file, you'll find that it sets a property on the `RootViewController` for a `managedObjectContext`. It is at this point that the chain is triggered to set up the managed object model, persistent store coordinator and finally the context.

> **NOTE**
>
> In earlier versions of Xcode, the template code may be slightly different; for example, setting up the managed object model by merging the models in the main bundle, and setting the `RootViewController`'s `managedObjectContext` property from within `application:didFinishLaunching:`.

Lastly, the `applicationWillTerminate:` method calls a `saveContext` method, which checks to see whether any changes have been made to objects in the managed object context, and tries to save those changes if so. This means that the persistent store will be updated with changes from the context when the application exits. Some versions of the project template also call `saveContext` from `applicationDidEnterBackground:`, so that the store will be updated if the user switches to a different application under iOS 4 multitasking.

You probably won't need to modify the code in these methods unless you need to work with multiple stores or custom store types. Once the managed object context has been set up, it's passed to the root view controller. This view controller has the code that actually performs the relevant fetches to display the data in a table view, and it's this sort of code that you will typically be writing most of the time when you're working with Core Data. In Chapter 4, "Basic Storing and Fetching," you'll start writing your own code to populate a table view with information from a Core Data store.

Running the Application

To see the functionality you get from the basic project template, build and run the application. You'll find that you can add to a list of `Events`; the table view shows these, outputting the values of the events' `timeStamp` attributes. Note that you can remove items from the table view using the Edit button, or by swiping your finger across a row.

A Quick Look at the RootViewController Code

To get an idea of how this all works, open up the `RootViewController.m` implementation file. The template application makes use of a *Fetched Results Controller* to simplify working with fetched objects and table views. This object is created lazily and told to fetch when it's needed by one of the table view data source methods.

> **NOTE**
>
> In earlier versions of Xcode, the template file creates the `FetchedResultsController` and executes a fetch at the end of the view controller's `viewDidLoad` method.

FIGURE 2.7   The Template Application in the Simulator

If you look at the code that generates the fetchedResultsController lazily, you'll see that it's set to use the Event entity and given sort descriptors to sort by the timeStamp attribute.

The methods to display the contents in the table view are the standard table view data source methods; for the numberOfSections... and numberOfRows... methods, the template code just queries the fetched results controller object. To display the information in the cellForRowAtIndexPath: method, a configureCell:atIndexPath: method is used. Notice how simple it is to get hold of the managed object at the selected index. The code to display the time stamp is shown in Listing 2.6.

LISTING 2.6   Displaying the timestamp in the cell

```
NSManagedObject *managedObject = [self.fetchedResultsController
                                       objectAtIndexPath:indexPath];


cell.textLabel.text = [[managedObject valueForKey:@"timeStamp"] description];
```

The fetched results controller returns the object at the specified index, and the code just queries that returned object for the description of its timeStamp key.

The commitEditingStyle:forRowAtIndexPath: method simply tells the managed object context to delete the object at the specified index path, and then asks the context to save.

This will mean that the object deleted from the table view will also be deleted from the persistent store.

Lastly, find the `insertNewObject` method that gets called when the user tries to add an object to the table view, and you'll see that the procedure is:

- ▶ Get a pointer to a managed object context.

- ▶ Decide which entity you need to use to create a new object.

- ▶ Insert a new object for that entity, into the managed object context.

- ▶ Set the relevant values on the new object.

- ▶ Tell the context to save.

When the context saves, the new object is written to the persistent store. It's as simple as that! Note that the template files are deliberately verbose—it's common to accomplish the above using only two or three lines of code.

Summary

Now that you have an idea of how a Core Data application is constructed, it's time to start learning how to use the individual parts of the Core Data framework. In the next chapter, you'll see best practices for constructing managed object models from the point of view of memory and performance considerations.

Although the Apple-provided template application makes use of a fetched results controller, it's a good idea to see how objects are fetched *manually*. Chapter 4, "Basic Storing and Fetching," demonstrates how to work directly with managed object contexts and fetch requests to display objects in a table view. Chapter 5, "Using NSFetchedResultsController," then shows how to take advantage of the memory optimization and performance benefits offered by the fetch results controller.

CHAPTER 3

Modeling Your Data

When writing an application that uses Core Data, your first step will normally be to design the *object graph*, using the Data Model editor in Xcode. In this chapter, you'll see how to build this visual representation of your *entities*, along with their *attributes* and *relationships*.

This chapter also covers general principles of data modeling, as they apply to Core Data. If you are familiar with data normalization for standard databases, you'll see how it's frequently better in performance terms **not** to over-normalize your data for a Core Data store, particularly on an iOS device.

Managed Objects and Entities

As you saw in Chapter 2, "A Core Data Primer," the basic data object in the Core Data framework is the *managed object*, and every managed object that you work with is an instance of an *entity*. You use the Xcode Data Modeler to describe your entities, specifying their *properties*, which are either *attributes* like strings, numbers and dates, or *relationships* to other entities.

Conceptually, this arrangement is similar to standard object-oriented programming. In Objective-C, a generic object is an instance of the NSObject class, where the class description defines the properties of the object (such as isa). Different *types* of object are instances of different *classes*, each with their own class description.

In Core Data, it is the *entity description* that defines the model data properties of the managed object instances. It's important to understand the difference between entities and Objective-C classes—although it is certainly common for each entity to be instantiated using a different Objective-C class, it's also perfectly possible for every entity to use the generic Core Data NSManagedObject class. NSManagedObject keeps track of the entity for any particular instance, so that it knows which properties are accessible from the underlying persistent store, as defined by the entity description.

Dividing Your Data into Entities

The first step in designing your data model is to decide how you'll divide the data into entities. In general, you follow similar principles as when working with database tables in database-driven web sites—you normally use an entity wherever you would use a table in a database. If you're not so familiar with database terminology, you might like to skip to *Core Data in Model-Object Terms*.

A big exception to this rule is *join tables*. Join tables are used in databases to indicate *many-to-many* relationships between tables (e.g., has_and_belongs_to_many in Rails terms). Because Core Data handles relationships for you, you should *not* use a separate join table entity for a many-to-many relationship. Instead, you simply specify the two related entities and create a relationship between those entities, specifying each end of the relationship as *To-many*. Core Data will figure out how to store the relationship in the persistent store; in the case of a SQLite database, it creates the relevant join tables behind the scenes and you never need to worry about how this is done.

The *columns* in a traditional database table translate into the attributes on an entity. The *rows*, of course, are the managed object instances of that entity.

Core Data in Model-Object Terms

If you're used to working with data in terms of archived or serialized dictionaries and arrays of model objects, the first step in a Core Data model is to create an entity for every basic model object. Each *instance variable* in those model objects becomes an attribute in the entity.

Where you have an *array* instance variable in a model object, containing references to several other model objects, you create a *one-to-many* relationship between the Core Data entities for the two model object types. If you have a CustomerOrder model object, for example, containing an NSArray of OrderItems, you would create a CustomerOrder entity and an OrderItem entity, with a to-many relationship between them.

This applies no matter what is contained within your array, even if you just need a simple array of NSString objects. Core Data does not have an array attribute type, so you would need to create an entity just to represent the string objects (such as a CustomerComment entity containing a single commentString attribute).

If it really doesn't make sense to create a whole new entity just for a string attribute, Core Data does have a plain data attribute type. You could write functionality to archive the basic array of strings into an NSData object and store that as an attribute of the entity. Whenever a CustomerOrder instance was fetched from the persistent store and the strings were needed, the information would need to be unarchived ready for display. Since this would normally introduce unnecessary performance overhead (not to mention additional code to maintain), it's probably easier just to model the extra entity.

Data Normalization

Data normalization refers to the process of separating data into related entities in order to minimize repeated information, and to make it easier to query the resulting data. If you were to model the CustomerOrder example from earlier, it would usually make sense to use a separate entity for a Customer, rather than duplicating the customer information in each order (e.g., having a customerName attribute on the CustomerOrder entity).

If a customer changes their name, you need only update the information held in one place, in a Customer managed object, which is much faster, easier and less error-prone than having to change the same string on every CustomerOrder object for that customer. It also means that to get a list of the orders from a particular customer, you can just ask a Customer managed object for all of its CustomerOrder objects, rather than having to search for all the CustomerOrder objects that have a specific customerName.

In traditional database design, there are various levels of normalization, referred to as *normal forms*. A complete discussion of normal forms is outside the scope of this book, but the principles that apply to designing a database for a web application also apply in general when working with Core Data.

If you were building a simple customer order application, you might decide to use three separate entities for a CustomerOrder, an OrderItem, and a Product, as shown in Figure 3.1.

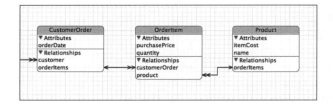

FIGURE 3.1   Relationship between customer orders, order items and products

When a customer places an order for various products, a CustomerOrder object is created, along with multiple OrderItem objects representing the products purchased. The OrderItem object stores the purchase price of the product at time of purchase so that if the price subsequently changes, the CustomerOrder still lists the correct price relevant to the order. The OrderItem does not store the name of the product, because this can be derived from the relationship between the OrderItem and the Product objects. In key-path terms, you would ask an OrderItem for its product.name.

In the example given in Figure 3.1, the CustomerOrder does not store the total amount for the order, because it is possible to generate that value on demand by adding together the prices (multiplied by the quantities) of all the OrderItems in the order.

If this was the data model design for an iOS application, you might decide to have a screen that listed recent orders, like the example shown in Figure 3.2. Each row of the table view represents one OrderItem object, and shows the date of the order along with the total amount.

FIGURE 3.2   A simple iPhone application screen, listing recent CustomerOrders

Because the order's total value is calculated for each row in the table view, you could suffer performance and memory usage issues on an iOS device. You'd need to fetch all the OrderItem objects for an order just to perform the calculation of (purchasePrice * quantity), and then calculate the sum of the results.

For an iOS Core Data application, it would make more sense to store an orderTotal amount in the CustomerOrder object. Although this might go against traditional normalization practice, the minimal additional time taken to store one extra value when the order is created or modified could offer great performance benefits in the future. You would no longer need to load any OrderItem objects or perform any calculations to display the table view in Figure 3.2.

You might also find a small performance benefit by caching the customerName in each CustomerOrder object, to avoid having to fetch a related Customer object just to display the name, but this would be at the expense of storing a duplicated string for every order.

When designing the data model for your Core Data project, you'll need to weigh the benefits of normalization and lack of data duplication against potential performance gains from *denormalization*.

Storing Binary Data

If you need to store binary data for a managed object, such as an image or audio clip, you can use a data attribute in an entity. Once again, there are performance and memory considerations whenever you work with this kind of data.

Consider an iOS application designed to keep track of names and addresses of contacts. If you wanted to be able to store a picture for each contact, you might come up with the entity design shown in Figure 3.3.

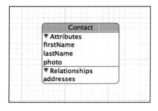

FIGURE 3.3   A basic data model for a contact-management application, with an attribute for a picture

This would work just fine if you were only displaying one contact on screen at a time. When you wanted to display a list of all your contacts, however, you would obviously need to fetch all the relevant contacts from the persistent store. If each contact has a 512 kb picture attached to it, you would very quickly run out of memory on an iOS device as you would be loading all of those contacts' images at once.

Core Data does offer you the ability to specify that only certain attributes are fetched, but this means you'd need to remember to specify that the picture attribute should be excluded for every fetch, except in the places where it will be needed.

The alternative is to have a dedicated entity for your large data objects, with a *one-to-one* relationship from the main entity to this data entity, as shown in Figure 3.4.

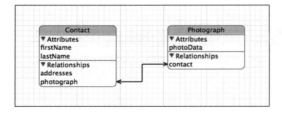

FIGURE 3.4   The basic contact-management data model, with a separate entity for the picture data

With this model design, you can safely load all the contacts from disk at once; when you've fetched the objects, all the picture relationships will be faults so no picture data will have been loaded. When you do need to display the picture for a contact and try to access the faulted relationship, the fault will fire and the picture will be fetched from the store.

The terminology and optimization suggestions covered briefly in this section are addressed throughout the rest of the book.

Working with Xcode's Data Modeler

Now that you've seen some of the best practices for iOS Core Data model design, let's look at how to use Xcode's Data Model editor to create your managed object models.

In order to follow along with the descriptions in the remainder of the chapter, create a new data model file in Xcode. Create a new Xcode 4 workspace (or an empty project), then choose File > New > New File (⌘-N) and select the Data Model option from the Core Data group, as shown in Figure 3.5.

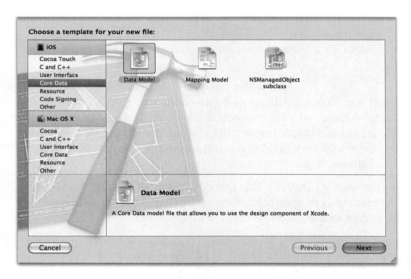

FIGURE 3.5   The New File sheet for a Data Model

> **NOTE**
>
> In Xcode 3, the Data Model file template is found under the Resource group in the New File window.

Click Next and enter a name to identify this model, along with a location on disk.

Once you create the file, the blank data model document will open in the Data Modeler, as shown in Figure 3.6.

FIGURE 3.6   A blank data model document in the Xcode 4 Data Modeler

In Xcode 4, there are two editor styles for the Data Model, table or graph. In Xcode 3, the data modeler window always shows both representations:

▶ The Graph editor style (the lower, main portion of the editor in Xcode 3) shows a visual representation of your entities and their relationships.

▶ The Table editor style (the upper portion of the editor in Xcode 3) allows you to view detailed information about the properties of a selected entity.

Creating Entities

To create an entity in Xcode 4, click the Add Entity button in the bottom bar of either editor style.[1] A new entity will be created, and appear in the Entity list on the left, as well as the graph representation, ready to add the attributes and relationships.

As an example, let's create the CustomerOrder entity from earlier in the chapter. Choose View > Utilities > Data Model Inspector (Option-⌘-3),[2] and you'll see further configuration options, as shown in Figure 3.7.

---

[1] In Xcode 3, click the + button at the bottom of the Entity table view in the top-left portion of the screen, or right-click (or Control-click) on the graph area and choose Add Entity from the contextual menu.

[2] This inspector is shown automatically in Xcode 3 whenever you select an entity.

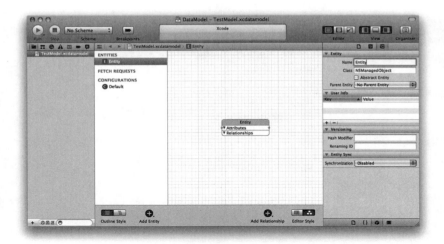

FIGURE 3.7   The Data Model Inspector in Xcode 4

Use this inspector to change the Name of the entity to CustomerOrder.

There are various requirements and conventions to keep in mind when naming entities. Just like an Objective-C class name, the name of an entity should start with a capital letter, contain no spaces, and use CamelCase. It should also be *singular*—although there will presumably be multiple orders in the store, you're creating the entity description to be used for each order object. An iOS application frequently has several view controllers, but the base Cocoa Touch class is named UIViewController, not UIViewControllers; a customer order entity should therefore be named CustomerOrder, not CustomerOrders. It's usually not necessary to prefix your entity names (e.g., AWCustomerOrder).

Note that the inspector also lets you specify a *Class* for the entity, a *Parent Entity*, and whether the entity is *Abstract*:

▶ The Class for an entity is set by default to NSManagedObject, which means that each object fetched from the store will be instantiated as an instance of the NSManagedObject class. If you create your own custom managed object classes, as described in Chapters 5 and 6, you will need to change this value to the name of your class.

Although you don't need to use a prefix for your entity names, it is a good idea to prefix your custom managed object *class* names. You might end up with a CustomerOrder entity that instantiates an AWCustomerOrder class, for example.

▶ The Parent Entity drop-down allows you to specify that one entity should inherit from another entity. As with Objective-C class inheritance, all the properties (i.e., attributes and relationships) from the parent are inherited by the child, and you cannot inherit from more than one Parent at a time.

▶ The Abstract checkbox is used to specify that an entity is designed purely for other entities to use as a Parent. No actual managed objects will be created for this entity, only for entities that inherit the abstract properties.

Leave the class of the entity as NSManagedObject for now, as we won't be creating any custom managed object subclasses in this chapter. Leave the inheritance options at the default values as well—inheritance is covered in more detail in Chapter 6, "Working with Managed Objects."

The Entity Inspector also allows you a number of other configuration options[3]:

▶ The User Info area is used to specify information for an *entity* (rather than any instances) that will be stored in the data model itself, rather than in attributes.

▶ The Versioning area is used to configure options used in versioned data models, as covered in Chapter 8, "Migration and Versioning."

▶ The Entity Sync area is used when working with Sync Services on the desktop and is not used for Core Data on iOS.

NOTE

In advanced Core Data applications with large data models and multiple persistent stores, you can make use of Configurations (listed by Xcode 4 in the left panel of the editor) to limit the included information when adding persistent stores to a persistent store coordinator. This is rare for an iOS application, and is beyond the scope of this book.

Creating Properties

Now that you have a brand new entity in your model, it's time to add some properties.

When using the Table editor style in the Data Modeler, you'll see the properties for the selected entity, with a property being an *attribute*, a *relationship*, or a *fetched property*. Attributes and relationships have been covered earlier in this chapter; a fetched property is a property defined on one entity whose value is actually fetched from another entity.

Make sure that your CustomerOrder entity is selected, and create a new attribute, by clicking the Add Attribute button in the bottom bar of the Editor.[4] A new attribute appears in the Attributes list in the Table, or in the Attributes section of the visual representation of the entity when using the Graph editor style, as shown in Figure 3.8.

---

[3] *Xcode 3 hides these options in various panels, which you can view using the four-icon segmented control at the top-right of the inspector.*
[4] *In Xcode 3, either click the Add (+) button at the bottom of the Properties table view and choose Attribute from the popup menu, or right-click (or Control-click) on the entity in the graph area and choose Add Attribute.*

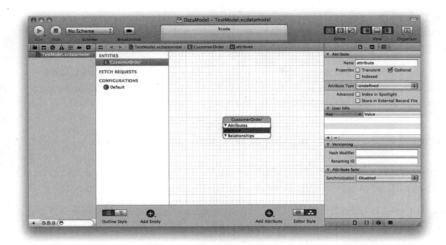

FIGURE 3.8   A new attribute in Xcode's Data Modeler

With an attribute selected, the Inspector lets you set the *Name* of the attribute, whether it
is *Transient*, *Optional*, or *Indexed*, and the *Attribute Type*:

► A Transient attribute is one that is not stored in the persistent store. It is used to
  specify an attribute generated in a custom managed object subclass, usually based on
  other attributes (such as a `fullName` transient attribute returning a string built from
  `firstName` and `lastName` attributes in a `Person` entity).

► If you specify that an attribute is Optional, you specify that a managed object
  instance of this entity can be saved with no value set for this particular attribute. If a
  value is required (i.e., this box is **not** checked), the managed object context will
  refuse to save a managed object unless it has a value set for this attribute (you will
  receive an `NSError` when you try and save the context).

► The Indexed checkbox is used to indicate that the underlying persistent store type
  should generate an index for this attribute; if you know that you will be fetching
  objects with queries based on one attribute more than others, specifying that the
  attribute should be indexed will speed up fetching when using predicates.

Change the name of your new attribute to `orderDate`. As with Entity names, there are
various requirements and conventions for attributes—attribute names *do not* start with a
capital letter, cannot contain spaces, and are normally singular. For Boolean attributes
(that are either true or false, `YES` or `NO`), you should follow conventions from Objective-C
instance variables—an attribute that specifies whether a `CustomerOrder` object has
shipped, for example, should be called `shipped`, rather than `isShipped`, `hasShipped`, etc.

> **NOTE**
>
> Some keywords can't be used as attribute names. At the time of writing, Apple doesn't publish a list of these, but Xcode 4 will generate a warning at compile time for some of them. It's worth bearing in mind that if your application is behaving strangely, or refusing to fetch, you may have a naming conflict. One common pitfall is to try and use an attribute called description, which clashes with the NSObject method of the same name.
>
> In general, it's best to avoid attribute names that match any of the most common Objective-C method names, and specifically any of NSObject's methods.

Next, change the type of the orderDate attribute to Date. When you change the type, additional fields appear to let you specify constraints and an initial value, as shown in Figure 3.9.

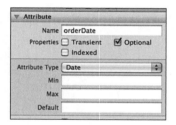

FIGURE 3.9   Changing the type of the orderDate attribute

The Default text field can be used to specify an initial value for the attribute, which will automatically be set whenever a new managed object instance is created. For a Date attribute, this field is used to set a date based on a natural language string, so you can either specify an unambiguous date such as "January 9, 2007 10:30 PST", or a more obscure date reference like "yesterday at lunchtime" (yes, this really does work!).

Sadly, at the time of writing, anything you put in this default field will be interpreted at compile time. This will work just fine for specific dates, but natural language strings won't behave as you'd expect. You might think that setting the initial value to "now" would ensure that whenever a new customer order object is created, the orderDate would automatically be set to the current date and time, but in fact it will be set to the *compile time of the project*.

NOTE

If you do need to set the date and time of a newly inserted managed object, you would either need to use a managed object subclass to set the date in `awakeFromInsert`, or set the date manually after inserting an object, just like the `timeStamp` property is set in the standard template project from the last chapter.

Core Data Attribute Types

The popup menu of available types for Core Data attributes is shown in Figure 3.10.

FIGURE 3.10   Available attribute types in Core Data

The *Undefined* type is the default type when you create a new attribute in the modeler; if you leave a persistent attribute type as undefined, you will receive errors when you try and compile your project.

The other attributes generally correspond to the data types typical for traditional databases; when working with currency amounts, it's worth noting that the *Decimal* type is usually the best option to avoid any problems with *Float* and *Double* rounding issues.

The *Transformable* attribute type is used to indicate that Core Data should use an `NSValueTransformer` to convert between the value to be stored and the actual binary data that gets persisted. If you don't specify the name of a value transformer, Core Data will use the `NSValueTransformer` defined as `NSKeyedUnarchiveFromDataTransformerName`. Chapter 6 covers Transformable attributes in more detail.

Creating Additional Entities

So that you have some additional entities ready for creating relationships in the next section, add a new entity to your model, called `OrderItem`, with the following attributes:

▶ A `Decimal` attribute called `purchasePrice` with a default value of 1.0.

▶ An `Integer16` attribute called `quantity` with a default value of 1.

Add another new entity called Product, with the following attributes:

▶ A String attribute called name.

▶ A Decimal attribute called itemCost with a default value of 1.0.

Click and drag the visual representations of your entities in the Graph editor style so your data model looks like Figure 3.11.

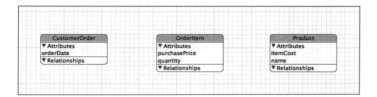

FIGURE 3.11   The data model with several entities defined

Creating Relationships

Now that you have multiple entities defined, it's time to add some relationships between them.

In Xcode 4, it's easiest to create relationships using the Table editor style. Select an entity then click the + button at the bottom of the Relationships list.[5] Start by creating a new relationship on the CustomerOrder entity. The general inspector panel for a relationship is shown in Figure 3.12.

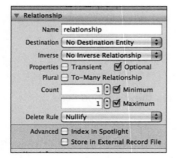

FIGURE 3.12   The Relationship inspector panel in the data modeler

[5] In Xcode 3, relationships are created in the same way as attributes—select an entity before clicking the + button in the Property list and choosing Relationship from the popup menu, or right-click (or Control-click) on an entity and choose Add Relationship.

Use the Name text field to change the name of the relationship to orderItems. The convention for relationship names is similar to attributes, but this time you *should* pluralize the name of the relationship for a *to-many* relationship. Generally, it's helpful to name a relationship so it indicates the name of the related entity; in this case, the OrderItem entity.

Use the Destination drop-down box to set the relationship destination to the OrderItem entity. The Inverse drop-down box is used to set the name of a relationship defined on the OrderItem entity that represents the opposite end of this orderItems relationship. Since you haven't yet defined any relationships for the OrderItem entity, you'll need to skip this step for now.

Because a CustomerOrder can have many orderItems, check the To-Many Relationship box. This will enable the Minimum and Maximum Count text fields, which are used to set constraints on relationships such as that a customer order must have at least 1 order item, but fewer than 50. Leave these blank to indicate that there are no constraints on the relationship.

The last drop-down in the inspector is used to set the Delete Rule; this sets what happens to any related managed objects when the object is deleted. The various values are described in Chapter 4, "Basic Storing and Fetching."

Next, select the OrderItem entity and create a new relationship called customerOrder. Set its destination to be the CustomerOrder entity. Since any particular order item belongs to only one customer order, this is *not* a to-many relationship; the name of the relationship is singular, and the To-Many Relationship box needs to remain unchecked.

If you use the Graph editor style to display the visual representation of your model, you'll find that there are currently two separate arrows joining the CustomerOrder and OrderItem entities, as shown in Figure 3.13.

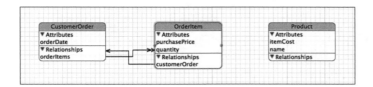

FIGURE 3.13   Two separate relationship arrows between entities in the data modeler

At the moment, the relationships are unidirectional, indicated by the fact that the arrows have their arrowheads on only one end. Note that the relationship from CustomerOrder to OrderItem has a double arrowhead, indicating that it is a to-many relationship.

Now that you have defined the two relationships, you can specify that one relationship is the inverse of the other. Click the customerOrder relationship, and use the Inverse drop-down to select the opposing relationship, orderItems. The two arrows in the visual representation will change into one arrow, with arrowheads on each end, indicating a one-to-one relationship between the entities.

Specifying the inverse relationship means that when you set a value on one side of a relationship, Core Data will handle the opposing side: when you add an order item to a customer order (i.e., add an `OrderItem` to the `orderItems` relationship), Core Data automatically sets the `OrderItem`'s `customerOrder` relationship as well.

Creating the Remaining Relationships

Now that you know how to set relationships between entities, finish the data model by creating additional relationships between the other entities so your model looks like Figure 3.14.

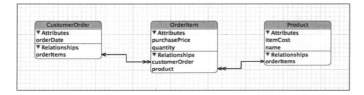

FIGURE 3.14   The data model with relationships set correctly between the entities in the data modeler

---

NOTE

The display of items in the graph is only an aid to help visualize entities and their relationships. It won't matter to Core Data whether you spend hours aligning all the entity boxes perfectly, or just leave them all piled on top of each other!

Summary

You should now have a complete understanding of the Data Modeler tool in Xcode. You've seen how to create entities and attributes, and how to define bidirectional relationships between the entities.

You've also seen that traditional normalization principles don't always apply when designing Core Data models; it's often the case that you'll need to denormalize your data model for performance and memory reasons.

In the next chapter, you'll put your Core Data model knowledge into practice by creating a new managed object model for a simple iOS application. You'll learn how to work with the Core Data framework to create new managed objects and save them into the persistent store. You'll then learn how to fetch those items back out again, ready for display in a table view.

PART II

Working with Core Data

The second part of the book focuses on a discussion of topics that apply to most applications wanting to make use of Core Data on iOS. Each facet of the framework or its related technologies is given a separate chapter so it is possible either to read this part of the book in order, building knowledge in incremental steps, or to pick out the chapters that are of particular interest. Each of these chapters is divided into two sections: the first introduces the particular feature or functionality, discusses why and when it might be useful, then walks through the relevant classes and methods; the second section is written in a tutorial format that starts by adding a basic feature to a simple application, before building on more advanced functionality. The aim of these tutorial sections is to enable you to learn by doing, but in such a way that you relate the same techniques to your own applications.

Basic Storing and Fetching

Back in Chapter 2, "A Core Data Primer," you learned the basic terms and underlying features in the Core Data framework. You saw how a persistent store coordinator is set up to talk to a SQLite persistent store, and how a managed object context can then be created to act as a *scratchpad* for the managed objects pulled from the store.

In this chapter you'll see how new managed objects are created in a managed object context, based on the entity descriptions you define in the managed object model. You'll learn how these new objects are stored on disk in the persistent store when the managed object context is told to save. Once you have some objects in the store, you'll learn how to fetch those objects, displaying them in a simple table view.

Creating New Managed Objects

Chapter 3, "Modeling Your Data," covered some best practices for designing a managed object model. Let's say that you have designed a document model for keeping track of patients and doctors. You might end up with a model that looks something like Figure 4.1.

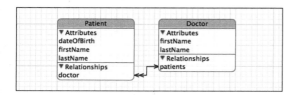

FIGURE 4.1   A simple object model

To create a new Patient object, you need to tell a managed object context to create a new object for the `Patient` entity. Core Data then returns a newly instantiated managed object, setting any default values specified in the model, ready for you to assign attributes as necessary.

When creating a managed object described by the information in the entity description, you can use the class method `insertNewObjectForEntityForName:inManagedObject Context:` provided by the `NSEntityDescription` class. Pass this method a string containing the name of the entity and a managed object context in which to create the new object. You will end up with code like Listing 4.1.

LISTING 4.1   Creating a new managed object

```
NSManagedObjectContext *context; // Taken from the application delegate

NSManagedObject *newPatient = [NSEntityDescription
                        insertNewObjectForEntityForName:@"Patient"
                            inManagedObjectContext:context];
```

If you insert an object using this call, it won't be saved to disk until you tell the managed object context to `save:`. Before the context is saved, the object exists only in memory.

Once you have created a managed object, set its attributes using Key-Value Coding. The code to set a patient's basic information would look something like Listing 4.2.

LISTING 4.2   Setting attributes for a managed object

```
NSManagedObject *practiceDoctor; // Assuming you have already fetched this

[newPatient setValue:@"John" forKey:@"firstName"];
[newPatient setValue:@"Doe" forKey:@"lastName"];
[newPatient setValue:practiceDoctor forKey:@"doctor"];
```

Notice that the patient-doctor *relationship* is set in exactly the same way as the patient *attributes*; simply by providing the Doctor object as a value to be set for the relationship's key.

Saving the Context

Once you've set the attributes on your managed object, you'll want to save it to the persistent store. This is as easy as calling `save:` on the managed object context. When you tell the context to save, any outstanding changes will be persisted (i.e., saved) to disk, whether they are newly-created objects, changes made to existing objects that you've fetched from the store, or objects deleted altogether. Until you choose to save the context, the underlying data remains unaffected by what's happening in the context.

It's important to note that it is your responsibility to decide when and how frequently to save changes from a context. If you were creating a document-based application on the desktop, it might make sense to save changes to disk when the user chooses the Save command in the application, or when the application exits. For an iOS application, however, the situation is a little different.

Under earlier iOS versions that don't support multitasking, it's absolutely essential for an application to be able to exit as quickly as possible, so you need to save the majority of changes *before* it's time to quit. If you have a large number of unsaved changes in a context when the application is exiting, it might take too long to write these changes to disk—the operating system might decide your app is taking too long to exit and kill it before the context has finished saving.

Under iOS 4+ multitasking on newer devices, your app may end up running indefinitely. If you don't save frequently, you run the risk of the phone crashing (obviously because of some other developer's application) and losing all unpersisted changes. Alternatively, your app may need to be terminated while it's suspended, and again you don't want to have to do very much work at this point.

Listing 4.3 shows the complete code necessary to create a new object, set its attributes and relationships, and save it to disk.

LISTING 4.3   Creating and saving a new object

```
NSManagedObject *practiceDoctor; // Assume you have already fetched this
NSManagedObject *newPatient = [NSEntityDescription
                        insertNewObjectForEntityForName:@"Patient"
                                   inManagedObjectContext:context];
[newPatient setValue:@"Jane" forKey:@"firstName"];
[newPatient setValue:@"Robinson" forKey:@"lastName"];
[newPatient setValue:practiceDoctor forKey:@"doctor"];

NSError *anyError = nil;
BOOL savedSuccessfully = [context save:&anyError];
if( !savedSuccessfully ) { /* do something with anyError */ }
```

If there is a problem in saving the context's changes, the call to save: will return NO, and provide you with an NSError object describing the problem. A save on a context might fail for a number of reasons, including validation failures or problems accessing the persistent store. If the save succeeds, the method will return YES.

Note that you should always check the Boolean value returned by save: to see if there is an error—don't just check to see whether anyError was set during the save attempt.

Fetching Saved Managed Objects

Once you've saved your objects into the persistent store, you'll need to be able to fetch them back again. Typically, you create a Fetch Request, specify which entity to fetch, and pass the request to a managed object context. The results are returned to you as an array of managed objects within that context, as shown in Listing 4.4.

LISTING 4.4   Creating and executing a Fetch Request

```
NSFetchRequest *request = [[NSFetchRequest alloc] init];

NSEntityDescription *entity =
                [NSEntityDescription entityForName:@"Patient"
                            inManagedObjectContext:context];
[request setEntity:entity];

NSError *anyError = nil;
NSArray *fetchedObjects = [context executeFetchRequest:request
                                                 error:&anyError];
[request release];
if( fetchedObjects == nil ) { /* do something with anyError */ }
```

The code in Listing 4.4 executes a fetch request that returns *all* the Patient objects from the persistent store. If you only want to fetch objects that match certain criteria, you can set a Fetch Predicate to specify the conditions to be met by any fetched objects. To return all the patients for a specified doctor, for example, you could use code similar to Listing 4.5.

LISTING 4.5   Using a Fetch Predicate

```
NSManagedObject *practiceDoctor; // Assuming you have already fetched this

NSFetchRequest *request = [[NSFetchRequest alloc] init];
NSEntityDescription *entity =
                [NSEntityDescription entityForName:@"Patient"
                            inManagedObjectContext:context];
[request setEntity:entity];

NSPredicate *predicate = [NSPredicate
        predicateWithFormat:@"doctor = %@", practiceDoctor];
[request setPredicate:predicate];

NSError *anyError = nil;
NSArray *fetchedObjects = [context executeFetchRequest:request
                                                 error:&anyError];
```

```
[request release];
if( fetchedObjects == nil ) { /* Do something with anyError */ }
```

Note that `executeFetchRequest:error:` will always return an array if the fetch succeeded. If no objects match the predicate, you'll receive an empty array; if an error occurs, the method will return `nil`. As with `save:`, don't assume that `anyError` will only be set if there's an error—always check for a `nil` return value before doing anything with `anyError`.

As you learned back in Chapter 2, Core Data does not maintain any order. When you execute a fetch request, the objects almost certainly won't be returned to you in the same order as they were inserted. Usually, you'll want to specify one or more sort descriptors for a fetch request, using code like that in Listing 4.6.

LISTING 4.6   Using sort descriptors

```
NSFetchRequest *request = [[NSFetchRequest alloc] init];
NSEntityDescription *entity =
                [NSEntityDescription entityForName:@"Patient"
                            inManagedObjectContext:context];
[request setEntity:entity];

NSSortDescriptor *sortLastName = [[NSSortDescriptor alloc]
                        initWithKey:@"lastName" ascending:YES];
NSSortDescriptor *sortFirstName = [[NSSortDescriptor alloc]
                        initWithKey:@"firstName" ascending:YES];
NSArray *sortDescriptors =
     [NSArray arrayWithObjects:sortLastName, sortFirstName, nil];
[request setSortDescriptors:sortDescriptors];
[sortLastName release]; [sortFirstName release];

NSError *anyError = nil;
NSArray *fetchedObjects = [context executeFetchRequest:request
                                                error:&anyError];
[request release];
if( fetchedObjects == nil ) { /* do something with anyError */ }
```

This time, the code in Listing 4.6 fetches *all* the `Patient` objects from the store, but sorts them in ascending alphabetical order by last name, then first name.

Deleting Managed Objects

Once you've fetched a managed object, you can delete it from its managed object context using the `deleteObject:` method provided by the context, as shown in Listing 4.7.

LISTING 4.7   Deleting a managed object

```
NSManagedObject *somePatient; // Assuming you have already fetched this

[context deleteObject:somePatient];

NSError *anyError = nil;
BOOL success = [context save:&anyError];

if( !success ) { /* Do something with anyError */ }
```

The object won't be removed from the underlying persistent store on disk until the context is saved, using the `save:` method.

When you delete an object, the Delete Rules that you set for the entity in the managed object model dictate how any relationships are affected:

▶ For a delete rule set to `Nullify`, any other objects with a relationship to the deleted object will have those relationships set to `nil`. For a to-many relationship, the deleted object will just be removed from the collection of related items.

▶ For a delete rule set to `Cascade`, any other objects with a relationship to the deleted object will also be deleted, as will related (with a Cascade delete rule) objects to the secondary object, and so on.

▶ For a delete rule set to `Deny`, if there are any related objects, the delete will be denied altogether.

▶ For a delete rule set to `No Action`, any other objects with a relationship to the deleted object will be left unchanged. This means that they will have a relationship pointing to a non-existent object, which is something best avoided without good reason!

Working with Table Views

Now let's look at how to implement a basic storing and fetching mechanism in a simple table view-based application. The application you'll create is shown in Figure 4.2.

This Random Dates application picks random dates when the + button is pressed. It displays both the date and the weekday name in a table view, and stores the date and day name information in a Core Data store. The Random Dates application isn't particularly useful, but it gives you the opportunity to work with the information from earlier in the chapter.

FIGURE 4.2   The Random Dates application in the simulator

DOWNLOAD THE XCODE PROJECT

An Xcode project for this application can be downloaded from **http://www.informit. com/title/9780321670427**.

It might help to get a feel for the application you're about to build, so download and open the Random Dates project in Xcode, then build it. Launch the app in the simulator and press the + button. A date will appear in the table view, along with the relevant weekday name. Each time you press the + button, additional random date objects will be created and displayed in the table view, sorted in ascending date order. You can remove dates either by using the Edit button and deleting rows, or by swiping your finger across a row and clicking the Delete button.

The date objects are saved to the store when they are added, so if you exit the application and re-launch, all the dates that were in the table view when you exited will reappear.

Close the simulator and the Random Dates Xcode project when you are finished.

The Random Dates Application Project

Now that you've seen how the Random Dates application works, let's create a new Xcode project and build it from scratch:

1. Create a new project in Xcode, using File > New > New Project (Shift-⌘-N).

2. Under iOS, select Navigation-based application.

3. Name the application Random Dates, and tick the Use Core Data checkbox.

You saw the template project created by Xcode back in Chapter 2; it makes use of a Fetched Results Controller object to handle fetching and displaying objects from the persistent store (you'll learn more about the fetched results controller in Chapter 5). Since the point of this chapter is to learn how to execute fetch requests yourself, you can delete the existing `RootViewController.h` and `.m` files from the Xcode project navigator to start from scratch.

Once you've removed the existing `RootViewController` files, select File > New > New File (⌘-N) to create a new `UIViewController` subclass. Choose to create a subclass of `UITableViewController`, so you end up with suitable table view data source and delegate methods in the implementation, and call the class `RootViewController`.

The Random Dates Data Model

The data model (that's the `Random_Dates.xcdatamodeld` file) provided by the template project contains a single entity, `Event`, with a single attribute, `timeStamp`. Delete this entity from the data model by selecting it in the Entity list and pressing the Delete key so you have a blank model slate to work with.

Add a new entity to the model, named `RandomDate`. Add in the following two attributes to this new entity:

▶ date, which is a Date attribute type

▶ dayName, which is a String attribute type

Your data model will look like Figure 4.3.

FIGURE 4.3   The Random Dates application data model

Basic RootViewController Behavior

To display the RandomDate objects in the table view, you'll need to fetch from the Core Data store. As you've already seen, you'll need to have access to a Managed Object Context, so add one to the @interface of the Root View Controller. You'll store the objects that you fetch into an array, so you'll also need to have access to an array object. With the relevant property declarations in place, the interface file will look like Listing 4.8.

LISTING 4.8   The RootViewController class description

RootViewController.h

```
@interface RootViewController : UITableViewController {
    NSManagedObjectContext *managedObjectContext;
    NSArray *datesArray;
}

@property (nonatomic, retain)
            NSManagedObjectContext *managedObjectContext;
@property (nonatomic, retain) NSArray *datesArray;

@end
```

> **NOTE**
>
> Don't forget to @synthesize the properties inside the RootViewController.m implementation, and release the instance variables in dealloc.

If you take a look in the template-generated Random_DatesAppDelegate.m file, you'll find that the awakeFromNib method uses standard behavior to get the root view controller from the top of the navigation stack, and sets its managedObjectContext property to the application delegate's managed object context, as shown in Listing 4.9.

LISTING 4.9   Passing around the managedObjectContext

Random_DatesAppDelegate.m

```
- (void)awakeFromNib {
    RootViewController *rootViewController =
      (RootViewController *)[navigationController topViewController];
    rootViewController.managedObjectContext =
                                      self.managedObjectContext;
}
```

That's great! You don't need to make any changes here since the template project is already set up for you. This also gives you a clue as to how you would work with multiple view controllers; you need to pass each controller a pointer to the managed object context.

Now that you know where the managed object context is coming from, you can use it to insert a new `RandomDate` managed object. Change back to the `RootViewController.m` file and find the `viewDidLoad` method (uncomment it if necessary). Also uncomment the line that adds an Edit button to the navigation items, changing it to the `leftBarButtonItem`, before adding code to display an Add button as well, that will call an `addNewRandomDate` method, as shown in Listing 4.10.

LISTING 4.10   Displaying the Add button

RootViewController.m

```
- (void)viewDidLoad {
    [super viewDidLoad];

    self.navigationItem.leftBarButton = self.editButtonItem;

    UIBarButtonItem *addButton = [[UIBarButtonItem alloc]
            initWithBarButtonSystemItem:UIBarButtonSystemItemAdd
                            target:self
                            action:@selector(addNewRandomDate)];

    self.navigationItem.rightBarButtonItem = addButton;
    [addButton release];
}
```

You'll need to write the `addNewRandomDate` method to insert a new managed object into the context, described by the `RandomDate` entity, using the code given in Listing 4.11. This listing also shows how to assign a random date value to the date attribute, and uses a date formatter to extract the full name of the day (i.e., Monday, Tuesday, Wednesday, etc.), which is then assigned to the `dayName` attribute.

LISTING 4.11   Adding a new RandomDate object

```
- (void)addNewRandomDate {
    NSManagedObject *newRandomDate = [NSEntityDescription
                insertNewObjectForEntityForName:@"RandomDate"
                        inManagedObjectContext:managedObjectContext];

    NSDateFormatter *dateFormatter = [[[NSDateFormatter alloc] init] autorelease];
    [dateFormatter setTimeStyle:NSDateFormatterNoStyle];
    [dateFormatter setDateFormat:@"EEEE"];

    NSDate *date = [NSDate dateWithTimeIntervalSince1970:arc4random()];
    NSString *dayName = [dateFormatter stringFromDate:date];

    [newRandomDate setValue:date forKey:@"date"];
    [newRandomDate setValue:dayName forKey:@"dayName"];
```

```
    NSError *anyError = nil;
    BOOL success = [managedObjectContext save:&anyError];
    if( !success ) { NSLog(@"Error = %@", anyError) };
}
```

Listing 4.11 also tells the managed object context to save:, checks that the save is successful and, if not, logs any error message to the Console.

Fetching the Random Date Objects

To display the random dates in the table view, the randomDates array needs to contain the
results of a fetch request. Add a new method at the top of the RootViewController.m
implementation, called fetchRandomDates. The method needs to create a new fetch
request for the RandomDate entity and, since it might be nice to display the dates in
ascending order, it should specify a suitable sort descriptor. The method then needs to
assign the results of the fetch to the datesArray instance variable. Your method will look
like Listing 4.12.

LISTING 4.12   Fetching the RandomDate objects

```
- (void)fetchRandomDates {
    NSFetchRequest *request = [[[NSFetchRequest alloc] init]autorelease];
    [request setEntity:[NSEntityDescription entityForName:@"RandomDate"
                        inManagedObjectContext:managedObjectContext]];

    NSSortDescriptor *sortDescriptor = [[NSSortDescriptor alloc]
                                        initWithKey:@"date"
                                        ascending:YES];
    [request setSortDescriptors:[NSArray
                                arrayWithObject:sortDescriptor]];
    [sortDescriptor release];

    // Release the datesArray, if it already exists
    if( datesArray ) {
        self.datesArray = nil;
    }

    NSError *anyError = nil;
    NSArray *results =
            [managedObjectContext executeFetchRequest:request
                                        error:&anyError];
    if( !results ) {
        NSLog(@"Error = %@", anyError);
    } else {
        self.datesArray = results;
```

```
    }

    [self.tableView reloadData];
}
```

This code checks to see whether an array was returned and, if not, displays the error in the console. It also tells the table view to reload its data. Assuming that you haven't changed anything in the `RootViewController.xib` file created by the original project template, the `tableView` outlet provided by `UITableViewController` should already be connected to the table view in the xib file.

You need to fetch the dates from the store when the view first loads, and whenever a new random date object is added. Add a call to `[self fetchRandomDates];` at the end of both the `viewDidLoad` method, and the `addNewRandomDate` method.

You should also release the array in the `viewDidUnload` method. In an application with multiple view controllers, you don't want each view controller to retain large arrays of information unless absolutely necessary, given the limited memory on an iOS device.

Displaying the RandomDate Objects

Start by changing the `numberOfSectionsInTableView:` method to return 1, and modify the `tableView:numberOfRowsInSection:` method to return the number of items in the `datesArray` array, as shown in Listing 4.13.

To display the `RandomDate` objects, you can make use of a `Subtitle`-style table cell, which allows you to display two different strings in one cell. If you wish, you can use an `NSDateFormatter` to display the date in the cell; the code in Listing 4.13 just uses the default date display provided by its `description` method for simplicity. To access the relevant object in the `datesArray`, you just need to ask for the object at the index of the current row.

LISTING 4.13   Displaying the RandomDate objects

```
- (NSInteger)tableView:(UITableView *)tableView
              numberOfRowsInSection:(NSInteger)section {

    return [datesArray count];
}

- (UITableViewCell *)tableView:(UITableView *)tableView
           cellForRowAtIndexPath:(NSIndexPath *)indexPath {

    static NSString *CellIdentifier = @"Cell";
```

```
UITableViewCell *cell =
    [tableView dequeueReusableCellWithIdentifier:CellIdentifier];
if (cell == nil) {
    cell = [[[UITableViewCell alloc]
                    initWithStyle:UITableViewCellStyleSubtitle
                 reuseIdentifier:CellIdentifier] autorelease];
}

// Configure the cell...
NSManagedObject *object =
                    [datesArray objectAtIndex:[indexPath row]];
cell.textLabel.text = [[object valueForKey:@"date"] description];
cell.detailTextLabel.text = [object valueForKey:@"dayName"];

return cell;
}
```

When you build and run the application this time, you should find that the objects are
displayed in the table view, as expected. Figure 4.4 shows the Random Dates application
in its current state.

FIGURE 4.4   The Random Dates application displaying the stored random dates

Deleting the RandomDate Objects

Since you enabled the Edit button in the navigation bar (see Listing 4.10), the view controller offers a default behavior to the user in deleting objects from the table view. At the moment, nothing happens when a user asks to delete a row from the table since you haven't written the relevant delegate methods. Let's correct this now.

Start by uncommenting the template file's tableView:commitEditingStyle:forRowAtIndexPath: method, and implement it with the code in Listing 4.14.

LISTING 4.14   Deleting RandomDate objects from the table view

RootViewController.m

```
- (void)tableView:(UITableView *)tableView
        commitEditingStyle:(UITableViewCellEditingStyle)editingStyle
        forRowAtIndexPath:(NSIndexPath *)indexPath {

    if (editingStyle == UITableViewCellEditingStyleDelete) {
        // Delete the row from the data source
        NSManagedObject *objectToDelete =
                        [datesArray objectAtIndex:[indexPath row]];

        [managedObjectContext deleteObject:objectToDelete];

        [self fetchRandomDates];
    }
}
```

You should now be able to delete dates either by using the Edit button, or by swiping across a row with your finger.

Custom Managed Object Sub-Classes

So far, you've seen how to work with an object's attributes using KVC methods, such as valueForKey: and setValue:forKey:. Each object you've created up until now has been an instance of NSManagedObject, and while the functionality provided by NSManagedObject is great for object persistence and fetching, in the real world you will probably need your model objects to do more than just persist into a store.

Core Data offers you the ability to specify your own custom classes for your managed objects, which need to inherit from NSManagedObject. Once you've defined the attributes in the data model, you can provide accessor methods on your custom subclass, or @property declarations, or even class factory methods to return a newly-created object in a provided managed object context. Chapter 6, "Working with Managed Objects," covers custom subclasses in more detail, showing you how you can define Transient attributes, or attributes that *aren't* persisted in the store, and how to do complicated *validation* based on multiple attributes or even across relationships.

As an introduction to custom subclasses, consider a class description like the one in Listing 4.15.

LISTING 4.15   The interface for a custom managed object subclass

```
@interface Patient : NSManagedObject
{
}

@property (nonatomic, retain) NSString *firstName;
@property (nonatomic, retain) NSString *lastName;
@property (assign) NSManagedObject *doctor;

+ (id)patientInManagedObjectContext:(NSManagedObjectContext *)context;

@end
```

By defining properties on the Patient object, you now have a number of options to access its attributes. Since your custom subclass inherits from NSManagedObject, you can still access its attributes and relationships using KVC. Assuming you have set up the @property declarations and synthesized the accessor methods for those properties, you also have the option of using either accessor methods, or dot syntax. Each of the statements in Listing 4.16 accomplishes the same thing.

LISTING 4.16   Setting the attributes on a custom managed object subclass

```
[somePatient setValue:@"John" forKey:@"firstName"];
[somePatient setFirstName:@"John"];
somePatient.firstName = @"John";
```

And, as an alternative to using NSEntityDescription whenever you want to insert new objects, you can place this code in a class factory method, like the one shown in Listing 4.17.

LISTING 4.17   A class factory method for a managed object

```
+ (id)patientInManagedObjectContext:(NSManagedObjectContext *)context
{
    return [NSEntityDescription insertNewObjectForEntityForName:@"Patient"
                                    inManagedObjectContext:context];
}
```

```
// Means you can create new Patient objects like this:
Patient *newPatient = [Patient patientInManagedObjectContext:context];
```

Notice that you don't need to do anything different for Core Data to instantiate your custom subclass rather than NSManagedObject. Provided you have set the name of the class used by your managed object in the data model, NSEntityDescription will always return the correct class of object for that entity.

Creating and Setting a Custom Class for a Managed Object

Let's use a custom subclass for the RandomDate objects in the application from the Working with Table Views section.

Open up the Random_Dates.xcdatamodeld file in the Xcode Data Modeler and select the RandomDate entity. In the Data Modeler, you'll find that you have the option to specify a Class in the Entity Inspector. Change the class from NSManagedObject to AWRandomDate (remember that it's best to prefix your class names, though not your entity names), as shown in Figure 4.5.

FIGURE 4.5   Setting the Entity's Class to RandomDate

There are several ways to define your custom subclass; you could obviously create a new class from scratch and add in the relevant property declarations, but Xcode provides you with an easier way. Make sure that the RandomDate entity is selected in the model editor, and select File > New > New File (⌘-N).

In the New File sheet (shown in Figure 4.6), select the NSManagedObject subclass template and click Next. You'll be asked for the location to save the file and to specify the relevant target information. Click Create to accept the default options.

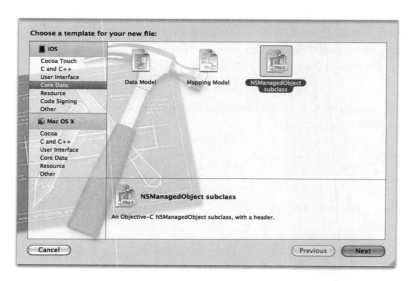

FIGURE 4.6   Creating a new Managed Object Class File

If you choose to create a Managed Object Class without selecting an entity in the model editor, you'll see a sheet asking you to select a data model file. Select the Random_Dates model and click Next, and you'll see the sheet shown in Figure 4.7. This sheet allows you to specify which entities you want Xcode to use when generating class files.

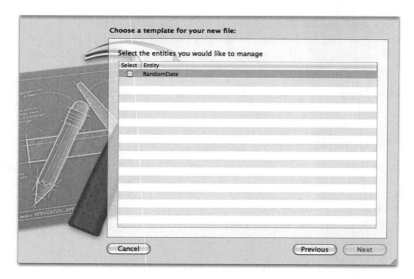

FIGURE 4.7   The Managed Object Class Generator

NOTE

Under Xcode 3, the Managed Object Class file template will only appear in the New File window if an entity was selected in the modeler prior to choosing File > New File.

When you specify and press Create, Xcode will auto-generate AWRandomDate.m and .h files, with the class description shown in Listing 4.18.

LISTING 4.18   The RandomDate class description

AWRandomDate.h

```
@interface AWRandomDate :  NSManagedObject {
@private
}

@property (nonatomic, retain) NSDate * date;
@property (nonatomic, retain) NSString * dayName;

@end
```

If you switch to the AWRandomDate.m file, you'll find that the properties are specified using the @dynamic keyword, which means the accessor methods will be available at runtime (provided automatically by NSManagedObject). This behavior is discussed further in Chapter 6, "Working with Managed Objects."

For a basic managed object subclass, the files generated by Xcode are all you will need. Let's make use of the new properties on our managed object subclass back in the RootViewController methods. You'll need to #import the AWRandomDate.h file at the top of the RootViewController.m file.

Start by changing the addNewRandomDate method so it uses the AWRandomDate class, as shown in Listing 4.19.

LISTING 4.19   Modifying the addNewRandomDate method

RootViewController.m

```
- (void)addNewRandomDate {
    AWRandomDate *newRandomDate = [NSEntityDescription
            insertNewObjectForEntityForName:@"RandomDate"
                    inManagedObjectContext:managedObjectContext];

    NSDateFormatter *dateFormatter = [[[NSDateFormatter alloc] init] autorelease];
    [dateFormatter setTimeStyle:NSDateFormatterNoStyle];
    [dateFormatter setDateFormat:@"EEEE"];
```

```
    NSDate *date = [NSDate dateWithTimeIntervalSince1970:rand()];
    NSString *dayName = [dateFormatter stringFromDate:date];

    newRandomDate.date = date;
    newRandomDate.dayName = dayName;

    NSError *anyError = nil;
    BOOL success = [managedObjectContext save:&anyError];
    if( !success ) NSLog(@"Error = %@", anyError);

    [self fetchRandomDates];
}
```

Next, change the `tableView:cellForRowAtIndexPath:` method, as shown in Listing 4.20.

LISTING 4.20   Modifying the cellForRowAtIndexPath: method

```
- (UITableViewCell *)tableView:(UITableView *)tableView
            cellForRowAtIndexPath:(NSIndexPath *)indexPath {

    static NSString *CellIdentifier = @"Cell";

    UITableViewCell *cell =
        [tableView dequeueReusableCellWithIdentifier:CellIdentifier];
    if (cell == nil) {
        cell = [[[UITableViewCell alloc]
                        initWithStyle:UITableViewCellStyleSubtitle
                        reuseIdentifier:CellIdentifier] autorelease];
    }

    // Configure the cell...
    AWRandomDate *object = [datesArray objectAtIndex:[indexPath row]];
    cell.textLabel.text = [object.date description];
    cell.detailTextLabel.text = object.dayName;

    return cell;
}
```

If you build and run the application, you should find that it behaves exactly as before, but now it uses the custom subclass instead of `NSManagedObject`.

You might like to test your understanding of managed object creation by adding a class factory method to the `AWRandomDate` class called `randomDateInManagedObjectContext:`. You could then move the code that provides the initial values for the random date object out of the `addNewRandomDate` method and into this new class factory method.

Summary

As far as performance in the Random Dates application is concerned, it's worth noting that it's not terribly efficient to fetch all the objects from the store *every* time a new object is added or deleted. You'll notice significant performance issues if you add large numbers of objects to the array, particularly on older iOS devices.

Ideally, you would only fetch in the rows necessary for display in the table view when they were needed. If you were only displaying the first 20 or so items, it doesn't make much sense to load in 6,000 items that might be in the persistent store. It would also be better to insert new objects directly into the table view, and remove objects on a row-by-row basis rather than reloading the whole table view every time a change is made.

In the next chapter, you'll see how to use a Fetched Results Controller to supply information to a table view as efficiently as possible, only loading in the rows necessary for display, and handling changes on a row-by-row basis.

CHAPTER 5

Using NSFetchedResults-Controller

In Chapter 4, "Basic Storing and Fetching," you saw how to fetch objects from the persistent store using an instance of NSFetchRequest. You created an application that displayed fetched objects in a table view; each time a new object was added, the fetch request was executed again in order to refresh the values to display. This is clearly not an efficient way to display large numbers of objects—having to re-fetch the data *and* refresh the entire table view any time information is changed could cause serious performance issues to arise.

One way of writing the application might be to make it so newly-created items are added directly into the cached array whenever the + button was tapped. The benefit here is that the app wouldn't have to reload the entire set of objects every time it was launched. You could then tell the table view to insert the new object at a specified index, which would make much better sense for performance in an iOS application.

If it is only possible to insert objects through a single button then this probably isn't a problem. If your application later adds functionality to insert objects in other ways, perhaps loading them in the background from a RESTful webservice, the application and code could soon get over-complicated and messy.

As an alternative solution, Apple offers iOS developers the NSFetchedResultsController, which keeps track of the results of a fetch request and provides suitable methods to act as a table view data source. The controller also notices when relevant objects are added or removed in its managed object context, and alerts the table view so that it can react accordingly.

Introducing NSFetchedResultsController

With iPhone OS 3.0, Apple added a new controller for the Core Data framework, currently available *only* under iOS, the NSFetchedResultsController. This controller is designed to act as an intermediary between a table view and a fetch request, behaving as efficiently as possible in serving the data required by the table view's data source methods. Rather than maintaining your own cached array of values fetched from the store, the fetched results controller keeps its own private cache of information. The benefit here is that you can just defer requests from the table view straight to the controller.

NSFetchedResultsController also has the benefit of loading rows in batches. Typically, a batch would contain the number of objects needed to fill the onscreen rows of a table view. For a table view that displays 20 rows out of a possible 6,000, this is obviously a huge advantage over the fetch suggested by the last chapter. When the table view first appears, the initial fetch would only be for the first 20 rows, rather than the entire 6,000.

If the user scrolls the table view, additional objects are fetched from the persistent store (in batches) as required. Naturally, this offers a sizeable performance benefit and if the application receives a low memory warning, the controller will react and automatically purge unnecessary objects from memory.

> **NOTE**
>
> It is possible to fetch in batches manually without using a fetched results controller, by specifying a fetchLimit and fetchOffset on a fetch request. Given the complication of working out which offset relates to which row in which batch, it's easier just to let NSFetchedResultsController do the hard work.

The other major benefit from using a fetched results controller is that it can recognize when changes have been made to objects in a managed object context and notify a delegate that it should insert, reload or remove certain rows in a table view. Again, rather than having to reload the entire table view when a new object is inserted, the fetched results controller can alert your UITableViewController that it should just deal with a single row at a specified index.

Creating an NSFetchedResultsController

As a fetched results controller is designed to provide data to a table view, you would typically create a controller as an instance variable in a UITableViewController, and generate it lazily as shown in Listing 5.1.

LISTING 5.1   Generating an NSFetchedResultsController

```
- (NSFetchedResultsController *)fetchedResultsController {
    if (!fetchedResultsController ) {
```

```
        NSFetchRequest *request = [[NSFetchRequest alloc] init];
        [request setEntity:[NSEntityDescription
                                      entityForName:@"Patient"
                           inManagedObjectContext:context]];

        [request setBatchSize:20];

        NSSortDescriptor *sortDescriptor = [[NSSortDescriptor alloc]
                                            initWithKey:@"lastName"
                                              ascending:YES];
        [request setSortDescriptors:[NSArray
                             arrayWithObject:sortDescriptor]];
        [sortDescriptor release];

        NSFetchedResultsController *newController =
                [[NSFetchedResultsController alloc]
                          initWithFetchRequest:request
                          managedObjectContext:context
                            sectionNameKeyPath:@"doctor.fullName"
                                     cacheName:@"patientsCache"];

        newController.delegate = self;
        self.fetchedResultsController = newController;
        [newController release];
        [request release];
    }

    return fetchedResultsController;
}
```

Notice from Listing 5.1 how you pass a standard fetch request to the fetched results controller. The fetch request is created in exactly the same way as before, but *must have at least one sort descriptor*. Listing 5.1 also sets the delegate on the fetched results controller; you'll need to implement some extra methods in your view controller, as shown later in this chapter in the *Handling Underlying Data Changes* section. The argument provided for cacheName: is discussed in *Caching Information*.

Once you've written the code to create the fetched results controller, you'll need to tell it to execute the fetch, either at the time the controller is created, or alternatively in the viewDidLoad: method of your view controller, using code similar to Listing 5.2.

LISTING 5.2   Executing the fetch

```
- (void)viewDidLoad {
    [super viewDidLoad];
```

```
    // Initial interface setup goes here

    NSError *anyError;
    BOOL success = [self.fetchedResultsController
                                     performFetch:&anyError];
    if( !success ) {
        // Handle the error...
    }
}
```

Supplying Information to Table Views

With the fetched results controller created and the fetch executed, you're ready to use it to supply information to the table view data source methods.

The three basic data source methods are those shown in Listing 5.3.

LISTING 5.3   The three basic data source methods

```
- (NSInteger)numberOfSectionsInTableView:(UITableView *)tableView;

- (NSInteger)tableView:(UITableView *)table
                    numberOfRowsInSection:(NSInteger)section;

- (UITableViewCell *)tableView:(UITableView *)tableView
                cellForRowAtIndexPath:(NSIndexPath *)indexPath;
```

An NSFetchedResultsController offers easy support of sectional table views, like the one shown in Figure 5.1.

If you look at Listing 5.1, you will notice that sectionNameKeyPath: is provided in the method to initialize the controller. If you pass nil for the key path, the fetched results controller won't bother to do anything about sections and you'll end up with a single-section table view similar to those in Chapter 4 (see Figure 4.2 for a specific example).

However, if you pass in a key path such as doctor.fullName, the fetched results controller will automatically configure itself to sectionalize the results according to that key path. The example in Figure 5.1 shows a list of patients sorted by doctor name, with each doctor having their patients listed underneath their full name.

FIGURE 5.1   A sectional table view

The Number of Sections and Rows

Keeping possible multi-section functionality in mind, the code for a typical
numberOfSectionsInTableView: method is shown in Listing 5.4. Rather than calculating
the number of sections manually, or returning 1 (for simple table views like the application in the last chapter), you can query the fetched results controller method for the
number of sections it will provide.

LISTING 5.4   The number of sections in a table view

```
- (NSInteger)numberOfSectionsInTableView:(UITableView *)tableView {
    return [[fetchedResultsController sections] count];
}
```

Similarly, to return the number of rows in a particular section, query the fetched results
controller as in Listing 5.5.

LISTING 5.5   The number of rows in a section

```
- (NSInteger)tableView:(UITableView *)table
                    numberOfRowsInSection:(NSInteger)section {
   id <NSFetchedResultsSectionInfo> sectionInfo =
        [[fetchedResultsController sections] objectAtIndex:section];
   return [sectionInfo numberOfObjects];
}
```

An Issue with iPhone OS 3.0

If you need to target iOS devices running iPhone OS 3.0, there's a problem between what the table view expects and the fetched results controller provides for a single-section table view. If you delete all the rows from a fetched-results-controller-backed table view, you'll get an exception thrown, saying:

> *Invalid update: invalid number of* sections. The number of sections contained in the table view after the update (0) must be equal to the number of sections contained in the table view before the update (1), plus or minus the number of sections inserted or deleted (0 inserted, 0 deleted).

If a fetched results controller has no results to display, it returns *zero* for the number of sections in the table view. As far as the table view is concerned, you simply deleted a row from "section 1." The table view expects there still to be a "section 1" after the row is deleted, but the controller states there are no sections at all.

The solution to this problem is to check whether there are zero sections (returning 1 instead), and to return the correct number of rows in a non-existent section, as shown below:

```
- (NSInteger)numberOfSectionsInTableView:
                    (UITableView *)tableView {
    NSUInteger count =
     [[fetchedResultsController sections]
                                    count];
    if (count == 0) count = 1;
    return count;
}


- (NSInteger)tableView:
                    (UITableView *)tableView
  numberOfRowsInSection:(NSInteger)section {
     NSArray *sections =
        [fetchedResultsController sections];
```

```
        NSUInteger count = 0;
        if ([sections count] > 0) {
            id <NSFetchedResultsSectionInfo>
              sectionInfo =
            [sections objectAtIndex:section];
            count =
                [sectionInfo numberOfObjects];
        }
        return count;
    }
```

Having said this, if you implement the fetched results controller delegate methods described later in this chapter, you should **not** implement the changed methods shown here, because the delegate methods will handle the table view row removal correctly. If you implement the methods in Listing 5.6, *and* implement the controller delegate methods to remove rows, you'll cause a number of exceptions to be raised when your app tries to add or remove objects.

If you only need to target iPhone OS 3.1 or later, you can safely ignore this sidebar.

Returning the Cell for an Index Path

The final basic data source method to implement is `tableView:cellForRowAtIndexPath:`, as shown in Listing 5.6. The implementation is very similar to the implementation from the last chapter (Listing 4.13), except that you query the fetched results controller for the object to display in the cell.

LISTING 5.6   Returning the cell for an index path

```
- (UITableViewCell *)tableView:(UITableView *)tableView
                cellForRowAtIndexPath:(NSIndexPath *)indexPath {

    static NSString *CellIdentifier = @"Cell";

    UITableViewCell *cell =
        [tableView dequeueReusableCellWithIdentifier:CellIdentifier];
    if (cell == nil) {
        cell = [[[UITableViewCell alloc]
                    initWithStyle:UITableViewCellStyleSubtitle
                reuseIdentifier:CellIdentifier] autorelease];
    }

    NSManagedObject *managedObject =
```

```
                [fetchedResultsController objectAtIndexPath:indexPath];
    cell.textLabel.text = [managedObject valueForKey:@"keyToDisplay"];

    return cell;
}
```

Returning Information about Sections

If you make use of the automatic grouping functionality to display multiple sections in a table view, there is at least one extra data source method that you'll need to implement to provide the header name for each section. Once again, you can simply query the fetched results controller, as shown in Listing 5.7.

LISTING 5.7   Providing section headers

```
- (NSString *)tableView:(UITableView *)tableView
                titleForHeaderInSection:(NSInteger)section {

    id <NSFetchedResultsSectionInfo> sectionInfo =
        [[fetchedResultsController sections] objectAtIndex:section];

    return [sectionInfo name];
}
```

The fetched results controller can also generate relevant section index titles for the table view. These are the small text values that appear on the right of a table view to let the user jump quickly to a particular section. For an example, look at the Contacts application running on an iPhone or iPod touch—the index titles are the letters A through Z.

If you defer responsibility for these to the fetched results controller, as shown in Listing 5.8, the default behavior uses the first letter of each section header as an index title, and you end up with a potentially disjointed list like the one shown earlier in Figure 5.1.

LISTING 5.8   Providing section index titles

```
- (NSArray *)sectionIndexTitlesForTableView:(UITableView *)tableView {
    return [fetchedResultsController sectionIndexTitles];
}

- (NSInteger)tableView:(UITableView *)tableView
                sectionForSectionIndexTitle:(NSString *)title
                                    atIndex:(NSInteger)index {
    return [fetchedResultsController
                sectionForSectionIndexTitle:title atIndex:index];
}
```

If you want to provide some other list for the index, such as the standard alphabet listing A–Z, it's usually best to subclass `NSFetchedResultsController`, giving you a choice of either overriding the `sectionIndexTitles` accessor method to return some custom array, or to override `sectionIndexTitleForSectionName:`. The standard implementation of `sectionIndexTitles` simply calls `sectionTitleForSectionName:` on every section, so you can override this method to provide one index string per section, but taken from something other than the first letter in the section name.

Handling Underlying Data Changes

You can specify a delegate for `NSFetchedResultsController` to be notified whenever the objects in the managed object context change. The methods that you need to implement to deal with these changes are shown in Listing 5.9.

LISTING 5.9   The NSFetchedResultsControllerDelegate methods

```
- (void)controllerWillChangeContent:
                        (NSFetchedResultsController *)controller;

- (void)controller:(NSFetchedResultsController *)controller
        didChangeSection:(id <NSFetchedResultsSectionInfo>)sectionInfo
              atIndex:(NSUInteger)sectionIndex
        forChangeType:(NSFetchedResultsChangeType)type;

- (void)controller:(NSFetchedResultsController *)controller
        didChangeObject:(id)anObject
            atIndexPath:(NSIndexPath *)indexPath
          forChangeType:(NSFetchedResultsChangeType)type
          newIndexPath:(NSIndexPath *)newIndexPath;

- (void)controllerDidChangeContent:
                        (NSFetchedResultsController *)controller;
```

The first and last methods in Listing 5.9 are called either side of the other change methods, and you typically use them to send the `beginUpdates` and `endUpdates` message to the table view, as shown in Listing 5.10.

LISTING 5.10   The WillChange and DidChangeContent methods

```
- (void)controllerWillChangeContent:
                        (NSFetchedResultsController *)controller {
    [self.tableView beginUpdates];
}

- (void)controllerDidChangeContent:
                        (NSFetchedResultsController *)controller {
```

```
    [self.tableView endUpdates];
}
```

If there are a lot of changes, such as from a background import of data, you might choose only to implement the final `controllerDidChangeContent:` method as you may find it better in performance terms just to reload the table view completely rather than one row at a time.

In normal usage, however, you would want to implement all four of the methods shown in Listing 5.9 to modify the table view on a row-by-row basis.

If a *section* will be changed in a table view based on changes to objects in the store, the delegate is sent the `controller:didChangeSection:atIndex:forChangeType:` message. There are two possible change types for this method:

▶ `NSFetchedResultsChangeInsert`, which indicates that a new section needs to be displayed in the table view

▶ `NSFetchedResultsChangeDelete`, which indicates that an existing section should be removed from the table view

Depending on which message is received, you tell the table view either to insert or to delete the relevant section, as shown in Listing 5.11.

The code in Listing 5.11 specifies a row animation of `UITableViewRowAnimationFade`; this will animate the inserted or deleted sections, fading them in or out. You could also specify `UITableViewRowAnimationNone` (meaning that the sections will just appear or disappear with no animation), or use one of the other `UITableViewRowAnimation` constants to specify that the rows should slide in, such as `UITableViewRowAnimationTop` (causing the sections to slide in from the top).

LISTING 5.11   Handling changes to the sections

```
- (void)controller:(NSFetchedResultsController *)controller
        didChangeSection:(id <NSFetchedResultsSectionInfo>)sectionInfo
              atIndex:(NSUInteger)sectionIndex
          forChangeType:(NSFetchedResultsChangeType)type {

    switch(type) {
        case NSFetchedResultsChangeInsert:
            [self.tableView insertSections:[NSIndexSet
                    indexSetWithIndex:sectionIndex]
                    withRowAnimation:UITableViewRowAnimationFade];
            break;

        case NSFetchedResultsChangeDelete:
            [self.tableView deleteSections:[NSIndexSet
                    indexSetWithIndex:sectionIndex]
```

```
                            withRowAnimation:UITableViewRowAnimationFade];
            break;
    }
}
```

Dealing with *object* changes requires a little more thought. The possible change types for objects are:

- ▶ NSFetchedResultsChangeInsert, which indicates that new managed objects have been inserted into the managed object context
- ▶ NSFetchedResultsChangeDelete, which indicates that existing managed objects have been deleted from the managed object context
- ▶ NSFetchedResultsChangeMove, which indicates that something has happened to affect the sort order of existing managed objects, such as a person's last name changing from Amargosa to Zabriskie in a list of contacts
- ▶ NSFetchedResultsChangeUpdate, which indicates that existing managed objects have been changed in the managed object context and need to be refreshed in the table view

For insert or delete changes, simply tell the table view to insert or remove the rows. If objects are moved from one section to another, tell the table view to remove the object from its old location and reload the section that it's been moved to. Finally, when objects are updated, you need to adjust the relevant text display for the cell to show those changes, as shown in Listing 5.12.

LISTING 5.12   Handling changes to the objects

```
- (void)controller:(NSFetchedResultsController *)controller
        didChangeObject:(id)anObject
          atIndexPath:(NSIndexPath *)indexPath
        forChangeType:(NSFetchedResultsChangeType)type
         newIndexPath:(NSIndexPath *)newIndexPath {

    switch(type) {

        case NSFetchedResultsChangeInsert:
            [self.tableView
        insertRowsAtIndexPaths:[NSArray arrayWithObject:newIndexPath]
            withRowAnimation:UITableViewRowAnimationFade];
            break;

        case NSFetchedResultsChangeDelete:
            [self.tableView
        deleteRowsAtIndexPaths:[NSArray arrayWithObject:indexPath]
```

```
                withRowAnimation:UITableViewRowAnimationFade];
            break;

        case NSFetchedResultsChangeMove:
            [self.tableView
          deleteRowsAtIndexPaths:[NSArray arrayWithObject:indexPath]
                withRowAnimation:UITableViewRowAnimationFade];

            [self.tableView
      reloadSections:[NSIndexSet indexSetWithIndex:newIndexPath.section]
     withRowAnimation:UITableViewRowAnimationFade];
            break;

        case NSFetchedResultsChangeUpdate: {
            // Change the content of the cell as appropriate
            UITableViewCell *cell = [self.tableView
                                  cellForRowAtIndexPath:indexPath];

            NSManagedObject *object = [controller
                                      objectAtIndexPath:indexPath];
            cell.textLabel.text = [object
                                  valueForKey:@"valueToDisplay"];
            break;
        }
    }
}
```

Caching Information

Earlier, in Listing 5.1, you saw that it's possible to specify the name of a cache to be used when initializing the fetched results controller.

If you specify nil for a cache name, all the information needed to display a table view (such as section header names, index titles, etc.) will be recalculated each time. If you do provide a cache name, NSFetchedResultsController will maintain a private cache of this information so it doesn't have to recalculate unless there are relevant changes. This cache persists even between application launches.

If you specifically need to purge a cache to display changes not automatically picked up by the fetched results controller, call NSFetchedResultsController's class method, deleteCacheWithName:. When developing an application, you may want to specify nil for the cache name to make sure you can see any changes, such as after adding a custom fetched results controller subclass to display custom section index titles. Once you're happy with the way the controller is working, you can then specify the name of the cache to speed up information display.

Using an NSFetchedResultsController in the Random Dates Application

Let's go back and modify the Random Dates application from Chapter 4 to use a fetched results controller rather than doing all the fetching manually. You might like to duplicate the project directory before proceeding so you can compare the performance and behavior once the changes are made.

The first step is to remove the cached array (datesArray) from the RootViewController.h interface, and replace it with a new NSFetchedResultsController attribute, as shown in Listing 5.13.

LISTING 5.13   Creating an NSFetchedResultsController instance variable

```
RootViewController.h

@interface RootViewController :
        UITableViewController <NSFetchedResultsControllerDelegate> {

    NSManagedObjectContext *managedObjectContext;
    NSFetchedResultsController *fetchedResultsController;
}

@property (nonatomic, retain) NSManagedObjectContext
                                        *managedObjectContext;
@property (nonatomic, retain) NSFetchedResultsController
                                        *fetchedResultsController;

@end
```

Notice that Listing 5.13 specifies that the RootViewController will implement the NSFetchedResultsControllerDelegate protocol, as you'll set the root view controller to be the delegate of the fetched results controller when you create it.

> **NOTE**
>
> You will also need to @synthesize the new fetchedResultsController instance variable (and release it in various places) instead of the existing datesArray in the RootViewController.m file.

Since the view controller will use the fetched results controller to handle all the fetching and updating, you can remove the entire fetchRandomDates method implemented back in Listing 4.12. You'll then need to implement an accessor method for the fetched results controller, to create it lazily when needed, with a suitable predicate and sort descriptor, as shown in Listing 5.14.

LISTING 5.14   Creating and returning the fetched results controller

RootViewController.m

```
- (NSFetchedResultsController *)fetchedResultsController {
    if (!fetchedResultsController ) {
        NSFetchRequest *request = [[NSFetchRequest alloc] init];
        [request setEntity:[NSEntityDescription
                            entityForName:@"RandomDate"
                    inManagedObjectContext:managedObjectContext]];
        NSSortDescriptor *daysDescriptor = [[NSSortDescriptor alloc]
                                            initWithKey:@"dayName"
                                            ascending:YES];
        NSSortDescriptor *dateDescriptor = [[NSSortDescriptor alloc]
                                            initWithKey:@"date"
                                            ascending:YES];
        [request setSortDescriptors:[NSArray
            arrayWithObjects:daysDescriptor, dateDescriptor, nil]];
        [daysDescriptor release];
        [dateDescriptor release];

        NSFetchedResultsController *newController =
        [[NSFetchedResultsController alloc] initWithFetchRequest:request
                            managedObjectContext:managedObjectContext
                            sectionNameKeyPath:@"dayName"
                                    cacheName:nil];

        newController.delegate = self;
        self.fetchedResultsController = newController;
        [newController release];
        [request release];
    }

    return fetchedResultsController;
}
```

This code uses two sort descriptors, sorting the objects first by the dayName attribute, then by the date. Sorting alphabetically by dayName will obviously not sort the days into the order that the user might expect; for now this is simply to aid in making use of the header names feature offered by the fetched results controller.

The viewDidLoad method needs to be changed so it tells the fetched results controller to fetch the objects, as shown in Listing 5.15.

LISTING 5.15   Fetching the results in viewDidLoad

```
- (void)viewDidLoad {
    [super viewDidLoad];

    self.navigationItem.leftBarButtonItem = self.editButtonItem;

    UIBarButtonItem *addButton = [[UIBarButtonItem alloc]
            initWithBarButtonSystemItem:UIBarButtonSystemItemAdd
                                target:self
                                action:@selector(addNewRandomDate)];
    self.navigationItem.rightBarButtonItem = addButton;
    [addButton release];

    NSError *anyError = nil;
    BOOL success = [self.fetchedResultsController
                                        performFetch:&anyError];

    if( !success ) NSLog(@"Error = %@", anyError);
}
```

Remove the call to fetchRandomDates from the end of the addNewRandomDate method; when a new row is inserted, the fetched results controller will inform the root view controller that it needs to update the table view.

Implement the basic data source methods for the table view as shown in Listing 5.16.

> **NOTE**
>
> Since you'll be implementing the fetched results controller delegate methods, you should *ignore* the instructions in the Sidebar about iPhone SDK 3.0 (i.e., don't change the number of sections returned if it's zero).

LISTING 5.16   Implementing the basic data source methods

```
- (NSInteger)numberOfSectionsInTableView:(UITableView *)tableView {
    return [[fetchedResultsController sections] count];
}

- (NSInteger)tableView:(UITableView *)table
                    numberOfRowsInSection:(NSInteger)section {
    id <NSFetchedResultsSectionInfo> sectionInfo =
        [[fetchedResultsController sections] objectAtIndex:section];
```

```
    return [sectionInfo numberOfObjects];
}

- (UITableViewCell *)tableView:(UITableView *)tableView
                cellForRowAtIndexPath:(NSIndexPath *)indexPath {
    static NSString *CellIdentifier = @"Cell";

    UITableViewCell *cell =
        [tableView dequeueReusableCellWithIdentifier:CellIdentifier];
    if (cell == nil) {
        cell = [[[UITableViewCell alloc]
                        initWithStyle:UITableViewCellStyleSubtitle
                      reuseIdentifier:CellIdentifier] autorelease];
    }

    // Configure the cell...
    AWRandomDate *object = [fetchedResultsController
                                  objectAtIndexPath:indexPath];
    cell.textLabel.text = [object.date description];
    cell.detailTextLabel.text = object.dayName;

    return cell;
}
```

You'll need to change the method `tableView:commitEditingStyle:forRowAtIndexPath:`
so it just deletes the object from the persistent store without making any changes to the
table view, as shown in Listing 5.17. Again, the fetched results controller calls the delegate methods you'll implement next when it detects an object has been deleted from
the context.

LISTING 5.17   Deleting objects

RootViewController.m

```
- (void)tableView:(UITableView *)tableView
        commitEditingStyle:(UITableViewCellEditingStyle)editingStyle
        forRowAtIndexPath:(NSIndexPath *)indexPath {

    if (editingStyle == UITableViewCellEditingStyleDelete) {
        // Delete the row from the data source
        NSManagedObject *objectToDelete =
                [fetchedResultsController objectAtIndexPath:indexPath];

        [managedObjectContext deleteObject:objectToDelete];
    }
}
```

If you build and run the app at this point, you'll find that clicking the + button will appear to have no effect. However, if you restart the app, you'll find that the relevant objects *were* created; it's just that you haven't yet implemented the fetched results controller delegate methods to update the table view with changes in the underlying objects.

To do this, add the delegate methods shown in Listing 5.18 first; these are identical to the code shown earlier in Listings 5.10 and 5.11.

LISTING 5.18   Basic fetched results controller delegate methods

```
- (void)controllerWillChangeContent:
                    (NSFetchedResultsController *)controller {
    [self.tableView beginUpdates];
}

- (void)controllerDidChangeContent:
                    (NSFetchedResultsController *)controller {
    [self.tableView endUpdates];
}

- (void)controller:(NSFetchedResultsController *)controller
        didChangeSection:(id <NSFetchedResultsSectionInfo>)sectionInfo
               atIndex:(NSUInteger)sectionIndex
          forChangeType:(NSFetchedResultsChangeType)type {
    switch(type) {
        case NSFetchedResultsChangeInsert:
            [self.tableView insertSections:[NSIndexSet
                    indexSetWithIndex:sectionIndex]
                     withRowAnimation:UITableViewRowAnimationFade];
            break;

        case NSFetchedResultsChangeDelete:
            [self.tableView deleteSections:[NSIndexSet
                    indexSetWithIndex:sectionIndex]
                     withRowAnimation:UITableViewRowAnimationFade];
            break;
    }
}
```

The third delegate method, `controller:didChangeObject:atIndexPath:forChangeType:newIndexPath:`, which handles changes to the objects in the managed object context, needs to insert or delete rows in the table view, or update an existing table view cell using code similar to that used in the `tableView:cellForRowAtIndexPath:` method, as shown in Listing 5.19.

LISTING 5.19   The didChangeObject delegate method

```objc
- (void)controller:(NSFetchedResultsController *)controller
        didChangeObject:(id)anObject
            atIndexPath:(NSIndexPath *)indexPath
          forChangeType:(NSFetchedResultsChangeType)type
           newIndexPath:(NSIndexPath *)newIndexPath {

    switch(type) {

        case NSFetchedResultsChangeInsert:
            [self.tableView
        insertRowsAtIndexPaths:[NSArray arrayWithObject:newIndexPath]
              withRowAnimation:UITableViewRowAnimationFade];
            break;

        case NSFetchedResultsChangeDelete:
            [self.tableView
         deleteRowsAtIndexPaths:[NSArray arrayWithObject:indexPath]
              withRowAnimation:UITableViewRowAnimationFade];
            break;

        case NSFetchedResultsChangeMove:
            [self.tableView
         deleteRowsAtIndexPaths:[NSArray arrayWithObject:indexPath]
              withRowAnimation:UITableViewRowAnimationFade];

            [self.tableView
       reloadSections:[NSIndexSet indexSetWithIndex:newIndexPath.section]
    withRowAnimation:UITableViewRowAnimationFade];
            break;

        case NSFetchedResultsChangeUpdate: {
            UITableViewCell *cell = [self.tableView
                                        cellForRowAtIndexPath:indexPath];

            AWRandomDate *object = [controller
                                        objectAtIndexPath:indexPath];
            cell.textLabel.text = [object.date description];
            cell.detailTextLabel.text = object.dayName;
            break;
        }
    }
}
```

Build and run the application again and you'll find that adding or removing random date objects is accompanied by animated changes in the table view.

When you coded the method to generate the `fetchedResultsController`, you specified a `sectionNameKeyPath` of `@"dayName"`. For the headers to appear on each section, you'll need to implement the *table view* data source method to return the relevant information, as shown in Listing 5.20.

LISTING 5.20   Table view data source method providing section information

```
- (NSString *)tableView:(UITableView *)tableView
                   titleForHeaderInSection:(NSInteger)section {
    id <NSFetchedResultsSectionInfo> sectionInfo =
        [[fetchedResultsController sections] objectAtIndex:section];
    return [sectionInfo name];
}
```

Also add the code from Listing 5.21 to display the default section index title information down the right-hand side of the table view.

LISTING 5.21   Table view data source method providing section index titles

```
- (NSArray *)sectionIndexTitlesForTableView:(UITableView *)tableView {
    return [fetchedResultsController sectionIndexTitles];
}

- (NSInteger)tableView:(UITableView *)tableView
                   sectionForSectionIndexTitle:(NSString *)title
                                       atIndex:(NSInteger)index {
    return [fetchedResultsController
                   sectionForSectionIndexTitle:title atIndex:index];
}
```

The app will now display the dates for each day name in sections, as shown in Figure 5.2. Notice how the default behavior has taken only the *unique* first letters of each day name for the section index titles, giving the rather unhelpful "F M S T W." Click the + button to add enough dates to the table view such that you have at least one date for each day name.

FIGURE 5.2   The Random Dates application with a sectional table view

Subclassing NSFetchedResultsController

Now let's provide a custom subclass of NSFetchedResultsController, which will be used to override its default behavior and specify more useful index title information.

Start by creating a new Objective-C class, specifying a subclass of NSFetchedResultsController, called AWDayNameFetchedResultsController. The interface should look like Listing 5.22.

LISTING 5.22   Subclassing NSFetchedResultsController

AWDayNameFetchedResultsController.h

```
@interface AWDayNameFetchedResultsController : NSFetchedResultsController {


}

@end
```

The first method to override is sectionIndexTitleForSectionName:, which is called for each section title. Let's return the first three letters of the section, as shown in Listing 5.23.

LISTING 5.23   Returning custom section index titles

AWDayNameFetchedResultsController.m

```
@implementation AWDayNameFetchedResultsController

- (NSString *)sectionIndexTitleForSectionName:(NSString *)sectionName {
    return [sectionName substringToIndex:3];
}

@end
```

You'll need to change the viewDidLoad method, in RootViewController.m to allocate and initialize an instance of the custom controller, as shown in Listing 5.24. You will also need to #import the AWDayNameFetchedResultsController.h file at the top of RootViewController.m.

LISTING 5.24   Instantiating the fetched results controller subclass

RootViewController.m

```
AWDayNameFetchedResultsController *newController =
  [[AWDayNameFetchedResultsController alloc]
                       initWithFetchRequest:request
                       managedObjectContext:managedObjectContext
                       sectionNameKeyPath:@"dayName"
                                cacheName:nil];
```

Build and run the application again and you'll find that it displays slightly more useful dayName index titles, as shown in Figure 5.3.

One last change you can make to the custom fetched results controller is to return the section index names in a different order than is displayed in the table view. The random dates are currently sorted by day name in *alphabetical* order, which means that Thursday appears before Tuesday, or worse, Friday before all the other days of the week. A better route to take here is to display the index names in *weekday* order (i.e., Sunday, Monday, Tuesday, etc.).

There are a couple of things to point out before doing this:

▶ Section index titles should really reflect their order in the table view to give the user a clue about where to scroll to find what they are looking for (ideally, the actual table view sections would be sorted in weekday order using a custom sort descriptor).

▶ The implementation that follows makes it more difficult to localize the application.

FIGURE 5.3   The Random Dates application displaying more useful section index titles

Treat this as an exercise in customizing behavior rather than a demonstration of good iOS interface design!

You've just overridden the `sectionIndexTitleForSectionName:` method to customize the index title on each section. The default behavior builds the array of section index titles calling this method in order on each section name. Since the section order is not the order you want for the custom index titles, you'll instead need to override the `sectionIndexTitles` accessor method to return a custom array of strings.

Listing 5.25 shows a very non-localized version of this method.

LISTING 5.25   Providing a custom order of section index titles

AWDayNameFetchedResultsController.m

```
- (NSArray *)sectionIndexTitles {
    return [NSArray arrayWithObjects:@"Sun", @"Mon", @"Tue", @"Wed",
                                     @"Thu", @"Fri", @"Sat", nil];
}
```

Because you're providing a custom order, you also need to override the method that checks to see which section is meant by a specific index title. One (non-localized) version of this method is shown in Listing 5.26.

LISTING 5.26   Returning the section for a given section index title

```
- (NSInteger)sectionForSectionIndexTitle:(NSString *)title
                              atIndex:(NSInteger)sectionIndex {
    NSArray *sectionsArray = [self sections];

    NSPredicate *predicate = [NSPredicate
              predicateWithFormat:@"name contains[cd] %@", title];

    NSArray *filteredArray = [sectionsArray
                        filteredArrayUsingPredicate:predicate];

    if( [filteredArray count] > 0 )
    {
        return [sectionsArray indexOfObject:[filteredArray
                                        objectAtIndex:0]];
    }
    else {
        return -1;
    }
}
```

This code uses a predicate to filter the array of section names to find one that contains the string in the index title. Objects returned by the call to [self sections] contain information about each section; the name attribute in this section information corresponds with the section header name, which in this application will be the full name of each weekday. In English, the first three characters of each weekday name are enough to identify uniquely the relevant day using this predicate.

If you build and run the application now, you'll see something like Figure 5.4. Tapping one of the section index titles should take you to the relevant section in the table view, even though the order of index titles is different from the section order in the table view.

FIGURE 5.4   The Random Dates application with custom section index titles

Once you're satisfied with the behavior, you can change the RootViewController's fetchedResultsController accessor, telling it to use a named cache, as shown in Listing 5.27.

LISTING 5.27   Specifying a cache for the fetched results controller

RootViewController.m

```
[request setSortDescriptors:[NSArray arrayWithObject:sortDescriptor]];
[sortDescriptor release];

AWDayNameFetchedResultsController *newController =
  [[AWDayNameFetchedResultsController alloc]
                    initWithFetchRequest:request
                    managedObjectContext:managedObjectContext
                      sectionNameKeyPath:@"dayName"
                              cacheName:@"daysCache"];
```

```
newController.delegate = self;
self.fetchedResultsController = newController;
```

Summary

Working with an NSFetchedResultsController offers great performance gains that would otherwise have to be coded on an application-by-application basis. Because it fetches in batches (usually loading only as many objects into memory as are necessary for display in a table view), there are potentially huge benefits in lower memory usage and decreased time taken when working with large data sets.

The implementation code and delegate methods to work with a fetched results controller are typically very similar from view controller to view controller so the development overhead is fairly minimal; if anything, it makes working with index paths and sections much easier and reduces the amount of code in many places.

If you do need to customize the default behavior, you either provide different code in the delegate methods, or subclass NSFetchedResultsController itself to override the section index title generation code.

5

Working with Managed Objects

At the end of Chapter 4, "Basic Storing and Fetching," you saw how to create a managed object subclass for an entity. You used the Xcode Managed Object Class Generator to create the relevant interface and implementation files for an AWRandomDate class, inheriting from NSManagedObject.

In this chapter, you'll look at the functionality provided automatically in these generated files, such as property declarations for the attributes on your entities. You'll see how to add *transient* attributes, which aren't persisted to the store but can still benefit from functionality like automatic Undo, and *transformable* attributes to persist properties with non-standard types. You'll also see how to work with custom validation code to validate supplied values for attributes and entire managed object instances, before they get persisted to disk.

Basic Managed Object Subclass Files

Through most of this chapter, you'll be working with a new demonstration application, called Random People. It works in a similar way to the Random Dates application from Chapter 4, but stores a list of people's names and dates of birth. The interface is shown in Figure 6.1.

When the + button is pressed, a first and last name are picked at random from two arrays of possible names; a random date of birth is also generated, and all three values are stored in a Person managed object instance. In the finished application, the names listed in the table view are sorted in ascending alphabetical order by last name, but the table view cells display each person's name in full. The displayed date of birth is also formatted correctly according to the current locale.

FIGURE 6.1   The Random People application in the simulator

Creating the Random People Project

Start by creating a new iOS Navigation-based Application project in Xcode. Call the project "Random People," and make sure you select the "Use Core Data" checkbox.

When the new project appears, open the `Random_People.xcdatamodeld` file and remove the existing `Event` entity by selecting it and pressing Delete.

Create a new entity called `Person`, with a Class name of `AWPerson`, and add three attributes:

- ▶ A String attribute called `firstName`
- ▶ A String attribute called `lastName`
- ▶ A Date attribute called `dateOfBirth`

None of these attributes should be marked as *Transient* since each value should be stored in the persistent store.

Your data model should look like Figure 6.2.

FIGURE 6.2   The initial data model for the Random People application

Once you've created the new Person entity, create a new managed object class for the entity:

▶ Make sure that your new Person entity is selected in the modeler and choose File > New > New File (⌘-N).

▶ Select NSManagedObject subclass from the iOS Core Data group and click Next.

▶ Click Create to have Xcode create your new AWPerson managed object subclass.

NOTE

Xcode 3 may place the AWPerson.h and .m files inside the data model bundle. If this happens, drag them up into the Classes group

Managed Object Class Interfaces

Open up the AWPerson.h file to view the generated interface for the class, shown in Listing 6.1.

LISTING 6.1   The auto-generated AWPerson class interface

```
@interface AWPerson :  NSManagedObject {
@private
}

@property (nonatomic, retain) NSString * firstName;
@property (nonatomic, retain) NSString * lastName;
@property (nonatomic, retain) NSDate * dateOfBirth;

@end
```

As you saw back in Chapter 4, these @property declarations mean you can access the attributes of an AWPerson object using either traditional accessor methods or dot syntax.

Notice from Listing 6.1 that Xcode has automatically picked what it thinks are the best Cocoa class matches to the attribute types set in the data model—in this case, NSString and NSDate. If the Person entity had any kind of integer or decimal number, the @property would be an NSNumber; for Binary Data attributes, Xcode would use NSData.

For a Boolean attribute, Xcode will still use an NSNumber object, rather than a BOOL scalar type. This can be a common cause of confusion—if the Person entity had a Boolean attribute called deceased, the AWPerson's deceased property type would be NSNumber. Listing 6.2 shows a common pitfall arising from this.

LISTING 6.2   Working with Boolean attributes

```
- (void)warnIfDeceased:(AWPerson *)person {
    if( person.deceased ) // This will be true for both YES or NO
        NSLog(@"Person is deceased");

    if( [person.deceased boolValue] ) // This will work as expected
        NSLog(@"Person is deceased");
}
```

Asking for the deceased property will return you an NSNumber object, not a BOOL value. The first condition in Listing 6.2 is actually checking whether the object pointer is "not nil." The first NSLog statement in Listing 6.2 will *always* be called, regardless of whether the actual Boolean value is true or false. The second condition extracts the YES or NO value from the NSNumber object, so works as expected.

Managed Object Class Implementations

Switch into the AWPerson.m implementation file (Ctrl-⌘-Up Arrow) to look at the auto-generated implementation for the AWPerson class, shown in Listing 6.3.

LISTING 6.3   The auto-generated AWPerson class implementation

```
@implementation AWPerson

@dynamic firstName;
@dynamic lastName;
@dynamic dateOfBirth;

@end
```

Rather than the traditional call to @synthesize the properties, this implementation makes use of the @dynamic keyword. This keyword indicates that the property accessors will be available at runtime, even though they are not specifically listed at compile time—they'll be provided automatically by NSManagedObject. These Core Data-provided accessors offer the added benefit of better performance than using either your own accessor methods, or KVC methods (i.e., valueForKey: and setValue:forKey:).

The information in these two class files is all that is required to use accessor methods or dot syntax, as you saw when you used the custom managed object subclass back in Chapter 4, in Listing 4.16.

If you don't need any of the other benefits from an entire NSManagedObject subclass, it's not strictly necessary to use a subclass at all. Core Data-provided property accessors are accessible from any NSManagedObject, so you can call [someObject someProperty] on a generic NSManagedObject instance and the value will be returned (obviously assuming that object's entity has someProperty defined in the data model). To make use of these accessors without subclassing NSManagedObject, you'll need to define a category on NSManagedObject to add your properties. If you don't, you'll get compiler warnings about unknown methods and won't be able to use dot syntax.

Implementing Custom Accessor Methods

It's also possible to implement your own accessor methods to provide custom behavior. Consider a Person entity that maintains not only a deceased attribute, but also a dateOfDeath attribute. You might decide to implement a setDateOfDeath: method in your AWPerson class that sets the deceased attribute to YES when a date of death is set.

The code to implement such a method is shown in Listing 6.4. It's important to note that by default, Core Data objects do not trigger automatic KVO notifications when an attribute is changed. This means that you need to include the KVO methods willChangeValueForKey: and didChangeValueForKey: manually.

NOTE

NSManagedObject implements the automaticallyNotifiesObserversForKey: class method to return NO for all modeled keys (overriding NSObject's implementation which returns YES by default). To trigger KVO notifications on your managed object accessor methods, you can either call the KVO will/didChangeValueForKey:, or alternatively override the automaticallyNotifiesObserversForKey: method in your NSManagedObject subclass and return YES for the relevant keys.

LISTING 6.4   Implementing a setter method in a managed object subclass

```
- (void)setDateOfDeath:(NSDate *)newValue {
    [self willChangeValueForKey:@"dateOfDeath"];
    [self setPrimitiveValue:newValue forKey:@"dateOfDeath"];
```

```
    [self didChangeValueForKey:@"dateOfDeath"];

    self.deceased = [NSNumber numberWithBool:YES];
}
```

Listing 6.4 makes use of a method provided by NSManagedObject,
setPrimitiveValue:forKey:, which works just like its setValue:forKey: counterpart, but
is used to set the internal value handled by the managed object (but, remember, nothing
is changed on disk in the persistent store until you tell that object's managed object
context to save:).

Should you need to *access* an object's primitive value, NSManagedObject also provides a
primitiveValueForKey: method. Like setPrimitiveValue:forKey:, this method doesn't
trigger any KVO notifications, so a custom accessor method needs to send notifications
about accessing the primitive value, as shown in Listing 6.5.

LISTING 6.5   Implementing a getter method in a managed object subclass

```
- (NSDate *)dateOfDeath {
    [self willAccessValueForKey:@"dateOfDeath"];
    NSDate *dateOfDeath = [self primitiveValueForKey:@"dateOfDeath"];
    [self didAccessValueForKey:@"dateOfDeath"];

    return dateOfDeath;
}
```

One way to avoid the potential problem shown earlier in Listing 6.2 is to redefine a
property with a different type from the one used for primitive storage. Listing 6.6 shows
the deceased property implemented using a scalar BOOL rather than an NSNumber. Note
that you'd also need to indicate this change by modifying the @property declaration in
the interface.

LISTING 6.6   Using a different property type for a persistent attribute

```
// AWPerson.h
@interface AWPerson : NSManagedObject {}

@property (assign) BOOL deceased;

@end


// AWPerson.m
@implementation AWPerson

- (BOOL)deceased {
```

```
    [self willAccessValueForKey:@"deceased"];
    NSNumber *deceasedNum = [self primitiveValueForKey:@"deceased"];
    [self didAccessValueForKey:@"deceased"];

    return [deceasedNum boolValue];
}

- (void)setDeceased:(BOOL)newValue {
    NSNumber *deceasedNum = [NSNumber numberWithBool:newValue];
    [self willChangeValueForKey:@"deceased"];
    [self setPrimitiveValue:deceasedNum forKey:@"deceased"];
    [self didChangeValueForKey:@"deceased"];
}

[...]

@end
```

By writing these custom accessor methods, you are now able to use the first conditional statement from Listing 6.2; if(person.deceased) will now work as expected.

Configuring the Random People Application

At this point, you should have a data model in your Xcode project, created at the beginning of the chapter, containing the Person entity. You should also have AWPerson.h and .m managed object files for the entity, with properties for the first and last names and date of birth.

Let's also add a readonly property for a fullName string. For simplicity, this just returns a string built by combining the firstName and lastName strings, ready for display in the table view later in this section.

You'll need to add both the readonly property declaration into AWPerson.h, along with the method implementation in AWPerson.m, as shown in Listing 6.7.

LISTING 6.7   A read-only fullName property

```
// AWPerson.h
@interface AWPerson :  NSManagedObject  {}

[...]
@property (nonatomic, readonly) NSString *fullName;

@end
```

```
// AWPerson.m
@implementation AWPerson

- (NSString *)fullName {
    return [NSString stringWithFormat:@"%@ %@",
            [self firstName], [self lastName]];
}

[...]
@end
```

Next, let's add a convenience method to the AWPerson class to create a new person, along with a method to generate a person with a random name and date of birth, as shown in Listing 6.8.

LISTING 6.8   Creating a new random person

```
+ (id)personInManagedObjectContext:(NSManagedObjectContext *)moc {
    return [NSEntityDescription
                    insertNewObjectForEntityForName:@"Person"
                            inManagedObjectContext:moc];
}

+ (id)randomPersonInManagedObjectContext:(NSManagedObjectContext *)moc {
    AWPerson *randomPerson = [self personInManagedObjectContext:moc];

    randomPerson.firstName = [self randomFirstName];
    randomPerson.lastName = [self randomLastName];
    randomPerson.dateOfBirth =
                    [NSDate dateWithTimeIntervalSince1970:arc4random()];

    return randomPerson;
}
```

The random date of birth is created in exactly the same way as it was back in Chapter 4. Add method signatures for both these methods into the @interface for the AWPerson class.

The methods to generate the random first and last names are shown in Listing 6.9; if you add these earlier in AWPerson.m than the methods in Listing 6.8, you don't need to add method signatures for randomFirstName or randomLastName in AWPerson.h.

LISTING 6.9   Generating random first and last names

```
+ (NSString *)randomFirstName {
    static NSArray *personFirstNamesArray = nil;
```

```
    if( !personFirstNamesArray )
    {
        personFirstNamesArray = [[NSArray alloc] initWithObjects:
            @"John", @"Jane", @"Adam", @"Amit", @"Peter",
            @"Mary", @"Susan", @"Anne", @"Jeffery", @"Mohammed", nil];
    }

    int randomIndex = arc4random() % [personFirstNamesArray count];

    return [personFirstNamesArray objectAtIndex:randomIndex];
}

+ (NSString *)randomLastName {
    static NSArray *personLastNamesArray = nil;

    if( !personLastNamesArray )
    {
        personLastNamesArray = [[NSArray alloc] initWithObjects:
            @"Smith", @"Patel", @"Jones", @"Adams", @"Peterson",
            @"Jackson", @"Ali", @"Jefferson", @"Dickens", nil];
    }

    int randomIndex = arc4random() % [personLastNamesArray count];

    return [personLastNamesArray objectAtIndex:randomIndex];
}
```

Displaying the Information

You'll need to write the table view delegate methods that display the stored person objects (using a subtitle cell). Use the fetched results controller in the template RootViewController to provide the data (following the code from Chapter 5, in Listings 5.13 through 5.19, if necessary), with the following changes:

▶ Set the fetched results controller to fetch the objects for the Person entity, specifying sort descriptors for last name and first name, as shown in Listing 6.10.

LISTING 6.10   Setting up the fetch results controller

```
[...]

NSFetchRequest *fetchRequest = [[NSFetchRequest alloc] init];
[fetchRequest setEntity:[NSEntityDescription
```

```
                    entityForName:@"Person"
            inManagedObjectContext:self.managedObjectContext]];

[fetchRequest setFetchBatchSize:20];

NSSortDescriptor *lastNameDescriptor = [[NSSortDescriptor alloc]
                 initWithKey:@"lastName" ascending:YES];
NSSortDescriptor *firstNameDescriptor = [[NSSortDescriptor alloc]
                 initWithKey:@"firstName" ascending:YES];
[fetchRequest setSortDescriptors:[NSArray arrayWithObjects:
                 lastNameDescriptor, firstNameDescriptor, nil]];
[lastNameDescriptor release];
[firstNameDescriptor release];

NSFetchedResultsController *aFetchedResultsController =
    [[NSFetchedResultsController alloc]
            initWithFetchRequest:fetchRequest
            managedObjectContext:self.managedObjectContext
              sectionNameKeyPath:nil
                       cacheName:@"Root"];

aFetchedResultsController.delegate = self;
self.fetchedResultsController = aFetchedResultsController;
[aFetchedResultsController release];
[fetchRequest release];

[...]
```

▶ Set the action for the Add button, created in the viewDidLoad method, to addNewPerson and implement it using the code in Listing 6.11.

LISTING 6.11   Adding a new person object

```
- (void)addNewPerson {
    AWPerson *newPerson = [AWPerson
        randomPersonInManagedObjectContext:self.managedObjectContext];
#pragma unused( newPerson )
    NSError *anyError = nil;
    BOOL success = [self.managedObjectContext save:&anyError];
    if( !success ) NSLog(@"Error = %@", anyError);
}
```

▶ Re-implement the `configureCell:atIndexPath:` method (used in the template file both in `tableView:cellForIndexPath:` and for the fetched results controller delegate's `didChangeObject:...` method for the `NSFetchedResultsChangeUpdate` case) so that it displays the full name of the person and their date of birth, as shown in Listing 6.12.

LISTING 6.12   Displaying a person's full name and date of birth

```
- (void)configureCell:(UITableViewCell *)cell
                        atIndexPath:(NSIndexPath *)indexPath {
    AWPerson *person =
      [self.fetchedResultsController objectAtIndexPath:indexPath];

    cell.textLabel.text = person.fullName;
    cell.detailTextLabel.text = [person.dateOfBirth description];
}
```

When you build and run the application, you'll find that a new random person is generated each time you press the Add button, as shown in Figure 6.3.

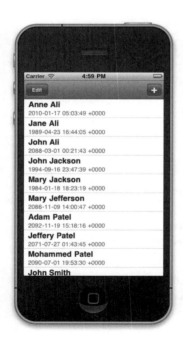

FIGURE 6.3   The Random People application showing random people and their dates of birth

At the moment, the date of birth is being displayed using NSDate's raw description. Let's add another readonly property to the Person entity to display a more localized version, excluding the time:

▶ Start by adding a new readonly NSString property, called dateOfBirthString, into the AWPerson class interface:

    @property (nonatomic, readonly) NSString *dateOfBirthString;

▶ Implement an accessor method for this property using the code in Listing 6.13.

LISTING 6.13   Generating a localized date of birth string

```
- (NSString *)dateOfBirthString {
    static NSDateFormatter *birthDateFormatter = nil;

    if( !birthDateFormatter ) {
        birthDateFormatter = [[NSDateFormatter alloc] init];

        [birthDateFormatter setTimeStyle:NSDateFormatterNoStyle];
        [birthDateFormatter setDateStyle:NSDateFormatterShortStyle];
    }

    NSString *bornString = NSLocalizedString(@"Born: ", @"Born: ");
    NSString *dateString = [birthDateFormatter
                                    stringFromDate:self.dateOfBirth];

    return [bornString stringByAppendingString:dateString];
}
```

▶ Modify the RootViewController's configureCell:atIndexPath: method to set the cell.detailTextLabel.text to use the new string property (i.e., set it to person.dateOfBirthString).

Listing 6.13 makes use of an NSDateFormatter, cached in a static variable, to generate a localized ShortStyle date without a time. Running this in the iPhone Simulator displays the output shown in Figure 6.4.

At the moment, the random birth dates are generated from 1970 onwards. Some dates are late into the 2090s. Let's use Core Data's validation functionality to fix this.

FIGURE 6.4   The Random People application showing a localized date of birth

Data Validation

In Chapter 3, "Modeling Your Data," you saw how to specify basic constraints in the Xcode Data Modeler. The Date attribute type and each of the different number attribute types, for example, can have minimum and maximum values; a String can have a minimum and maximum length, and can also be validated against an entered Regular Expression string, perhaps to check that an emailAddress attribute matches the correct address format. Relationships can also have validation specified in the model, such as that a Person must always have two parents.

Sometimes, you'll need to perform validation manually. You might, for example, need to validate one value based on some other value generated at runtime—like not setting a Person's dateOfBirth as being greater than the current date and time. Or, you might need to validate one value against another, such as making sure a Person's dateOfBirth isn't later than their dateOfDeath.

Validating Individual Properties

The Core Data framework provides programmatic validation by calling certain methods, if they exist in your subclasses, when the managed object context tries to save. You can also ask to validate properties manually by calling validateValue:forKey:error:.

For iOS applications, it's often a good idea to validate data as it's being entered, such as in a `UITextField`'s `textFieldShouldEndEditing` delegate method; this allows you to display an error to the user at a time when they can easily do something about it. If you wait until you save the managed object context, perhaps after allowing a user to edit multiple values on multiple objects, it's not going to be a great user experience to be greeted with a string of errors listing all the incorrect values over multiple view controllers!

When a managed object is validated, either when a managed object context is being saved, or on an individual key basis using the `validateValue:forKey:error:` method, the Core Data framework will call a method named `validate<KeyName>:error:`, if it exists. The `<KeyName>` should be replaced with the capitalized attribute name.

NOTE

If you want to validate a particular value for which you have provided a validation method, you should still call the `validateValue:forKey:error:` method, rather than calling any `validate<KeyName>:error:` method directly, so that any constraints specified in the data model are also validated.

The first argument to the validation method is a reference to the proposed new value; the second argument is a reference to an `NSError` pointer. If the proposed value meets your validation criteria, you just return `YES`. If the proposed value is not valid, you can return `NO` and pass back an `NSError` object, by reference, describing the problem.

Because the new value is supplied by reference, you can also change the value so that it validates correctly without generating an error. If you store telephone numbers in a certain format, for example, you might change a string of numbers like "13105559450" into "+1 (310) 555 9450."

Listing 6.14 shows a method to validate that a date of birth is not greater than the current date. If the supplied value is greater, that value is changed to be the current date.

LISTING 6.14   Validating a date

```
- (BOOL)validateDateOfBirth:(id *)ioValue error:(NSError **)outError {
    NSDate *proposedDate = *ioValue;
    NSDate *currentDate = [NSDate date];

    if( [proposedDate compare:[NSDate date]] == NSOrderedDescending ) {
        *ioValue = currentDate;
    }

    return YES;
}
```

By changing the value of the `*ioValue`, the managed object itself will be marked as having a change (i.e., *dirty*) and will be validated again. This means that you shouldn't do anything in a validation method that might cause an infinite loop. One example of this would be to try and use a validation method to force a specific value for a particular property, regardless of the proposed `ioValue`, as shown in Listing 6.15.

LISTING 6.15 Causing an infinite loop from a validation method

```
- (BOOL)validateDateOfBirth:(id *)ioValue error:(NSError **)outError {
    *ioValue = [NSDate date]; // don't do this!

    return YES;
}
```

The method in Listing 6.15 would keep changing the `ioValue`, causing the validation method to be called again and again until Core Data gives up and terminates the application with the exception:

```
'Failed to process pending changes before save. The context is
 still dirty after 100 attempts. Typically this recursive dirtying
 is caused by a bad validation method, -willSave, or notification
 handler.'
```

Validation Based on Other Properties

There are two ways to validate one property based on another:

▶ Perform a conditional check in a `validate<KeyName>:error:` method.

▶ Implement `validateFor<Action>:` methods:

  (`validateForUpdate:`, `validateForInsert:`, `validateForDelete:`).

The first option is shown in Listing 6.16.

LISTING 6.16 Making sure a date of birth isn't after a date of death

```
- (BOOL)validateDateOfBirth:(id *)ioValue error:(NSError **)outError {
    NSDate *proposedDate = *ioValue;
    NSDate *checkDate = self.dateOfDeath;

    if( [proposedDate compare:checkDate] == NSOrderedDescending ) {
        *ioValue = checkDate;
    }

    return YES;
}
```

The code in Listing 6.16 checks whether the proposed date is later than the dateOfDeath, and if so, it changes *ioValue to the dateOfDeath.

This would be useful if you are going to be calling the validateValue:ForKey:error: method while the user is changing a Person's information. You might decide, however, only to validate the values when the whole record is saved, perhaps when a particular view controller is about to be popped off the navigation stack. In this instance, you would implement the validateForUpdate: and validateForInsert: methods, as shown in Listing 6.17.

LISTING 6.17   Validating a managed object before it is saved

```
- (BOOL)validateForInsert:(NSError **)error {
    if( ![super validateForInsert:error] ) {
        return NO;
    }

    if( [self.dateOfBirth compare:self.dateOfDeath] ==
                                        NSOrderedDescending ) {
        self.dateOfBirth = self.dateOfDeath;
    }

    return YES;
}

- (BOOL)validateForUpdate:(NSError **)error {
    if( ![super validateForUpdate:error] ) {
        return NO;
    }

    if( [self.dateOfBirth compare:self.dateOfDeath] ==
                                        NSOrderedDescending ) {
        self.dateOfBirth = self.dateOfDeath;
    }

    return YES;
}
```

If you create a new managed object, make some changes to its attributes, and then save the object's managed object context, the validateForInsert: method will be called. If the object already exists in the persistent store, the validateForUpdate: method will be called.

Note that changing values of the object in either of these methods will cause the method to be called again because the object has changed, so the potential infinite loop problem illustrated in Listing 6.15 must be avoided here, too.

It's also important to note that you should call NSManagedObject's implementation of the validateFor<Action> method before continuing; this will perform any individual property validation first, by validating each property that has unsaved changes using the validateValue:forKey:error: method.

If you choose to return NO and need to supply an error message, note that you should amalgamate multiple errors into one error object with an NSValidationMultipleErrorsError code, as shown in Listing 6.18.

LISTING 6.18   Generating multiple errors for validation failure

```
- (BOOL)validateForUpdate:(NSError **)error { // and validateForInsert:
    BOOL valid = [super validateForUpdate:error];

    NSMutableArray *errorsArray = [NSMutableArray array];
    NSMutableDictionary *userInfoDictionary =
                                [NSMutableDictionary dictionary];

    // Check to see if there are existing errors
    if( error && [*error code] == NSValidationMultipleErrorsError ) {
        [userInfoDictionary addEntriesFromDictionary:[*error userInfo]];
        [errorsArray addObjectsFromArray:
                [userInfoDictionary objectForKey:NSDetailedErrorsKey]];
    } else if( error ) {
        [errorsArray addObject:*error];
    }

    if( [self.dateOfBirth compare:self.dateOfDeath] ==
                                        NSOrderedDescending ) {
        valid = NO;

        NSString *localizedDesc = NSLocalizedString(
                @"Date of birth must be before date of death",
                @"Date of birth must be before date of death");
        NSDictionary *errorUserInfo = [NSDictionary
                    dictionaryWithObject:localizedDesc
                                forKey:NSLocalizedDescriptionKey];
        NSError *dateOfBirthError =
            [NSError errorWithDomain:kAWPersonDomain
                            code:kAWPersonInvalidDateOfBirthError
                        userInfo:errorUserInfo];

        [errorsArray addObject:dateOfBirthError];
    }

    if( [self.firstName length] == 0 && [self.lastName length] == 0 ) {
```

```
        valid = NO;
        NSError *noNameError = // generate as dateOfBirthError
        [errorsArray addObject: noNameError];
    }

    if( error && [errorsArray count] > 1 )
    {
        [userInfoDictionary setObject:errorsArray
                            forKey:NSDetailedErrorsKey];

        NSError *multipleError = [NSError
                    errorWithDomain:NSCocoaErrorDomain
                            code:NSValidationMultipleErrorsError
                        userInfo:userInfoDictionary];

        *error = multipleError;
    }
    else if( error && [errorsArray count] == 1 )
    {
        *error = [errorsArray objectAtIndex:0];
    }

    return valid;
}
```

This code shows several points:

- ▶ It starts by checking whether there are any existing errors from the call to the overridden validation method, storing them if so, and they are ready to be added again at the end of the method.

- ▶ It checks that the date of birth is before any date of death, creating a localized error if not.

- ▶ It checks whether both the person's first name and last name are missing, creating an error describing that problem (i.e. a person could potentially have just a last name or just a first name, but must have at least one of those).

- ▶ If there is only one error at the end of the method, it sets the *error reference to this one error. If there are multiple errors, it creates an NSValidationMultipleErrorsError.

Validation Prior to Deletion

If you need to disallow an object from being deleted, depending on certain criteria, you implement the validateForDelete: method. In a data records application, for example, you might decide that an object can only be deleted if it was created at least 5 years ago.

Again, you should also call the overridden implementation before doing any custom validation. The `NSManagedObject` implementation checks to see whether the object has any relationships to other objects specified on a relationship with a delete rule set to Deny. If so, the `validateForDelete:` will return `NO` to prevent the object from being deleted.

Fixing the Random People Application

Let's make sure that no people are created with dates of birth greater than the current date; this is simply a matter of implementing the validation code for `AWPerson` that you saw earlier in Listing 6.14, repeated here in Listing 6.19 for convenience.

LISTING 6.19   Validating the date of birth

```
- (BOOL)validateDateOfBirth:(id *)ioValue error:(NSError **)outError {
    NSDate *proposedDate = *ioValue;
    NSDate *checkDate = [NSDate date];

    if( [proposedDate compare:checkDate] == NSOrderedDescending ) {
        *ioValue = checkDate;
    }

    return YES;
}
```

Working with Transient Attributes

A transient attribute defined for an entity behaves just like any other modeled attribute, except that it won't be persisted to disk. This allows you to take advantage of Core Data features (like change management and automatic Undo) on properties that you don't need to persist, such as cached information, references to objects that exist only at runtime, or objects you need to save outside the Core Data persistent store.

Transient properties can also be used to work with non-standard attribute types (i.e., objects or structures that Core Data cannot handle automatically).

Let's look at an example of adding an `eyeColor` property to our `Person` entity. As with the existing names and dates of birth, each person will be given a random `eyeColor` from an array of possibilities. A person's `eyeColor` can then be set as the background color for the relevant table view cell. This is going to require a `UIColor` object to set as the background color, but `UIColor` isn't one of the supported Core Data attribute types.

Since you might expand this application to allow a user to change a person's eye color using a color picker, it doesn't make sense just to store a string like `@"blue"` or `@"green"`. Instead, you'll need to convert the `UIColor` into binary data, so that Core Data can store it.

In order not to have to keep archiving and unarchiving the color data every time you want to use the color property, it would be useful to have a dedicated UIColor property as well as the raw data property. And, if you were to expand the application to allow the user to make changes to a person's eyeColor, it would be good to have Core Data's change management look after the UIColor property, even though it won't be persisted.

This is where transient attributes come in. You can define two separate attributes on the Person entity; one is an eyeColorData property, persisted as binary data by Core Data, the other is a transient eyeColor property, used to deal directly with the UIColor.

Modifying the Data Model

Start by opening up the Random_People.xcdatamodeld file again and add these two new attributes:

▶ A Binary Data attribute called eyeColorData (optional but not transient)

▶ A transient attribute called eyeColor (leave the type as Undefined)

Because they aren't persisted in the store, transient properties are the exception to the rule that you must specify an attribute's type. Since none of Core Data's types correspond to a UIColor, you can leave the transient eyeColor attribute's type as Undefined.

Adding to the AWPerson Interface and Implementation

Once a transient property has been defined, you'll need to add some information to the managed object class files. Xcode offers some help in implementing the relevant @property declarations and accessor methods.

NOTE

Xcode 3 makes this functionality available by right-clicking on an attribute in the data model design area, as shown in Figure 6.5. At the time of writing, Xcode 4 does not have any contextual menus when using the Graph editor style, although it seems likely that this functionality will be made available in the future.

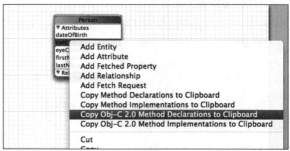

FIGURE 6.5   Xcode 3's contextual menu for an attribute

The Xcode 3 commands generate additional code compared to the current Xcode 4 Copy and Paste commands; just delete the extra text as necessary.

Open the data model and select the `eyeColorData` property. Choose Edit > Copy (⌘-C), then open `AWPerson.h`. Click after the existing property declarations and choose Edit > Paste Attribute Interface (Opt-⌘-V). You'll end up with the code shown in Listing 6.20.

LISTING 6.20   Auto-generated method declaration for the eyeColorData attribute

```
@interface AWPerson :   NSManagedObject
[...]
@property (nonatomic, readonly) NSString * dateOfBirthString;
@property (nonatomic, retain) NSData * eyeColorData;



@end
```

Next, you need to add the relevant implementation information for this attribute in `AWPerson.m`. Click just before the final `@end` keyword, and choose Edit > Paste Attribute Implementation (Opt-⌘-V), to paste the `@dynamic` property information shown in Listing 6.21.

LISTING 6.21   Auto-generated method implementation for the fullName attribute

```
@implementation AWPerson

[...]

@dynamic firstName;
@dynamic dateOfBirth;
@dynamic lastName;

@dynamic eyeColorData;

@end
```

If you were working with a to-many relationship, and used the Edit > Paste Relationship Implementation command, the pasted code would include methods to add and remove other managed objects from the relationship set; Listing 6.22 shows the method declarations you would see for a to-many relationship from an `EmailAccount` entity.

LISTING 6.22   Auto-generated method declarations for a relationship

```
- (void)addEmailAccountsObject:(NSManagedObject *)value {
    [...]
}
```

```
- (void)removeEmailAccountsObject:(NSManagedObject *)value {
    [...]
}

- (void)addEmailAccounts:(NSSet *)value {
    [...]
}

- (void)removeEmailAccounts:(NSSet *)value {
    [...]
}

@end
```

These methods are actually provided automatically at runtime; if you don't need to modify the default behavior, you could simply add a category to the class specifying that it implements these methods, without having to use any of the code shown in Listing 6.22.

In order to make use of the eyeColor transient property, you'll need to write code to convert the eyeColorData into a UIColor, and back again.

Let's start with the eyeColor property declaration; select the eyeColor property in the Data Modeler, Copy it, then open AWPerson.h and Paste the Attribute Interface after the other properties.

You'll need to change the property type from UNKNOWN_TYPE to UIColor*, as shown in Listing 6.23.

LISTING 6.23   Adding the transient eyeColor property declaration

```
@interface AWPerson :   NSManagedObject
[...]
@property (nonatomic, retain) NSData * eyeColorData;
@property (nonatomic, retain) UIColor * eyeColor;

@end
```

Adding a Getter Method for the Transient Property

There are several strategies for accessing the color; you could preload the UIColor whenever a Person is fetched (i.e. in awakeFromFetch), or generate it lazily when required. Let's use the second approach.

At the time of writing, Xcode 4 won't paste anything more than the @dynamic attribute "implementation". For the eyeColor property, you'll also need to type the code yourself for the custom accessor method. If `eyeColor` was a normal, non-transient attribute, the accessor method would look like Listing 6.24.

LISTING 6.24   An accessor method implementation for a non-transient property

```
- (UIColor *)eyeColor {
    [self willAccessValueForKey:@"eyeColor"];
    UIColor *tmpValue = [self primitiveEyeColor];
    [self didAccessValueForKey:@"eyeColor"];

    return tmpValue;
}
```

Because `eyeColor` is a transient property, nothing is stored in the persistent store. Unless you specifically set a primitive value, the `primitiveEyeColor` method will return nil. So, you need to generate the `UIColor` from the `eyeColorData` raw data property when necessary, storing the result as the managed object's primitive value for `eyeColor`, as shown in Listing 6.25.

LISTING 6.25   The lazy accessor for the transient eyeColor property

```
- (UIColor *)eyeColor {
    [self willAccessValueForKey:@"eyeColor"];
    UIColor *tmpValue = [self primitiveEyeColor];
    [self didAccessValueForKey:@"eyeColor"];
    if( tmpValue ) return tmpValue;

    NSData *colorData = [self eyeColorData];
    if( !colorData ) return nil;

    tmpValue = [NSKeyedUnarchiver unarchiveObjectWithData:colorData];
    [self setPrimitiveEyeColor:tmpValue];

    return tmpValue;
}
```

If the primitive `eyeColor` has previously been set, this method returns it straightaway. Otherwise, it gets the `eyeColorData`, unarchives it and sets it as the primitive `eyeColor` value.

NOTE

The method checks to make sure the data is not nil. `NSKeyedUnarchiver` will raise an exception if the data is invalid.

In order to avoid compiler warnings, you'll need to add a category to indicate that an AWPerson instance can respond to the primitive accessor methods. Since these are only used internally within the AWPerson.m file, add the category shown in Listing 6.26 to top of AWPerson.m.

LISTING 6.26   Adding the PrimitiveAccessors category

```
#import "AWPerson.h"

@interface AWPerson (PrimitiveAccessors)

- (UIColor *)primitiveEyeColor;
- (void)setPrimitiveEyeColor:(UIColor *)value;
- (NSData *)primitiveEyeColorData;
- (void)setPrimitiveEyeColorData:(NSData *)value;


@end

@implementation AWPerson
[...]
```

Adding a Setter Method for the Transient Property

As far as *archiving* the UIColor is concerned, there are once again several options. One strategy would be to implement a setEyeColor: method, and archive the color every time it's changed. This might be fine for a simple color, but if your archival procedure is more complex or time consuming, it's preferable to perform it only once—when the object is saved. Let's use the second approach.

Make sure that you have pasted (or typed) the @dynamic eyeColor; line in the implementation file. The behavior provided automatically by NSManagedObject for setEyeColor: will be fine.

When a managed object is about to be saved, it will receive a willSave message, which you can use to archive transient attributes. Implement the method as shown in Listing 6.27.

LISTING 6.27   Implementing willSave to archive a transient value

```
- (void)willSave {
    UIColor *color = [self primitiveEyeColor];
    if( color ) {
        [self setPrimitiveEyeColorData:
                [NSKeyedArchiver archivedDataWithRootObject:color]];
    } else {
```

```
        [self setPrimitiveEyeColorData:nil];
    }

    [super willSave];
}
```

This method will also be called when an object is about to be deleted, so if your archival operation is particularly expensive, you may want to check isDeleted before proceeding.

Note that this method makes use of the primitive accessors. If for some reason you need to trigger change notifications in willSave by using the standard accessors, like setEyeColorData:, Core Data will notice the change, and willSave will be called again. If you continually set a new value using a standard accessor, you'll end up with an infinite loop (as with validation, you'll get an exception after 100 attempts). To avoid this you'd need to add a conditional check to make sure you're not just setting the same value again.

CHANGES TO THE PERSISTENT PROPERTY

If you want to be able to set the *persistent* property directly, i.e. eyeColorData in this example, and have it update the transient eyeColor as well, you'd also need to implement a custom setter method for setEyeColorData:. If you use lazy generation for the transient property, this method can simply set the transient attribute to nil, i.e. using setEyeColor:nil, clearing the cached primitive UIColor, and triggering change notifications.

Using the UIColor Property

Now that you have the eyeColor and eyeColorData properties set up for archival, let's assign a random eyeColor to new Person objects, and display that color as the background of the relevant cell in the table view.

Start by adding a new randomColor class method to AWPerson.m, as shown in Listing 6.28.

LISTING 6.28   Generating a random color

```
+ (UIColor *)randomColor {
    static NSArray *colorsArray = nil;

    if( !colorsArray ) {
        colorsArray = [[NSArray alloc] initWithObjects:
                        [UIColor lightGrayColor],
                        [UIColor blueColor],
                        [UIColor greenColor], nil];
    }
```

```
    int randomIndex = arc4random() % [colorsArray count];

    return [colorsArray objectAtIndex:randomIndex];
}
```

Use this to assign an `eyeColor` to a newly generated person, as in Listing 6.29.

LISTING 6.29   Setting the eyeColor for new people

```
+ (id)randomPersonInManagedObjectContext:(NSManagedObjectContext *)moc {
    AWPerson *randomPerson = [self personInManagedObjectContext:moc];

    [...]

    randomPerson.eyeColor = [self randomColor];

    return randomPerson;
}
```

All that's left is to set the background color on each cell before it gets displayed in the table view. The easiest way to do this is to implement the table view delegate method `tableView:willDisplayCell:forRowAtIndexPath:`, as shown in Listing 6.30.

LISTING 6.30   Setting the background color of the cell

```
- (void)tableView:(UITableView *)tableView
            willDisplayCell:(UITableViewCell *)cell
           forRowAtIndexPath:(NSIndexPath *)indexPath {
    AWPerson *person = [[self fetchedResultsController]
                          objectAtIndexPath:indexPath];

    [cell setBackgroundColor:person.eyeColor];
}
```

Before you build and run the project, you'll need to delete the existing data store (the `Random_People.sqlite` file in the app's Documents directory) because the data model has changed (you added a new persistent attribute) and the app isn't set up for automatic migration (described in Chapter 8, "Migration and Versioning"). If you don't delete the store before running the app, you'll get an exception. The easiest way is just to delete the whole app from the Simulator or from an iOS device (press and hold the app icon until it jiggles, then press the X).

When you run the project, you'll find that new people will be added to the table view with a randomly selected eye color, used as the background color of the table view cell.

A note about fetching and sorting

It is worth bearing in mind that it isn't possible to create a fetch request that either fetches or sorts its results based on a transient attribute. In the Random People application, for example, you would receive an error and the fetch would fail if you tried to use a predicate or set a sort descriptor involving the eyeColor attribute.

If you have a situation where you need to be able to sort or fetch based on a non-standard property, you'll either need to cache a derived standard value (suitable for sorting or a predicate) in the data model as another persistent attribute, updating it whenever its value is affected by other properties changing, or filter/sort an array of results after it has been fetched.

Working with Transformable Attributes

The eyeColor example used above is very simple in terms of transformation between the transient UIColor and the persistent data attributes—it's just a case of standard archiving and unarchiving using the relevant archivedDataWithRootObject: and unarchiveObjectWithData: methods on NSKeyedArchiver and NSKeyedUnarchiver.

If you don't need to perform any complex transformation, you may find it easier to make use of another Core Data timesaver, *transformable attributes*. These make use of a value transformer to convert automatically between the non-standard attribute type and the persisted NSData, meaning you can achieve the same functionality as you've just seen, but without the need for a transient attribute. Because this value transformer is specified in the model, you don't even need to subclass NSManagedObject.

Let's replace the existing eyeColor and eyeColorData attributes and methods in Random People with a single transformable eyeColor attribute:

▸ Start by removing the eyeColorData attribute from the data model.

▸ Change the eyeColor attribute type to Transformable, and uncheck the Transient checkbox.

▸ A Name option will appear to specify a value transformer. If you need to use a custom transformer, you can set it here; if you don't specify a value transformer, Core Data will use the NSKeyedUnarchiveFromData option. This uses NSKeyedArchiver and NSKeyedUnarchiver to transform the data, and will work just fine for UIColor, so leave the field blank.

▸ Remove the eyeColorData property from AWPerson.h, along with its @dynamic entry in AWPerson.m.

▸ Remove the eyeColor accessor method, and the willSave method.

This means that you're left with just an eyeColor property (still a UIColor) in AWPerson.h, and an @dynamic entry for eyeColor in AWPerson.m—you don't need to implement any accessor methods. If you were working without a subclass of NSManagedObject, you'd need to add these to a category, as described earlier in the chapter.

Once again, you've made changes to the data model so you'll need to erase the persistent store before continuing (just delete the app from the simulator or the device). When you build and run the project, you'll find it behaves just as it did before. The UIColor transformation now happens automatically through a value transformer.

In practice, you'll often find that you can get away with a value transformer rather than writing custom code for transient attributes. It's worth going the transient attribute route, however, if you don't want the value to be transformed every time it's accessed, such as for a complex archival process. You'll also need to use the transient property approach to work with non-standard scalar attributes, like custom structures.

The Managed Object Lifecycle

You've seen how to add transient properties (which aren't persisted in the data store) to an entity by specifying them in the Xcode Data Modeler. It's also perfectly acceptable to have properties on a managed object that aren't listed in the entity description.

In an application that downloaded information from the internet based on a saved search string, you might have an entity called SavedSearch, with its various persistent properties specified in the model, but also need access to an object property for an NSURLConnection object on each active search. This might be to enable searches to run independently from each other, perhaps so that important searches can run on a more frequent timer than less important searches. In this case, you can just treat your NSManagedObject subclass like any other object, creating additional properties for an NSURLConnection and NSTimer in the class description and implementation, but not specifying these as properties in the data model.

The only reason to specify these properties as transient in the data model is if you need to make use of change management or Undo. Specifying a transient property in the data model means that a managed object will be marked as having changes if the value of that property is changed; if you specified the NSURLConnection attribute in the data model, for example, the managed object would be marked as dirty when you first created that connection.

Initializing Non-persistent Properties

If you need to allocate or release objects used during the lifetime of a managed object instance, and would traditionally use init or dealloc methods to do this, you need instead to make use of managed object lifecycle methods. It's important to note that you should *not* override init or dealloc in a subclass of NSManagedObject.

Because of the way that Core Data works with faults, the time to allocate any necessary objects that need to be retained by a managed object is during the awakeFromFetch, awakeFromInsert, and awakeFromSnapshotEvents: methods:

▶ awakeFromInsert will be called when a new object is created and inserted into a managed object context.

▶ awakeFromFetch will be called when an object that already exists in the persistent store is fetched (and a fault triggered).

▶ awakeFromSnapshotEvents: will be called when an object is reset, for example following an Undo. You might use this method to recalculate instance variables derived from persistent attributes.

Each of these methods requires you to call the overridden implementation before your own.

The time to release any retained objects, or do any other necessary tidying work for a managed object, is either in its willTurnIntoFault or its didTurnIntoFault method. You do not need to call the overridden implementation of either of these methods because the default methods—provided by NSManagedObject—do nothing. You should, however, set any released instance variables to nil to avoid dangling pointers if the object's fault is later fired.

If you need to set any initial state for a new object using default values that cannot be specified in the data model, you should do this in awakeFromInsert. Change notifications are disabled for both this method and awakeFromFetch, so you can safely make changes to an object's properties using its setter methods without marking the object as dirty. This also means that any properties you change won't be noticed by the managed object context's undo manager. You could set a persistent creationDate property, for example, without worrying what happens if the user shakes the phone to Undo immediately after creating the object (which would otherwise just undo the creation date setting but not the object insertion).

The downside to disabling notifications during these methods is that any relationships set during awakeFromFetch or awakeFromInsert won't have their inverse set automatically.

Listing 6.31 shows sample implementations of methods that set an initial creationDate persistent attribute on a new object and allocate a string object (declared in the @interface) to be retained for the lifetime of managed object instances, created or fetched.

LISTING 6.31   Working with the lifecycle of a managed object

```
- (void)awakeFromFetch {
    [super awakeFromFetch];

    usefulString = [[NSString alloc] initWithString:@"Hello!"];
}

- (void)awakeFromInsert {
```

```
    [super awakeFromInsert];

    self.creationDate = [NSDate date];

    usefulString = [[NSString alloc] initWithString:@"Hello!"];
}

- (void)didTurnIntoFault {
    [usefulString release]; usefulString = nil;
}
```

Summary

This chapter has shown you some of the power achievable through Core Data and its managed objects. Aside from the fact that you need to use the awakeFrom... and ...TurnIntoFault methods rather than init and dealloc, you can generally use managed objects like any other object, but with added persistence mechanisms.

You've seen how to work with transient properties, which are not persisted to disk, and also how to accomplish validation both on an individual property-level and for an object as a whole to make sure its properties are valid in combination as well as individually.

So far, any fetch requests and fetched results controllers have worked with *all* the managed object instances for any given entity in the data model. The next chapter covers NSPredicate, allowing you to specify that a fetch should only return objects matching certain requirements.

CHAPTER 7

Working with Predicates

IN THIS CHAPTER

- ▶ Predicate Basics
- ▶ Comparing Strings
- ▶ Compound Predicates
- ▶ Sets and Relationships
- ▶ Examining SQL Queries
- ▶ Adding a Search Display Controller

Although predicates are not unique to the Core Data framework, they are such key ingredients to fetch requests that it's important to have a thorough understanding of predicate syntax. Predicates are the way you specify constraints on what is returned from a fetch request. If you don't use a predicate, *all* the objects for a specified entity will be returned.

This chapter begins with the basics of creating an NSPredicate, discussing simple predicate format strings. You'll learn how to use predicates to match against scalar values like numbers or dates, and also how to match objects, particularly across relationships, such as when fetching employees who work in a specific department. There's a whole section dedicated to working with strings, including information on case sensitivity, and you'll see how to examine the raw SQL that Core Data generates to query a SQLite store.

The last part of the chapter demonstrates how to add a Search Display Controller to the Random People application, to enable searching for people by first and last name, as well as filtering on past and future birth dates.

Predicate Basics

If you create a fetch request for a given entity but don't specify a predicate, Core Data will return *all* managed objects for that entity. If you only need to return managed objects that satisfy certain conditions, you need to use a predicate.

A predicate is a statement that evaluates as true or false, such as deceased == NO or lastName == 'Smith'. When fetching objects from a persistent store, Core Data checks the condition specified by the predicate against each object, and returns only those for which the predicate evaluates as true. In relational database terms, adding a predicate to a fetch request is like adding a WHERE clause to a standard SQL SELECT query.

The simplest predicates contain a single comparison, like those shown in the previous paragraph. Later in this chapter, however, you'll learn about predicates involving multiple conditions, and compound predicates built by combining two or more predicates together.

Creating Predicates Using Format Strings

The NSPredicate class offers a number of factory methods, most of which involve a format string. The simplest of these is this method:

```
+ (NSPredicate *)predicateWithFormat:(NSString *)format, ...
```

The format string is similar to that used by NSString's stringWithFormat: method, where you either provide a self-contained string, like this:

```
NSPredicate *predicate =
    [NSPredicate predicateWithFormat:@"lastName == 'Smith'"];
```

or use token substitution, like this:

```
NSString *testName = @"Smith";

NSPredicate *predicate =
    [NSPredicate predicateWithFormat:@"lastName == %@", testName];
```

> **NOTE**
>
> If you specify a string inline (as in the first example), you need to surround that string with quotation marks. If you insert a string using the %@ token, you don't need to include quotation marks because the predicate string parser will insert them automatically.
>
> If you do include quotation marks around the %@ characters, or any other substitution token, the token characters will be used—no substitution will occur.

Scalar values, by contrast, do not need quotation marks:

```
NSPredicate *predicate =
    [NSPredicate predicateWithFormat:@"deceased == NO"];
```

The tokens used in the parser are the standard tokens used by NSLog() and described in the *Format Specifiers* section of the *String Programming Guide*,[1] so you can substitute scalar variables directly, like this:

---

[1] Apple's String Programming Guide can be found at: http://bit.ly/eovaWQ

```
BOOL testDeceased = NO;

NSPredicate *predicate =
    [NSPredicate predicateWithFormat:@"deceased == %d", testDeceased];
```

Alternatively, you can substitute an NSNumber object instead of the scalar value, using the %@ token:

```
NSNumber *testDeceased = [NSNumber numberWithBool:NO];

NSPredicate *predicate =
    [NSPredicate predicateWithFormat:@"deceased == %@", testDeceased];
```

The predicate parser will figure out that the object isn't a string, and so won't include quotation marks.

The same holds true for dates; if you need to perform a date comparison, it's usually easiest to create an NSDate object and substitute it into a format string, like this:

```
NSDate *currentDate = [NSDate date];

NSPredicate *predicate =
    [NSPredicate predicateWithFormat:@"dateOfBirth < %@", currentDate];
```

Substituting Strings Without Quotation Marks

There's one additional token available for predicate format strings, %K (that's a capital K). This token is used to substitute a string *without* surrounding it with quotation marks. Typically, you'd use this if you need to specify a property name at runtime:

```
NSString *propertyToTest = @"deceased";
BOOL testDeceased = NO;

NSPredicate *predicate =
    [NSPredicate predicateWithFormat:@"%K == %d",
                              propertyToTest, testDeceased];
```

Building the Predicate as a String

It's also possible to build your predicate as an NSString and then use that NSString as the predicate format. You'll need to insert all the necessary quotation marks yourself, because NSPredicate only inserts quotes when processing substitution tokens in a format string supplied directly. In this case, you build the predicate using normal NSString methods and pass the string to predicateWithFormat: with no token values:

```
NSString *propertyToTest = @"deceased";
BOOL testDeceased = NO;
```

```
NSString *predicateFormat = [NSString stringWithFormat:@"%@ == %d",
                                     propertyToTest, testDeceased];
NSPredicate *predicate =
                [NSPredicate predicateWithFormat:predicateFormat];
```

Predicate Variables

It's also possible to include substitution *variables* in a predicate. Substitution variables allow you to re-use a predicate for multiple fetches that have the same format but different values. You specify a substitution variable in a predicate by using the $ sign, like this:

```
NSPredicate *predicateWithVariables =
        [NSPredicate predicateWithFormat:@"lastName == $LAST_NAME"];
```

This creates a template predicate that can be used to create new predicates with the same format and different values for LAST_NAME. In order to make use of these substitution variables you need to provide a dictionary of key/value pairs to substitute for the variables, like this:

```
NSDictionary *substitutionVariables = [NSDictionary
                dictionaryWithObject:@"Smith" forKey:@"LAST_NAME"];

NSPredicate *predicate =
   [predicateWithVariables predicateWithSubstitutionVariables:
                                        substitutionVariables];
```

> **NOTE**
>
> The leading $ sign is only used in the predicate format string. When you create your dictionary of substitution variables and their values, you should not include the $ in the dictionary key names.

Substitution variables are also useful when working with fetch requests stored in the data model, as covered in the next section.

Storing Fetch Requests in the Data Model

The Core Data Model Editor allows you to create fetch requests "visually" for a given entity: click and hold the + icon in the bottom bar, and choose "Add Fetch Request."

> **NOTE**
>
> Under Xcode 3, you'll need to select an entity before you can add a fetch request. When you click the + button under the property list and choose "Add Fetch Request," the property list view will change to show *only* fetch requests; to show the properties again, use the triangle button next to the – button and choose "Show All Properties."

When editing a fetch request in Xcode 4's Data Model Editor, you'll only be able to use the Table editor style, as shown in Figure 7.1.

FIGURE 7.1   Editing a Fetch Request stored in the data model

Storing Fetch Requests with Substitution Variables

The **Xcode 3** Data Modeler offers the ability to switch between typed *constant values* in fetch request predicates, and *variables* or *keys*. Right-click (or Control-click) in the area to the right of the value text field, as shown in Figure 7.2, and you'll be able to select the type of information to supply on the right hand side of the predicate.

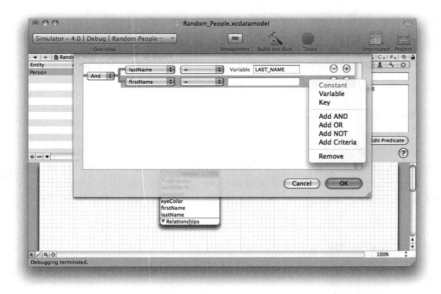

FIGURE 7.2   Editing a Fetch Request in the Data Modeler under Xcode 3

If you use this feature to specify a Variable, you only need to enter the name of the variable; don't include the $ sign or the parser will fail to understand the predicate.

At the time of writing, this functionality hasn't yet made it into Xcode 4, and if you open a data model in Xcode 4 with a variable in a fetch request created by Xcode 3, you'll see the predicate displayed as an expression. If the feature hasn't made it into Xcode 4 by the time you read this, it's important to note that when using an *expression* in the model, you do need to include the $ sign.

Once you have successfully stored a fetch request in the model, you can execute it using the code shown in Listing 7.1.

LISTING 7.1   Executing a stored fetch request with substitution variables

```
NSManagedObjectModel *managedObjectModel =
   managedObjectContext.persistentStoreCoordinator.managedObjectModel;

NSError *anyError = nil;
NSDictionary *substitutionVariables = [NSDictionary
                 dictionaryWithObject:@"Smith" forKey:@"LAST_NAME"];

NSFetchRequest *fetchRequest =
     [managedObjectModel
          fetchRequestFromTemplateWithName:@"PeopleWithLastName"
                    substitutionVariables:substitutionDictionary];
NSArray *results =
          [self.managedObjectContext executeFetchRequest:fetchRequest
                                    error:&anyError];
```

Predicate Comparison Operators

When creating predicates using format strings, you can use any of the standard logical comparison operators, like <, > and !=, etc.

To check equality, you can use either = or ==. It can be confusing at first when deciding which is correct (= or ==), especially since their meanings in C/Objective-C are very different. In this case though, they're equivalent. If you use one of these equality operators with an object, it's important to remember that the predicate parser will substitute the object's *value*:

```
NSNumber *testDeceased = [NSNumber numberWithBool:NO];

NSPredicate *predicate =
    [NSPredicate predicateWithFormat:@"deceased == %@", testDeceased];
```

This code snippet checks to see whether the value of deceased is equal to the value of the testDeceased number object (i.e., the scalar Boolean NO). It does not check that deceased is the exact same NSNumber *object* as testDeceased.

The exception to this is when specifying Core Data managed objects, like this:

```
NSManagedObject *department = ...; // Assume you've fetched this

NSPredicate *predicate =
    [NSPredicate predicateWithFormat:@"department == %@",
                                                department];
```

If you execute a fetch request based on this predicate in an employee/department application, Core Data will return all the employees whose department is represented by the actual department object.

NOTE

In this particular example, you don't need to execute a fetch. Assuming you've modeled a bidirectional relationship between employees and departments, you can simply ask the department for its set of employees.

Bitwise Operators

Although it's not documented at the time of writing, it's possible to use bitwise operators with NSPredicate and Core Data. If you've defined an integer value on an entity, which you are using as a bit field, you can use the & operator to return only managed objects whose integer has a specific bit set:

```
NSPredicate *predicate =
    [NSPredicate predicateWithFormat:
        @"(integerValue & %i) == %i",
                    1 << 2, 1 << 2];
```

This predicate checks each integerValue by performing a bitwise AND operation against the provided bit mask (in this case, 0b100).

Key Paths

If you are fetching objects with relationships to other objects, you can generate a fetch request using key paths, like this:

```
NSPredicate *predicate =
   [NSPredicate predicateWithFormat:
                        @"department.name == 'Sales'"];
```

This would fetch employee objects whose related department is named "Sales."

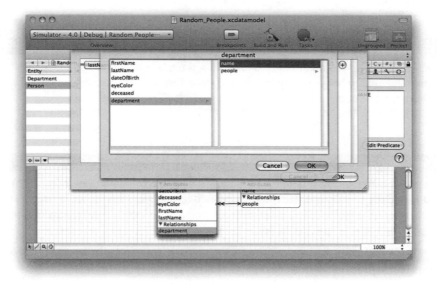
Comparing Strings

There are a number of operators specifically for use with strings. The basic equality operator (= or ==) will evaluate as true in a predicate only if the strings match exactly. As an example, the following predicate:

```
NSPredicate *predicate =
    [NSPredicate predicateWithFormat:
                        @"department.name == 'Sales'"];
```

will only match a department with the exact name "Sales." It won't match against "sales," "SALES," or "Domestic Sales."

To indicate that you want a case-insensitive match, you can append [c] to the operator:

```
NSPredicate *predicate =
    [NSPredicate predicateWithFormat:
                @"department.name ==[c] 'Sales'"];
```

This will now match "sales," "SALES" and "Sales," but still not "Domestic Sales."

If you need to match the beginning or end of a string, you can use BEGINSWITH or ENDSWITH:

```
NSPredicate *predicate =
    [NSPredicate predicateWithFormat:
                @"department.name ENDSWITH 'Sales'"];
```

The predicate will still match "Sales," but now also matches "Domestic Sales." As with any of the string operators in this section, you can specify that you want a case insensitive search by appending [c] to the operator:

```
NSPredicate *predicate =
    [NSPredicate predicateWithFormat:
                @"department.name ENDSWITH[c] 'Sales'"];
```

This time, the predicate will evaluate as true for any string ending with the upper or lower case "sales," such as "DOMESTIC SALES," "saLES" or "sales."

By default, a string is matched *diacritically*, which means that the character é will only match é and not e or ë. To indicate a diacritic-insensitive search, append [d] to the operator:

```
NSPredicate *predicate =
    [NSPredicate predicateWithFormat:
            @"department.name BEGINSWITH[d] 'Département'"];
```

This predicate will match against "Departement," "Departement des Transports" and "Département."

If you need to indicate both case and diacritic insensitivity, specify both inside the square brackets:

```
NSPredicate *predicate =
    [NSPredicate predicateWithFormat:
            @"department.name BEGINSWITH[cd] 'Département'"];
```

The predicate will still match both "Departement" and "Département," but also "departement" and "département."

To check whether one string contains another, use the CONTAINS operator:

```
NSPredicate *predicate =
    [NSPredicate predicateWithFormat:
            @"department.name CONTAINS 'Shipping'"];
```

This predicate will match against both "Shipping Department" and "International Shipping and Domestic Delivery."

The LIKE operator allows you to indicate wildcard characters using * and ?. A ? will match one character, a * will match one or more characters:

```
NSPredicate *predicate =
    [NSPredicate predicateWithFormat:
            @"department.name LIKE 'De?i*n'"];
```

This will match "Design" and "Dedication," but not "Deportation."

Finally, the MATCHES operator allows you to perform a regular expression-style comparison, like this:

```
NSPredicate *predicate =
    [NSPredicate predicateWithFormat:
            @"department.name MATCHES 'S[ao]les'"];
```

This predicate will evaluate true for both "Sales" and "Soles."

NOTE

If you're also developing for the Mac desktop, it's not possible to use the MATCHES operator for SQLite stores under desktop versions prior to OS X 10.6 Snow Leopard.

Keep in mind that string matching will be slower than numerical comparisons, which could lead to slow fetches. Performance implications of NSPredicate expressions are discussed in Chapter 11, "Optimizing for iOS Performance and Memory Requirements."

Compound Predicates

Up to this point, the examples in this chapter have all assumed you need to specify only a single condition in a predicate. If you need to specify multiple conditions, such as specifying both a first name *and* a last name, you have two options.

It's perfectly acceptable to include both conditions within a single format string, like this:

```
NSPredicate *predicate =
    [NSPredicate predicateWithFormat:
        @"firstName == 'John' AND lastName == 'Smith'"];
```

When Core Data executes a fetch request for this predicate, it first evaluates the left side; objects that don't meet the left condition are immediately disregarded. Only objects that do satisfy the left side criteria will be tested against those on the right.

In a predicate that's testing against both a numeric value and a text comparison, it's best to put the numeric comparison first, thereby avoiding unnecessary overhead checking last names if the faster numeric comparison fails:

```
NSDate *currentDate = [NSDate date];
NSPredicate *predicate =
    [NSPredicate predicateWithFormat:
            @"dateOfBirth < %@ AND lastName == %@",
                                currentDate, @"Smith"];
```

To specify that a predicate should evaluate as true if either of two conditions is met, use the OR operator:

```
NSDate *currentDate = [NSDate date];
NSPredicate *predicate =
    [NSPredicate predicateWithFormat:
            @"dateOfBirth < %@ OR lastName == %@",
                                currentDate, @"Smith"];
```

Again, put any numeric comparisons first—if the left side evaluates as true, Core Data won't bother checking the right side. Once the numeric condition is met, an object is included in the fetch results without checking the string comparison.

You can also use && and ¦¦ in place of AND and OR, respectively. To negate an expression, use NOT or !, like this:

```
NSDate *currentDate = [NSDate date];
NSPredicate *predicate =
    [NSPredicate predicateWithFormat:
            @"dateOfBirth < %@ AND NOT lastName == %@",
                                currentDate, @"Smith"];
```

This predicate is equivalent to the following:

```
NSDate *currentDate = [NSDate date];
NSPredicate *predicate =
    [NSPredicate predicateWithFormat:
            @"dateOfBirth < %@ AND lastName != %@",
                                currentDate, @"Smith"];
```

As with Objective-C conditional statements, it can be useful to add parentheses to clarify the operator precedence. The following predicate is equivalent to the previous two examples, but may be easier to read:

```
NSDate *currentDate = [NSDate date];
NSPredicate *predicate =
    [NSPredicate predicateWithFormat:
            @"(dateOfBirth < %@) AND (NOT lastName == %@)",
                            currentDate, @"Smith"];
```

NSCompoundPredicate

It's also possible to create a predicate with multiple sub-predicates using
NSCompoundPredicate. This class offers three factory methods. Two of these take an array
of sub-predicates to be combined with the relevant AND, or OR operators:

```
+ (NSPredicate *)andPredicateWithSubpredicates:(NSArray *)subpredicates
+ (NSPredicate *)orPredicateWithSubpredicates:(NSArray *)subpredicates
```

The third negates an existing predicate:

```
+ (NSPredicate *)notPredicateWithSubpredicate:(NSPredicate *)predicate
```

The following code creates a compound predicate to check both first and last names:

```
NSPredicate *firstNamePredicate = [NSPredicate
                    predicateWithFormat:@"firstName == 'John'"];
NSPredicate *lastNamePredicate = [NSPredicate
                    predicateWithFormat:@"lastName == 'Smith'"];

NSPredicate *predicate =
        [NSCompoundPredicate andPredicateWithSubpredicates:
            [NSArray arrayWithObjects:firstNamePredicate,
                                lastNamePredicate, nil]];
```

If you need a predicate to check whether a property has one of several values, you can set
up a compound predicate using code like that in Listing 7.2:

LISTING 7.2   Building a compound predicate using a for loop

```
NSArray *firstNamesToTest = [NSArray
            arrayWithObjects:@"James", @"Jim", @"Jimmy", nil];

NSMutableArray *namePredicatesArray = [NSMutableArray array];

for( NSString *eachName in firstNamesToTest) {
    [namePredicatesArray addObject:
            [NSPredicate predicateWithFormat:
                    @"firstName == %@", eachName]];
}
```

```
NSPredicate *predicate = [NSCompoundPredicate
                orPredicateWithSubpredicates:namePredicatesArray];
```

In this example, the for loop creates one predicate per first name, and adds each predicate to a mutable array. The final compound predicate is built by combining all of those first name predicates using the OR operator.

Sets and Relationships

As an alternative to using multiple sub-predicates to test whether a property matches one of several different values, you can use one of NSPredicate's aggregation operators: IN.

The example compound predicate created in Listing 7.2 could be replaced with a simple predicate using the IN operator, like this:

```
NSArray *firstNamesToTest = [NSArray
              arrayWithObjects:@"James", @"Jim", @"Jimmy", nil];

NSPredicate *predicate = [NSPredicate predicateWithFormat:
                           @"firstName IN %@", firstNamesToTest];
```

The collection object you provide for substitution in this predicate can be an array, a set, or a dictionary.

NOTE

There's a problem when using dictionaries with Core Data predicates under iOS. If you supply a dictionary as the collection object, the documented behavior is that the predicate should use the *values* in the dictionary (this is what happens on the desktop, and in any non-Core Data predicate use under iOS, such as filtering a dictionary in memory). At the time of writing, it actually uses the *keys*.

If you need to use a dictionary with IN, it's best to specify that the predicate should use the values, like this:

```
NSPredicate *predicate =
  [NSPredicate predicateWithFormat:
                @"firstName IN %@",
      [someDictionary allValues]];
```

On the other hand, if you need to use the keys, don't assume that this problem won't be fixed in the future to make it consistent with the expected behavior. Instead, use the same code as above, but substitute allKeys in place of allValues.

It's also possible to create a predicate to filter objects based on properties of their related objects using the ANY, SOME, ALL, or NONE aggregate operator keywords.

In an employee/department application, for example, you might wish to fetch a set of departments that have any employees with a salary greater than a specified amount:

```
NSPredicate *predicate = [NSPredicate predicateWithFormat:
                          @"ANY employees.salary > 50000"];
```

Executing a fetch request for departments with this predicate will return any departments that have at least one employee with a salary above $50,000. You could also use SOME in place of ANY and still have the same behavior.

ALL and NONE behave as you would expect. The following examples both match any department where an employee earns at least $10,000 and no less (i.e., you won't see results for employees that earn less than $10,000):

```
NSPredicate *predicate = [NSPredicate predicateWithFormat:
                          @"ALL employees.salary >= 10000"];
```

```
NSPredicate *predicate = [NSPredicate predicateWithFormat:
                          @"NONE employees.salary < 10000"];
```

Examining SQL Queries

When using predicates with SQLite stores, it's possible to find out the raw SQL queries generated by Core Data. You'll need to pass an argument at runtime to enable a Core Data debug option, as described in detail in Chapter 11, "Optimizing for iOS Performance and Memory Requirements," in the section "Monitoring SQLite Stores."

It can be helpful to check the raw SQL to make sure your predicates convert to SQL queries with constraints included in the best possible order, such as when performing numerical comparisons before textual searches. See Chapter 11 for more information.

It's important to remember, though, that neither the internal structure of the SQL tables of a Core Data SQLite store, nor the conversion process from an NSPredicate into a raw SQL query, are documented. Apple may change the underlying implementations in the future, so don't expect the same SQL query or entity table name to be used under every version of iOS.

Adding a Search Display Controller

Let's put all this NSPredicate knowledge into practice by adding a Search Display Controller to the Random People application from Chapter 6. This adds a search field to the top of the table view, allowing users to filter the list of people based on matched names, as shown in Figure 7.4.

Start by opening the RootViewController.xib file from the Random People project.

FIGURE 7.4   The Random People application with a Search Display Controller

Make sure you can see the Object Library (Control-Option-⌘-3), and find the "Search Bar and Search Display Controller object" (its icon shows a view with a search bar and a yellow circle). Drag out an instance and drop it onto the table view object, as shown in Figure 7.5.

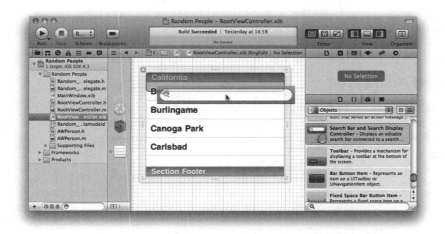

FIGURE 7.5   Dropping the Search Display Controller on the table view

The new item in the table view is just a Search Bar; if you look at the left bar of the Interface Editor, you'll find the new Search Display Controller object listed. Right-click (or Control-click) this object, and you'll see that the relevant connections have been pre-populated, as shown in Figure 7.6.

FIGURE 7.6   The Search Display Controller, with pre-populated connections

Note that the Delegate object has automatically been set to the File's Owner. You'll need to implement a couple of delegate methods:

```
searchDisplayController:shouldReloadTableForSearchString:
searchDisplayControllerWillEndSearch:
```

You'll use these methods to adjust the items displayed in the search results table view whenever the user taps to enter something in the search bar, or cancels the search completely.

Setting a Fetch Predicate

If the user taps inside the search bar and enters a search term, the Search Display Controller's delegate (the RootViewController object) will be sent the message searchDisplayController:shouldReloadTableForSearchString:. This method reloads the search results table view.

There are various ways to filter the displayed results; you might, for example, choose to maintain two separate fetched results controllers (one for normal display, one for search results). For simplicity, let's just use one fetched results controller.

It is *possible* to change the predicate on a fetch request used by a fetched results controller as long as you're careful about deleting any cache. Since it would be good to use the cache to speed up the initial loading of the table view contents when no predicate is specified, let's replace the fetched results controller each time the predicate needs to change. If no predicate is included, the cache name will be set, otherwise it will be left as nil.

There are several places you'll need to do this, so let's move the code that generates the fetched results controller into a dedicated method, with an optional predicate, as shown in Listing 7.3.

LISTING 7.3   Creating a fetched results controller with optional predicate

```
- (NSFetchedResultsController *)fetchedResultsControllerWithPredicate:
                                        (NSPredicate *)aPredicate {
    NSFetchRequest *fetchRequest = [[NSFetchRequest alloc] init];
    NSEntityDescription *entity = [NSEntityDescription
                    entityForName:@"Person"
              inManagedObjectContext:self.managedObjectContext];
    [fetchRequest setEntity:entity];

    [fetchRequest setFetchBatchSize:20];

    [fetchRequest setPredicate:aPredicate];

    // Edit the sort key as appropriate
    NSSortDescriptor *lastNameDescriptor = [[[NSSortDescriptor alloc]
                initWithKey:@"lastName" ascending:YES] autorelease];
    NSSortDescriptor *firstNameDescriptor = [[[NSSortDescriptor alloc]
                initWithKey:@"firstName" ascending:YES] autorelease];

    [fetchRequest setSortDescriptors:[NSArray arrayWithObjects:
                    lastNameDescriptor, firstNameDescriptor, nil]];

    NSString *cacheName = @"Root";
    if( aPredicate ) cacheName = nil;

    NSFetchedResultsController *aFetchedResultsController =
            [[NSFetchedResultsController alloc]
                    initWithFetchRequest:fetchRequest
                    managedObjectContext:self.managedObjectContext
          sectionNameKeyPath:nil cacheName:cacheName];

    aFetchedResultsController.delegate = self;
    [fetchRequest release];

    NSError *anyError = nil;
    if (![aFetchedResultsController performFetch:&anyError]) {
        NSLog(@"Error fetching: %@", anyError);
    }
```

```
    return [aFetchedResultsController autorelease];
}
```

Note that this method sets the predicate as provided. If no predicate is supplied (i.e., all objects should be displayed), the fetched results controller is created with a cache as before. If a predicate is supplied (i.e., the search results are displayed), no cache is used.

Change the fetchedResultsController lazy accessor to use this method to create the controller, as shown in Listing 7.4.

LISTING 7.4   Creating the fetched results controller lazily using the new method

```
- (NSFetchedResultsController *)fetchedResultsController {
    if (__fetchedResultsController != nil) {
        return __fetchedResultsController;
    }

    self.fetchedResultsController =
            [self fetchedResultsControllerWithPredicate:nil];

    NSError *error = nil;
    [...]
}
```

Next, you're ready to implement the searchDisplayController:shouldReloadTableForSearchString: method. This method needs to create a suitable predicate to include only people whose firstName or lastName matches the characters in the search string. Start by adding the method shown in Listing 7.5.

LISTING 7.5   Setting a simple fetch predicate

```
- (BOOL)searchDisplayController:(UISearchDisplayController *)controller
            shouldReloadTableForSearchString:(NSString *)searchString {
    NSPredicate *searchPredicate = [NSPredicate
                                predicateWithFormat:
            @"firstName CONTAINS[c] %@ OR lastName CONTAINS[c] %@",
                                searchString, searchString];

    self.fetchedResultsController = [self
            fetchedResultsControllerWithPredicate:searchPredicate];

    return YES;
}
```

The predicate in Listing 7.5 performs a case-insensitive check to see whether the firstName or lastName contain the characters in the searchString. This comparison could also be accomplished using two separate "... CONTAINS[c] %@" predicates combined into an OR compound predicate, but for this simple check a single predicate with an inline OR is fine.

Clearing the Fetch Predicate

There's one additional method you'll need to implement, the search display controller delegate method searchDisplayControllerWillEndSearch:. If you don't implement this method, your application will crash at runtime if the user enters a search string and then presses the Cancel button (the fetched results controller will still be set up to display search results, when it should be displaying *all* the objects).

To avoid this problem, implement searchDisplayControllerWillEndSearch: to replace the fetched results controller using a nil predicate when the search finishes, as shown in Listing 7.6.

LISTING 7.6   Clearing the fetch predicate when the search ends

```
- (void)searchDisplayControllerWillEndSearch:
                       (UISearchDisplayController *)controller {
    self.fetchedResultsController = [self
            fetchedResultsControllerWithPredicate:nil];
}
```

If you test the application at this point, you'll find that you can search for people by *either* first name *or* last name. If you enter a Space after a name, no results are shown, as the predicate attempts to match the entire string, including the Space. It would be better to be able to type both a first and last name in the search field, and have the relevant results displayed. These improvements are covered in the next section.

There's also a hidden problem that arises when using only one fetched results controller. Because the Search Display Controller maintains a separate table view for the search results (which it displays over the top of the non-filtered table view), the fetched results controller is effectively used to serve two different table views. If you delete an entry in the search results table view, you'll trigger an exception when the NSFetchedResultsControllerDelegate methods are called to perform updates on the main table view (because the number of rows will be given relevant to the filtered table view, and won't match what's expected for the unfiltered table view).

To avoid this, you have several options:

▶ Don't use the Fetched Results Controller delegate methods to make changes on a line-by-line basis, but instead just implement controllerDidChangeContent: to call reloadData for the entire table view any time there is a change.

▶ Switch to using *two* fetched results controllers, one for the unfiltered table view, and a separate one for the search results. You'd need to modify every table view data source/delegate method, and every fetched results controller delegate method to check which table view is involved, then return the information or make changes using the relevant fetched results controller.

▶ Disable changes to cells in the search results table view.

For simplicity, let's just disable changes by implementing the `tableView:canEditRowAtIndexPath:` method to return YES only if the relevant table view is the main, unfiltered table view, as shown in Listing 7.7.

LISTING 7.7   Preventing edits to the search results table view

```
- (BOOL)tableView:(UITableView *)tableView
           canEditRowAtIndexPath:(NSIndexPath *)indexPath {
    return (tableView == [self tableView]);
}
```

If the table view isn't the primary table view, the method returns NO, disabling any edits to the search results table view.

The sample code for this book includes an additional project for this chapter, showing how to make use of two separate fetched results controllers. This is the approach to take if you'd like the user to be able to make changes in the search results table view, and you would prefer to use `NSFetchedResultsControllerDelegate` methods to perform updates on a per-row basis rather than just reloading the entire table view.

Now let's fix the search behavior, and allow the user to search by both first name and last name.

Modifying the Search Predicate

There are various ways to implement a better search procedure. You might be tempted to try adding a transient `fullName` attribute to the `Person` entity, to return a single string containing both `firstName` and `lastName`, ready for use in the search predicate.

The problem with this approach is that Core Data cannot execute a fetch with a predicate that references transient properties, so the fetch would fail.

NOTE

It's possible to get an array of results returned from some Core Data fetch request, and then filter that array *in memory* based on a transient property, but this is obviously no use for fetched results controllers.

Filtering in memory can also lead to problems in the limited memory environment of an iOS device, where it's advisable to minimize the number of results returned wherever possible.

The solution offered here is to check whether the search string contains more than one search word; if not, the original predicate is fine, otherwise the search string needs to be split into its component parts ready to generate a suitable predicate to check first and last names separately.

Let's start by implementing a method to return a predicate for a given search string, as shown in Listing 7.8.

LISTING 7.8   Generating a predicate for a given search string

```
- (NSPredicate *)predicateForSearchString:(NSString *)searchString {
    searchString = [searchString
            stringByTrimmingCharactersInSet:[NSCharacterSet
                                        whitespaceCharacterSet]];

    NSArray *stringComponents =
                [searchString componentsSeparatedByString:@" "];

    if( [stringComponents count] > 1 )
        return [self predicateForSearchComponents:stringComponents];
    else
        return [NSPredicate predicateWithFormat:
    @"firstName CONTAINS[c] %@ OR lastName CONTAINS[c] %@",
                                    searchString, searchString];
}
```

This method starts by trimming any whitespace characters from the search string. This avoids the situation where a leading or trailing space would affect search results. It then separates the string into its individual word components. If there is only one search word, it uses the same predicate as before; otherwise, it calls the predicateForSearchComponents: method, which you'll need to implement next, as shown in Listing 7.9.

LISTING 7.9   Constructing a predicate for multiple search words

```
- (NSPredicate *)predicateForSearchComponents:
                                    (NSArray *)stringComponents {
    if( [stringComponents count] < 1 ) return nil;

    NSString *firstComponent = [stringComponents objectAtIndex:0];
    NSString *lastComponent = [stringComponents lastObject];

    NSPredicate *firstAndLastInOrderPredicate =
    [NSCompoundPredicate andPredicateWithSubpredicates:
        [NSArray arrayWithObjects:
            [NSPredicate predicateWithFormat:
```

```
            @"firstName CONTAINS[c] %@", firstComponent],
        [NSPredicate predicateWithFormat:
            @"lastName CONTAINS[c] %@", lastComponent],
        nil]];

    NSPredicate *firstAndLastInReverseOrderPredicate =
    [NSCompoundPredicate andPredicateWithSubpredicates:
        [NSArray arrayWithObjects:
            [NSPredicate predicateWithFormat:
                @"firstName CONTAINS[c] %@", lastComponent],
            [NSPredicate predicateWithFormat:
                @"lastName CONTAINS[c] %@", firstComponent],
            nil]];

    return [NSCompoundPredicate orPredicateWithSubpredicates:
                [NSArray arrayWithObjects:
                    firstAndLastInOrderPredicate,
                    firstAndLastInReverseOrderPredicate, nil]];
}
```

This method makes use of several compound predicates to check firstName and lastName against the first and last items in the array of components:

▶ The first compound predicate checks whether the firstName contains the first search word AND the lastName contains the last search word, so that entering "jo smit" would match "John Smith".

▶ The second compound predicate checks the reverse (i.e., that firstName contains the last search word AND lastName the first), so that entering "jon mary" would match "Mary Jones".

▶ The final predicate is a compound OR predicate to check against both AND predicates. This means that "jo m" will match both "John Smith" and "Mary Jones".

Because these predicates only make use of the first and last search words, any other search terms are disregarded. The search uses anything before the first Space and anything after the last Space; if there are multiple spaces, the intervening text is ignored. You might like to decide whether it makes sense to use an alternative solution that matches these other search components.

Finally, you'll need to modify the searchDisplayController:shouldReloadTableForSearchString: method to use predicateForSearchString:, as shown in Listing 7.10.

LISTING 7.10   Using the predicateForSearchString: method

```
- (BOOL)searchDisplayController:(UISearchDisplayController *)controller
            shouldReloadTableForSearchString:(NSString *)searchString {
  NSPredicate *searchPredicate =
                      [self predicateForSearchString:searchString];
  self.fetchedResultsController = [self
            fetchedResultsControllerWithPredicate:searchPredicate];

  return YES;
}
```

Build and run the application to make sure that you can specify (in any order) both first and last names to search.

Adding a Search Scope Bar Filter

One further feature to add is the ability to filter search results based on date of birth. Assuming that dates of birth can be in the past or in the future (you may need to remove any validation test to prevent new people being created with a date of birth in the future, if you added one in Chapter 6, "Working with Managed Objects"), let's add search scope buttons to limit the results accordingly.

Open RootViewController.xib and select the Search Bar (at the top of the table view). Check the Shows Scope Bar option in the Attributes Inspector (Option-⌘-4), then add three Scope Button Titles: "All," "Past," and "Future" as shown in Figure 7.7.

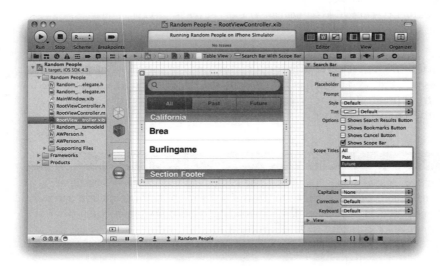

FIGURE 7.7   Adding scope buttons to the search bar

You'll need a method that generates a suitable predicate given a search string and a type of date filter; implement this after the existing `predicateForSearchString:` method, using the code shown in Listing 7.11.

LISTING 7.11 Generating a predicate with a date filter, if necessary

```
- (NSPredicate *)predicateForSearchString:(NSString *)searchString
                         dateFilter:(NSInteger)dateFilter {
    NSPredicate *searchStringPredicate =
                [self predicateForSearchString:searchString];

    if( !dateFilter ) return searchStringPredicate;

    NSPredicate *dateFilterPredicate = nil;
    switch ( dateFilter ) {
        case 1: // Past
            dateFilterPredicate = [NSPredicate predicateWithFormat:
                    @"dateOfBirth < %@", [NSDate date]];
            break;
        case 2: // Future
            dateFilterPredicate = [NSPredicate predicateWithFormat:
                    @"dateOfBirth > %@", [NSDate date]];
            break;
    }

    return [NSCompoundPredicate andPredicateWithSubpredicates:
            [NSArray arrayWithObjects:
                dateFilterPredicate, searchStringPredicate, nil]];
}
```

The number passed as the `dateFilter` argument corresponds to the index of the selected scope button. If `dateFilter` is 0 (which is the All button), the method just returns the standard search string predicate. Otherwise, a suitable date comparison predicate is generated, and the method returns another compound AND predicate.

NOTE

The `dateFilterPredicate` is specified first in the compound predicate—a date comparison is a numeric comparison, so is faster than a text search. Any objects that don't match the date filter should be disregarded immediately to avoid any unnecessary string testing.

All that remains is to make use of this method both in the existing
searchDisplayController:shouldReloadTableForSearchString: delegate method, and in
a new searchDisplayController:shouldReloadTableForSearchScope: method which will
be called when the scope changes. Since the arguments to these methods only provide the
search string, you'll need to query the search display controller for the date filter type, as
shown in Listing 7.12.

LISTING 7.12   Implementing both shouldReloadTableFor... methods

```
- (BOOL)searchDisplayController:(UISearchDisplayController *)controller
            shouldReloadTableForSearchString:(NSString *)searchString {
  NSPredicate *searchPredicate =
    [self predicateForSearchString:searchString
          dateFilter:controller.searchBar.selectedScopeButtonIndex];
  self.fetchedResultsController = [self
          fetchedResultsControllerWithPredicate:searchPredicate];

  return YES;
}

- (BOOL)searchDisplayController:(UISearchDisplayController *)controller
            shouldReloadTableForSearchScope:(NSInteger)searchOption {
  NSPredicate *searchPredicate =
    [self predicateForSearchString:controller.searchBar.text
                    dateFilter:searchOption];
  self.fetchedResultsController = [self
          fetchedResultsControllerWithPredicate:searchPredicate];

  return YES;
}
```

If necessary, remove any validation logic in AWPerson.m that prevents a person from
having a date of birth in the future, then build and run the application to make sure you
can search as before, and filter search results based on past and future birth dates.

Summary

In order to work with Core Data for anything beyond the most trivial data fetching needs,
you'll need to make use of predicates. You've seen how to create these using format
strings, substitution tokens and substitution variables, and how to combine multiple predicates into a single compound predicate to specify more than one condition.

You've seen how to store fetch requests in the data model, and how to work with a Search Display Controller in combination with a Fetched Results Controller to filter the objects displayed in a table view for a given search string or scope.

In Chapter 8, you'll learn how to implement versioning for your data model so that if you change the structure of your entities once you've shipped an application, your user's existing data can be migrated easily and automatically.

CHAPTER 8

Migration and Versioning

When using the code provided by Apple in the Core Data project templates at the time of writing, a Core Data-based iOS application will only be able to work with a persistent store created using the current data model version. During the development of an application, you typically go through several different revisions of the data model. If you make a change to the data model, such as adding a new attribute on an entity, the Core Data framework will raise an exception and refuse to load the persisted data.

In order to support changes and multiple versions in data models, Core Data provides support for automatic and custom migration. In this chapter you'll learn how to enable *Lightweight Migration*, the simplest option to enable automatic migration between data model versions, before seeing how to work with manual migration using *Mapping Models* that define how one model version relates to another through *Entity Migration Policies*.

The Migration Problem

So that you have an idea of what happens without migration and versioning, let's start by creating a very simple Core Data iOS project.

▶ Create another new Navigation-based iPhone application, making sure the Use Core Data checkbox is ticked, and call it "MigrationTest."

▶ When the project window appears, build and run the application in the simulator.

You've seen this template application several times already in the book; it looks like Figure 2.7 in Chapter 2, "A Core Data Primer." When the application has loaded in the simulator, press the + button several times to add some time-stamped entries in the table view so that you have some information saved in the persistent store.

Exit the application, then run it once again to check that the persisted information has been stored successfully, and that the table view is re-populated with the timestamp entries.

Changing the Data Model

Now that you have some persisted information based on the current data model in the project, let's make a simple change to that data model:

▶ Open up the `MigrationTest.xcdatamodeld` file and add a new attribute to the `Event` entity.

▶ Call this new attribute `testAttribute` and set its type to `String`.

Save the updated data model file and try to build and run the application in the Simulator. You'll find that the application fails to launch. Look in the Debugger Console (part of Xcode 4's Debug Area, Shift-⌘-Y, or as a separate window in Xcode 3, Shift-⌘-R) for the project and you'll see an unresolved error, looking like Listing 8.1.

LISTING 8.1   An unresolved error for incompatible data model versions

```
Unresolved error Error Domain=NSCocoaErrorDomain Code=134100 "The operation couldn't
 be completed. (Cocoa error 134100.)" UserInfo=0x5e2ec80 {[...]
reason=The model used to open the store is incompatible with the one used to create
the store}, {
    metadata =      {
        NSPersistenceFrameworkVersion = 320;
        NSStoreModelVersionHashes =        {
            Event = <5431c046 d30e7f32 c2cc8099 58add1e7 579ad104 a3aa8fc4
846e97d7 af01cc79>;
        };
        NSStoreModelVersionHashesVersion = 3;
        NSStoreModelVersionIdentifiers =          (
        );
        NSStoreType = SQLite;
        NSStoreUUID = "3E3BEF8E-DCA5-4748-8FFF-CD50DFF47BA7";
        "_NSAutoVacuumLevel" = 2;
    };
    reason = "The model used to open the store is incompatible with the one used to
create the store";
}
```

The important piece of information is the reason at the end of the error description. When Core Data opens an existing persistent store from disk, it first checks the *hash* of the stored model schema to make sure it matches the current version of the data model schema in the application.

The data model describes the structure of the information, and is used to determine how managed objects should relate to the stored data. If the data model used to create a store is different from the data model you try to use to open a store, Core Data will complain with this error of incompatibility.

The persistent store on disk (containing those timestamp entries that you created only a few minutes ago) was created using the initial version of the data model. Because you added the extra attribute to the Event entity, the hash of the existing persistent store's model schema won't match the hash of the model schema now in the application.

Multiple Data Model Versions and Lightweight Migration

To avoid the incompatible stores problem, you need to ask Core Data to migrate an existing persistent store from one data model version to another. So that Core Data can work out what has changed between two data model versions, you must keep a copy of those different data models in your Xcode project.

To demonstrate, let's create a completely new project, identical to the first one in this chapter, but this time called "LightweightMigrationTest."

When you've created this new project, build and run it in the simulator. As before, click the + button several times to create some entries in the persistent store before you exit the application.

Creating Data Model Versions

Before making any changes to the Event entity, you need to add a new data model version:

▶ Click once on the LightweightMigrationTest.xcdatamodeld file to select it.

▶ Choose Editor > Add Model Version.

Xcode will ask you for a name for the new file, and offer a dropdown box menu to select the model version it should use as a base. Click Finish to accept the default options; you'll rename the file later.

> **NOTE**
>
> Under Xcode 3, the menu command is Design > Data Model > Add Model Version, and the file will just be created without you having to specify any additional options.

You'll find that a new .xcdatamodel file is added, called LightweightMigrationTest 2.xcdatamodel file, inside the enclosing .xcdatamodeld bundle, as shown in Figure 8.1.

FIGURE 8.1   An expanded xcdatamodeld bundle

Notice that the LightweightMigrationTest.xcdatamodel file has a green tick in its icon; this indicates that it is the current model version for the application.

The other file, LightweightMigrationTest 2.xcdatamodel, has no green tick, indicating that it's there for versioning purposes only. Rename this file to LightweightMigrationTest01.xcdatamodel to help identify it as the version used for a persistent store created from the first design iteration of your project.

Open up the current data model file, the one with the green tick, and add in the same additional attribute as before to the Event entity—a String attribute called testAttribute.

Don't run the application yet, as you'll need to make a simple code modification to the application delegate to enable migration.

Enabling Lightweight Migration

In order to migrate information between two different data model versions, Core Data needs mapping information that describes how entities and attributes in one model relate to the entities and attributes in another model. For some data model changes, you'll need to create a separate mapping model file for each model version relationship. For some simple changes, however, Core Data offers what's called *lightweight migration*.

If you have added or removed an entity, or added or removed an attribute, Core Data can infer its own mapping information without you needing to provide a mapping model file. All that you need to do is ensure that the relevant data model files are included in the project, and enable a couple of options when the persistent store is created.

Because the change you've made to the LightweightMigrationTest data model is a simple one (adding a new attribute), and you've kept both data model versions in the project, the only change you need to make is to the code that creates the persistent store.

Open the LightweightMigrationTestAppDelegate.m file and find the persistentStoreCoordinator method. Change the code that adds the persistent store so it matches Listing 8.2.

LISTING 8.2   Enabling migration

```objc
- (NSPersistentStoreCoordinator *)persistentStoreCoordinator {
    if (__persistentStoreCoordinator != nil) {
        return __persistentStoreCoordinator;
    }

    NSURL *storeURL = [[self applicationDocumentsDirectory]
        URLByAppendingPathComponent:@"LightweightMigrationTest.sqlite"];

    NSError *error = nil;
    __persistentStoreCoordinator = [[NSPersistentStoreCoordinator alloc]
                initWithManagedObjectModel:[self managedObjectModel]];

    NSDictionary *optionsDictionary =
        [NSDictionary dictionaryWithObjectsAndKeys:
          [NSNumber numberWithBool:YES],
                    NSMigratePersistentStoresAutomaticallyOption,
          [NSNumber numberWithBool:YES],
                    NSInferMappingModelAutomaticallyOption, nil];

    if (![__persistentStoreCoordinator
            addPersistentStoreWithType:NSSQLiteStoreType
                configuration:nil URL:storeUrl
                    options:optionsDictionary error:&error]) {

        NSLog(@"Unresolved error %@, %@", error, [error userInfo]);
        abort();
    }

    return __persistentStoreCoordinator;
}
```

The code in Listing 8.2 specifies two options when the persistent store is added:

▶ NSMigratePersistentStoresAutomaticallyOption specifies that Core Data should attempt to migrate persistent stores either by using any provided mapping models or, if the next option is also set, by inferring its own mapping information.

▶ NSInferMappingModelAutomaticallyOption specifies that Core Data should attempt to infer its own mapping models between versions, using lightweight migration.

Lightweight migration and the NSInferMappingModelAutomaticallyOption are available on all iOS versions, from iPhone OS 3.0 onward. On the desktop, lightweight migration is only available under Mac OS X 10.6 Snow Leopard and later, and automatic migration itself is only available from Mac OS X 10.5 Leopard onward.

Once you've made the changes in Listing 8.2, build and run the application and you'll find that the application launches correctly and the timestamp entries you created previously are displayed as before. Core Data has mapped the old persistent store over to the new data model version, automatically.

NOTE

If you're running an earlier version of Xcode, or setting up the managed object model using `mergedModelFromBundles:`, you may need to choose Build > Clean (Shift-⌘-K) first to remove any existing compiled data model information from your project. If you don't do this, you'll receive an error when you try to run your application, saying that Core Data `Can't merge models with two different entities named 'Event.'`

Changes Supported by Lightweight Migration

While you're developing an application, lightweight migration will usually be sufficient to handle changes as you extend the data model. Specifically, lightweight migration will work for:

▶ Adding or removing an entity.

▶ Adding or removing an attribute.

  ▶ Note that if you're adding an attribute, and want to use a value other than the default value, you'll need to use a mapping model, described later in this chapter.

▶ Marking an optional attribute as required, specifying a default value, or marking a required attribute as optional.

If you need to rename an entity or an attribute, you'll need to provide some extra information in your data model versions.

Renaming Entities and Attributes

If you rename an entity without providing any additional information, Core Data won't be able to work out which entity in a previous version corresponds to which entity in the current version. Instead, it will assume that you've removed the old entity altogether, and created a new entity with the new name; as a result, it will **remove** all the persistent data for the old entity.

To test this, let's add another model version to the `LightweightMigrationTest` project:

▶ Select the current `LightweightMigrationTest.xcdatamodel` version (with the green checkmark).

▶ Choose Editor > Add Model Version.

▶ Specify the name as `LightweightMigrationTest02`, and check that it's based on the model called `LightweightMigrationTest`.

Before you proceed, it's a good idea to duplicate the existing persistent store file on disk so that you have a copy of the data before you test what happens when you rename an entity.

If you use the Finder to navigate to `~/Library/Application Support/iPhone Simulator/<iOS Version>/Applications`, you'll find a directory containing a series of unique IDs for the applications you've used in the simulator. Use the Finder's Browser view to see which of these directories contains the `LightweightMigrationTest` application, as shown in Figure 8.2.

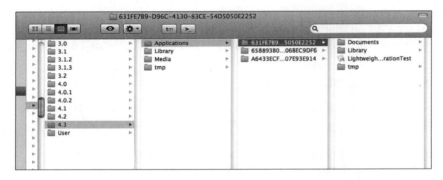

FIGURE 8.2   Locating the support files for iPhone simulator applications

The Documents directory inside the application's support directory contains the `.sqlite` store file. Hold down the Option key and drag the Documents directory to the desktop to create a copy.

Return to Xcode, open the current data model version, `LightweightMigrationTest.xcdatamodel`, and rename the `Event` entity to `Occurrence` using the Data Model Inspector (Option-⌘-3).

You'll also need to modify any code that specifically mentions the entity by name. For the `LightweightMigrationTest` application, the only place the old `Event` entity is mentioned is in the `RootViewController.m` file's `fetchedResultsController` method. Change the code that generates the fetch request to use the new entity name, as shown in Listing 8.3.

LISTING 8.3   Using a different entity name

```
// Create the fetch request for the entity.
NSFetchRequest *fetchRequest = [[NSFetchRequest alloc] init];
NSEntityDescription *entity = [NSEntityDescription
```

8

```
        entityForName:@"Occurrence"
    inManagedObjectContext:managedObjectContext];
[fetchRequest setEntity:entity];

// Set the batch size to a suitable number.
[fetchRequest setFetchBatchSize:20];
```

Build and run the application; you'll find that the table view is empty, containing none of the previous timestamp entries. As predicted, Core Data has decided that the old Event entity has been deleted, so it's removed all the old Event data from the persistent store, ready to create instances of what it thinks is an entirely new Occurrence entity.

Exit the application in the simulator and switch over to the Finder; locate the application data directory again (you'll find that the unique ID for the application has changed), and drag the copied Documents directory so that it replaces the one with the wiped data.

Supplying Renaming Identifiers

In order for Core Data to migrate the old Event data using the newly-renamed Occurrence entity, you need to supply a *renaming identifier* in the Xcode data modeler:

▶ Open the LightweightMigrationTest02.xcdatamodel file in the modeler (that's the version of the model used by the old data in the Documents directory).

▶ Select the Event entity and find the Versioning section of the inspector, as shown in Figure 8.3.

▶ Set the Renaming ID to eventEntity.

▶ Open the LightweightMigrationTest.xcdatamodel file (the green-ticked current version), and set the renaming identifier of the Occurrence entity to eventEntity as well.

NOTE

If you're using Xcode 3, you'll find the Renaming Identifier under the Configurations and Versioning panel in the entity inspector; it's the one with the wrench icon.

Build and run the application to check that it works. Now that you've supplied a renaming identifier, Core Data knows that the Event entity is the same entity as the Occurrence entity, and so migrates across all the old data.

FIGURE 8.3   Setting the renaming identifier for an entity

Renaming Attributes

The same process applies if you need to rename an attribute; you'll need to use the data modeler to set a unique renaming identifier in both the old model version and the new one.

If you test this out for the LightweightMigrationTest project, for example by creating yet another data model version and renaming the timeStamp attribute to startTime, you'll need to make a number of changes to the RootViewController.m file. The easiest way is to use Find and Replace to replace all occurrences of @"timestamp" with @"startTime".

Keeping Track of Multiple Versions

It's worth pointing out that you only need to keep data model versions for the versions that are actually required for any existing persistent stores. While you're developing an application, you may need to add several model versions for multiple iterations of the data model.

When it's time to release a *new* application to other people, you can remove all the previous model versions. If you're releasing an *update* to a previously released application, you can remove all the temporary, development-only model versions, leaving only those used by previous release versions of your application.

Model-Naming Conventions

I tend to follow strict naming conventions when working with multiple data model versions. I leave the *current* model version un-numbered, as with the earlier LightweightMigrationTest.xcdatamodel file.

Once I release an application and start working on an upgrade, I rename the previously released model using its application version number, adding letters to the names of any subsequent model iterations.

If I release MyApp 1.01, for example, and start working on version 1.02, I rename the model version that went out in the 1.01 release to MyApp101.xcdatamodel, and name any subsequent versions while I'm developing as MyApp101a.xcdatamodel, MyApp101b.xcdatamodel etc. When it comes time to release the updated MyApp 1.02, the only model versions that are needed are the current model version (unnumbered) and the previous number-only version, MyApp101.xcdatamodel. All the versions with letters can be removed, either manually or even automatically using a build script.

Mapping Models

If you need to perform more complex migration, such as setting a new attribute in one version to a value derived from an attribute in an old version (like taking a fullName attribute and converting it into separate firstName and lastName attributes), you'll need to customize the migration process. Lightweight migration won't help you in this instance, so you'll need to create a mapping model file between the relevant versions, specifying exactly how instances of an entity in an older *source* model relate to instances of an entity in the current *destination* model.

In this section, you'll modify the Random People application from Chapter 6, "Working with Managed Objects," to store a new attribute, yearOfBirth. This will mean that the application's main table view can show an alphabetical list of people born in each year, as shown in Figure 8.4; this wouldn't be possible just by sorting on dateOfBirth.

Open up the Random People project in Xcode, and build and run the application to make sure that you have 30 or so random people stored in the persistent store before continuing.

Start by setting up versioning for the application:

▶ Select Random_People.xcdatamodeld in the Project Navigator and create a new model version using Editor > Add Model Version.

▶ Call the file Random_People101.xcdatamodel.

▶ Open the current version, Random_People.xcdatamodel, and add a new Integer 32 attribute to the Person entity, called yearOfBirth.

▶ Change the code that sets up the persistent store in Random_PeopleAppDelegate.m so it sets the migration options used earlier in the chapter in Listing 8.2.

▶ If you're using an older Xcode version or setting up your managed object model using mergedModelFromBundles:, clean the project using Build > Clean (Shift-⌘-K).

FIGURE 8.4   The Random People application in the simulator, showing people arranged alphabetically by year of birth

Next, create the mapping model between the two data model versions:

▶ Choose File > New > New File (⌘-N) and select the Mapping Model template, listed under iOS > Core Data, as shown in Figure 8.5.

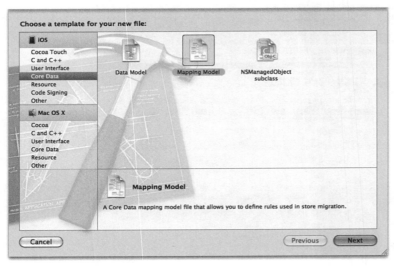

FIGURE 8.5   Creating a mapping model file

▶ Select the `Random_People101.xcdatamodel` file as the Source Data Model, as shown in Figure 8.6. Set the current `Random_People.xcdatamodel` file as the Target Data Model.

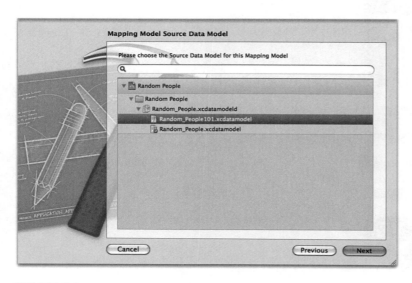

FIGURE 8.6   Setting the source for a mapping model

▶ Call the file `101to101a.xcmappingmodel`.

The new mapping model file will be created, and open in the Mapping Model editor, shown in Figure 8.7.

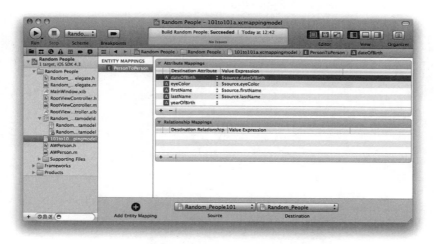

FIGURE 8.7   The mapping model editor

This window specifies entity and property mappings between the old
Random_People101.xcdatamodel and the Random_People.xcdatamodel versions.

Examining the Differences

Xcode 3 offers a helpful option to show a summary of what needs to be migrated;
when you click the Show Differences button, a FileMerge-style change window appears,
as shown in Figure 8.8.

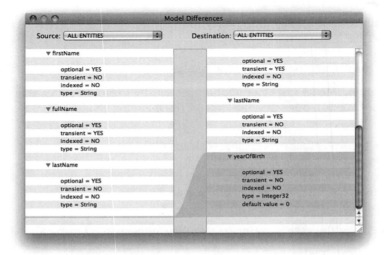

FIGURE 8.8   Displaying the differences between data models in Xcode 3

At the time of writing, this feature has not yet made it into Xcode 4.

The Value Expression column of the Attribute Mappings list for the Person entity shows
how Core Data will map the earlier version onto the current version. In the case of the
dateOfBirth attribute, the Value Expression column specifies a value expression of
$source.dateOfBirth, meaning that the destination entity's dateOfBirth attribute will
take the value of the source entity's dateOfBirth.

In the case of the new yearOfBirth attribute, Core Data is unable to determine a direct
mapping between the source and destination entities, so the value expression is blank.

Unfortunately, it isn't possible to extract the year from the date of birth using expressions,
so you can't use the Value Expression field to handle the migration. Instead, you'll need
to define a custom property mapping by creating an entity migration policy object.

Custom Entity Migration Policies

When Core Data migrates data between model versions, it uses a series of different objects to handle entity and property mappings. One of these objects is an NSEntityMigrationPolicy object.

An entity migration policy object determines how a source entity will be migrated to a destination entity; in order to derive and set the yearOfBirth attribute, you'll need to specify a custom subclass of NSEntityMigrationPolicy for the Person entity to define the custom behavior.

First of all, set the name of the custom migration policy in the 101to101a.xcmappingmodel file:

▶ Select the PersonToPerson mapping in the Entity Mappings list.

▶ In the Core Data Mapping Model inspector (Option-⌘), set the Custom Policy value to AWPersonMigrationPolicy. Notice that the Type of the mapping changes to Custom.

Next, you'll need to create the AWPersonMigrationPolicy class files:

▶ Choose File > New > New File (⌘-N) and create a new Cocoa Touch Objective-C Class, set to inherit from NSEntityMigrationPolicy, called AWPersonMigrationPolicy.

▶ Check that the contents of the AWPersonMigrationPolicy.h file match Listing 8.4.

LISTING 8.4   Inheriting from NSEntityMigrationPolicy

```
@interface AWPersonMigrationPolicy : NSEntityMigrationPolicy {

}

@end
```

In order to provide your custom migration behavior, you'll need to override the NSEntityMigrationPolicy method createDestinationInstancesForSourceInstance:entityMapping:manager:error:.

This method will be invoked by the migration manager object for each source instance in the original persistent store. The default implementation uses the information in the mapping model file to determine how the instances will be migrated across.

By overriding this method, you'll be able to supply additional mapping information beyond what's specified in the mapping model file. In order to set the yearOfBirth attribute, the method will need to do the following:

▶ Access the dateOfBirth attribute from the source managed object instance, and extract the year as an integer value.

▶ Find the NSPropertyMapping that relates to the yearOfBirth property by requesting the relevant mapping in the supplied entity mapping's attributeMappings array.

▶ Change the value expression for that property mapping to an expression representing the year.

▶ Call the overridden implementation to perform the actual migration, now using the modified mapping.

Listing 8.5 shows the code to achieve all this.

LISTING 8.5   Changing a specific mapping

```
- (BOOL)createDestinationInstancesForSourceInstance:
                                (NSManagedObject *)sInstance
              entityMapping:(NSEntityMapping *)mapping
                  manager:(NSMigrationManager *)manager
                  error:(NSError **)error {
    NSArray *attributeMappings = [mapping attributeMappings];
    NSPredicate *mappingNamePredicate =
        [NSPredicate predicateWithFormat:@"name == %@", @"yearOfBirth"];

    attributeMappings = [attributeMappings
                  filteredArrayUsingPredicate:mappingNamePredicate];
    if( [attributeMappings count] > 0 )
    {
        NSDate *dateOfBirth = [sInstance valueForKey:@"dateOfBirth"];
        NSDateFormatter *dateFormatter =
                    [[[NSDateFormatter alloc] init] autorelease];
        [dateFormatter setDateFormat:@"yyyy"];
        int yearOfBirth =
                [[dateFormatter stringFromDate:dateOfBirth] intValue];

        NSPropertyMapping *yearOfBirthMapping =
                [attributeMappings objectAtIndex:0];

        [yearOfBirthMapping setValueExpression:
            [NSExpression expressionForConstantValue:
                        [NSNumber numberWithInt:yearOfBirth]]];
    }

    return [super createDestinationInstancesForSourceInstance:sInstance
                entityMapping:mapping manager:manager error:error];
}
```

The code in Listing 8.5 uses a predicate to filter the attribute mappings and find the one for the yearOfBirth attribute. It then sets the value expression for that mapping to a constant value, built from the extracted year integer value.

Create a copy of the Random People application's Documents directory (as you did earlier for the LightweightMigrationTest application) before proceeding, just in case you've made any mistakes and the migration fails.

Before you build and run the application, you might want to make a few changes to the existing code so any new people you add will have their years of birth set correctly:

▶ Copy the yearOfBirth attribute from the data model and paste an NSNumber @property declaration into AWPerson.h.

▶ Paste an @dynamic declaration for the yearOfBirth property into AWPerson.m.

▶ Implement the methods shown in Listing 8.6 to set the yearOfBirth attribute whenever the dateOfBirth is changed. The listing also implements a KVO method to notify observers of the yearOfBirth attribute whenever the dateOfBirth attribute is changed. These methods won't do anything if some future code modifies the yearOfBirth attribute directly, meaning that the two attributes would be out of sync. You'd need to implement a setYearOfBirth: method as well to correct this.

LISTING 8.6   Changing the yearOfBirth when the dateOfBirth property is modified

```
- (void)setDateOfBirth:(NSDate *)newDate {
    static NSDateFormatter *yearOfBirthDateFormatter = nil;

    if( !yearOfBirthDateFormatter ) {
        yearOfBirthDateFormatter = [[NSDateFormatter alloc] init];

        [yearOfBirthDateFormatter setDateFormat:@"yyyy"];
    }

    [self willChangeValueForKey:@"dateOfBirth"];
    [self setPrimitiveValue:newDate forKey:@"dateOfBirth"];
    [self didChangeValueForKey:@"dateOfBirth"];

    int tmpYear =
        [[[yearOfBirthDateFormatter stringFromDate:newDate] intValue];

    [self setValue:[NSNumber numberWithInt:tmpYear]
            forKey:@"yearOfBirth"];
}
```

```
+ (NSSet *)keyPathsForValuesAffectingYearOfBirth
{
    return [NSSet setWithObject:@"dateOfBirth"];
}
```

Finally, change the RootViewController.m method that creates the fetched results controller to sort the random people by their years of birth, and set the relevant section index information, as shown in Listing 8.7.

LISTING 8.7   Setting up the fetched results controller to sort by year of birth

```
[...]
[request setEntity:[NSEntityDescription
                      entityForName:@"Person"
            inManagedObjectContext:managedObjectContext]];
NSSortDescriptor *yearOfBirthDescriptor = [[NSSortDescriptor alloc]
                initWithKey:@"yearOfBirth" ascending:YES];
NSSortDescriptor *lastNameDescriptor = [[NSSortDescriptor alloc]
                      initWithKey:@"lastName" ascending:YES];
NSSortDescriptor *firstNameDescriptor = [[NSSortDescriptor alloc]
                     initWithKey:@"firstName" ascending:YES];
[request setSortDescriptors:[NSArray arrayWithObjects:
                yearOfBirthDescriptor, lastNameDescriptor,
                firstNameDescriptor, nil]];
[yearOfBirthDescriptor release];
[...]
NSFetchedResultsController *aController =
[[NSFetchedResultsController alloc] initWithFetchRequest:request
                      managedObjectContext:managedObjectContext
                        sectionNameKeyPath:@"yearOfBirth"
                                 cacheName:nil];
[...]
```

When you build and run the application, you'll find that people are sorted into birth year sections, before being sorted by last name then first name, as shown in Figure 8.9.

FIGURE 8.9   The modified Random People application, sorting using the new yearOfBirth attribute

Depending on which version of the Xcode project template you are using, you may need to implement the method shown in Listing 8.8 to display the section name headers.

LISTING 8.7   Setting up the fetched results controller to sort by year of birth

```
- (NSString *)tableView:(UITableView *)tableView
                        titleForHeaderInSection:(NSInteger)section {
    id <NSFetchedResultsSectionInfo> sectionInfo =
        [[self.fetchedResultsController sections] objectAtIndex:section];
    return [sectionInfo name];
}
```

Summary

In this chapter, you've seen how Core Data provides automatic support for migrating existing persistent stores created using one version of a data model over to a new data model version. For simple addition or removal of entities and attributes, lightweight migration will handle the changes automatically, provided you keep each model version in your project and specify the migration options in the code that creates the persistent store.

For more complicated migration, you can make use of Mapping Models and custom entity migration policies to deal with migrating managed object instances from a source model version to their destination version.

The next chapter looks in greater detail at managed object contexts. You'll learn how to work with contexts across multiple view controllers, and see how to make use of multiple contexts, and their individual undo managers.

CHAPTER 9

Working with Multiple View Controllers and Undo

Up until this point in the book, you've been working with example iOS applications that use only a single view controller containing a single table view. In this chapter, you'll see how to pass managed objects and managed object contexts to additional view controllers to allow you to edit values on existing managed objects.

You'll also see how to make use of Core Data's built-in undo functionality, seeing how to support the Shake to Edit feature to undo changes to managed objects.

Editing Managed Objects

This chapter adds some additional functionality to the Random People application, enabling the user to edit individual people stored in the persistent store, or change the information for people about to be added. Let's start by creating an additional view controller to edit a person's details.

Open the Random People project from the last chapters, and choose File > New > New File (⌘-N) to use the Xcode template window to create new files for a UIViewController subclass. Tick the *With XIB for user interface* checkbox and specify the subclass as UIViewController. Call the class AWPersonEditorViewController.

Once Xcode has created the files, open the AWPersonEditorViewController.xib file and add the user interface items shown in Figure 9.1, using the following settings:

▶ The `UIDatePicker` mode is set to *Date*

▶ Each `UITextField` has its *Clear when editing begins* checkbox unticked and is set to capitalize *Words*

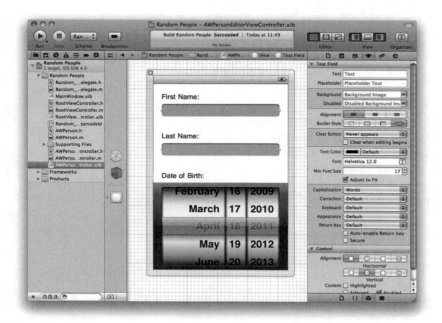

FIGURE 9.1   The new view controller to edit a person

Keeping Track of the Managed Object to Edit

In order to display the values of the managed object in this new view controller, you'll need a way to set the initial values of the interface items when the view appears, and set the relevant managed object properties using the values from those interface items when the view disappears.

The view controller will need to keep an instance variable to refer to the managed object currently being edited, which will need to be set before the view controller is pushed. So, open the `AWPersonEditorViewController.h` file and add in outlets for the interface items you created earlier, along with a `currentPerson` property (you'll need to include a forward declaration for the `AWPerson` class), as shown in Listing 9.1.

LISTING 9.1   Adding outlets to the new view controller, along with a property for the managed object

```
@class AWPerson;
```

```
@interface AWPersonEditorViewController : UIViewController {
    UITextField *firstNameTextField;
    UITextField *lastNameTextField;
    UIDatePicker *dateOfBirthPicker;

    AWPerson *currentPerson;
}

@property (nonatomic, retain) IBOutlet UITextField *firstNameTextField;
@property (nonatomic, retain) IBOutlet UITextField *lastNameTextField;
@property (nonatomic, retain) IBOutlet UIDatePicker *dateOfBirthPicker;
@property (nonatomic, retain) AWPerson *currentPerson;

@end
```

You'll also need to import the AWPerson.h file at the top of
AWPersonEditorViewController.m, synthesize all four of the properties, and connect the
outlets in the .xib.

In order to display the correct values for the current managed object, any object that
opens this view controller will need to set the currentPerson object before the view is
pushed. When the editing view is about to appear, the interface needs to be updated with
the values from the current person object. Split the code to update the interface into a
separate method so it can be re-used in other methods, later in the chapter, as shown in
Listing 9.2.

LISTING 9.2   Setting the currentPerson property and updating the interface

```
- (void)updateInterfaceForCurrentPerson {
    firstNameTextField.text = currentPerson.firstName;
    lastNameTextField.text = currentPerson.lastName;
    dateOfBirthPicker.date = currentPerson.dateOfBirth;
}

- (void)viewWillAppear:(BOOL)animated {
    [super viewWillAppear:animated];

    [self updateInterfaceForCurrentPerson];
}
```

You'll also need a text field delegate method to hide the keyboard when the user finishes
editing. Set File's Owner as the delegate for each text field in
AWPersonEditorViewController.xib, and then implement the method shown in Listing 9.3.

LISTING 9.3   Hiding the keyboard when the user finishes editing

```
- (BOOL)textFieldShouldReturn:(UITextField *)textField {
    [textField resignFirstResponder];
    return YES;
}
```

Next, you'll need to write the code to load this new view controller when a person is tapped in the root view controller. Open the `RootViewController.h` file and add a readonly property for the `AWPersonEditorViewController`; you'll generate this lazily, when first requested, so add in an instance variable to hold the view controller once it's been allocated (as before, you'll need a forward declaration for the view controller class), as shown in Listing 9.4.

LISTING 9.4   Adding a property for the new view controller in RootViewController.h

```
@class AWPersonEditorViewController;

@interface RootViewController : UITableViewController
                        <NSFetchedResultsControllerDelegate> {
    [...]
    AWPersonEditorViewController *personEditorViewController;
}

@property (nonatomic, retain) NSFetchedResultsController
                                    *fetchedResultsController;
@property (nonatomic, retain) NSManagedObjectContext
                                    *managedObjectContext;
@property (readonly, retain) AWPersonEditorViewController
                                    *personEditorViewController;

@end
```

Switch to the `RootViewController.m` file, import the `AWPersonEditorViewController.h` file at the top, and then implement the method that returns the new view controller, as shown in Listing 9.5.

LISTING 9.5   Generating the new view controller, lazily when required

```
- (AWPersonEditorViewController *)personEditorViewController {
    if( !personEditorViewController ) {
        personEditorViewController =
                [[AWPersonEditorViewController alloc]
                    initWithNibName:@"AWPersonEditorViewController"
                        bundle:nil];
```

```
    }

    return personEditorViewController;
}
```

Next, configure the code that displays the table view cells so that each cell has a disclosure indicator, as shown in Listing 9.6.

LISTING 9.6   Setting the detail disclosure indicator for the table view cells

```
- (UITableViewCell *)tableView:(UITableView *)tableView
                  cellForRowAtIndexPath:(NSIndexPath *)indexPath {
    static NSString *CellIdentifier = @"Cell";

    UITableViewCell *cell =
       [tableView dequeueReusableCellWithIdentifier:CellIdentifier];
    if (cell == nil) {
       cell = [[[UITableViewCell alloc]
                      initWithStyle:UITableViewCellStyleSubtitle
                    reuseIdentifier:CellIdentifier] autorelease];
       cell.accessoryType =
                 UITableViewCellAccessoryDisclosureIndicator;
    }
    [...]
}
```

You'll need to implement the table view delegate method
tableView:didSelectRowAtIndexPath: to fetch the selected person from the fetched results controller, set that person as the currentPerson for the editing view controller, and then push the controller onscreen, as shown in Listing 9.7.

LISTING 9.7   Displaying the new view controller to edit a selected person

```
- (void)tableView:(UITableView *)tableView
              didSelectRowAtIndexPath:(NSIndexPath *)indexPath {
    AWPerson *selectedPerson =
       [self.fetchedResultsController objectAtIndexPath:indexPath];

    [self.personEditorViewController setCurrentPerson:selectedPerson];

    [self.navigationController
              pushViewController:self.personEditorViewController
                        animated:YES];
}
```

9

In order for the navigation to work correctly, you'll need to set a title for the **root** view controller in its `viewDidLoad` method, as shown in Listing 9.8. If you don't do this, you won't get the default *navigate back* behavior for the navigation bar in the **editing** view controller.

LISTING 9.8   Setting a title for the root view controller

```
- (void)viewDidLoad {
    [super viewDidLoad];

    self.title = @"Random People";

    [...]
}
```

Build and run the project in the simulator to check that you can tap on a person to edit their details. The two text fields should be populated with that person's name, and the date picker should display the person's date of birth.

Although you can edit the information on screen, the changes won't be saved since you haven't yet done anything about updating the properties on the managed object. Let's correct that now.

Updating a Managed Object's Properties

There are several ways that you might implement code to update an edited managed object based on the changed values in the user interface. You could set the values of the object whenever a text field finished editing or the date picker's value changed, but the easiest way is just to set the managed object's properties in the `viewWillDisappear:` method.

It's also a good idea to take this opportunity to save the managed object context that contains the `AWPerson` object. Since an `NSManagedObject` keeps track of its managed object context, you can use the code shown in Listing 9.9.

LISTING 9.9   Setting the managed object's values before the editing view disappears

```
- (void)viewWillDisappear:(BOOL)animated {
    [super viewWillDisappear:animated];

    currentPerson.firstName = firstNameTextField.text;
    currentPerson.lastName = lastNameTextField.text;
    currentPerson.dateOfBirth = dateOfBirthPicker.date;

    NSError *anyError = nil;
    BOOL success = [[currentPerson managedObjectContext]
                                        save:&anyError];
```

```
    if( !success ) {
        NSLog(@"Error saving: %@", anyError);
    }
}
```

Build and run and you'll find that you can now change the first and last names of people in the persistent store.

The code in Listing 9.9 might be sufficient for a very simple application but it doesn't allow anything to be done about warning the user if the save fails. If any validation tests for the person object fail, it's too late to let the user know when the view is about to disappear. You can't stop the view disappearing, so any error message you display will appear after the editing view has gone.

One solution is to offer a Done button in the navigation bar; if the object is saved without validation errors, you can pop the view controller. If the save fails, you can display a suitable error message, and leave the view on screen.

There's also another problem, which involves the NSFetchedResultsController in the RootViewController object. As of the time of writing, NSFetchedResultsController and UITableView don't allow you to update a managed object in such a way that the number of table view sections needs to change, when using the NSFetchedResultsController delegate methods (described in Chapter 5 in the section "Handling Underlying Data Changes"). The only time the number of sections can change is when you either *insert* or *delete* a managed object.

NOTE

It's almost certain that this problem will have been fixed by the time this book goes to press, but it's worth keeping these points in mind if you need to maintain backwards compatibility with earlier iOS versions.

As always, it's important to test your code under each previous iOS version you support.

In the Random People application, this will manifest if you change the date of birth for a person in a section that currently has several people, setting the year to a value that doesn't currently appear as a section header in the root view controller. The application will crash with an error like this:

Exception was caught during Core Data change processing: Invalid
update: invalid number of rows in section 0. The number of rows
contained in an existing section after the update (2) must be equal
to the number of rows contained in that section before the update
(1), plus or minus the number of rows inserted or deleted from that
section (0 inserted, 0 deleted).

There are several ways to avoid this in the Random People application. The simplest way
is to specify the section key path as `nil` on the fetched results controller, instead choosing
to sort people by date of birth in just a single section.

If you wanted to keep the people sorted into sections by year, you have a couple of
other options:

- Set the maximum and minimum dates in the editing view controller's `UIDatePicker`
  to be January 1 and December 31 in the year currently set for the date of birth so
  that the user cannot change the year.

- Change the `RootViewController` implementation so that it doesn't use the fetched
  results controller delegate methods to handle individual objects or sections being
  inserted or updated.

Let's use the second option. You'll need to remove the `controllerWillChangeContent:`,
`controller:didChangeSection:atIndex:forChangeType:`, and
`controller:didChangeObject:atIndexPath:forChangeType:newIndexPath:` methods, and
change the `controllerDidChangeContent:` method to reload the table view completely.
You'll also need to reload the table view whenever the view is about to appear, as shown
in Listing 9.10.

LISTING 9.10   Ignoring fetched results controller notifications of individual changes

```
- (void)viewWillAppear:(BOOL)animated {
    [super viewWillAppear:animated];

    [self.tableView reloadData];
}


- (void)controllerDidChangeContent:
                    (NSFetchedResultsController *)controller {
    [self.tableView reloadData];
}
```

Build and run the application to make sure that you can now change the year without the
application crashing.

Validating Managed Objects

As noted earlier in the chapter, waiting until viewWillDisappear: to set the changed values for the object doesn't give you a chance to notify the user in such a way that they have the option to change the values. One solution is to offer a Done button, allowing the properties to be changed before the view disappears.

Let's modify the AWPersonEditorViewController.m file so its navigation bar has a Done button on the right and a Cancel button on the left. The Cancel button replaces the default back navigation behavior. Add the code shown in Listing 9.11 to set the two buttons.

LISTING 9.11   Adding a Done and a Cancel button to the editing view controller's navigation bar

```
- (void)viewDidLoad {
    [super viewDidLoad];

    UIBarButtonItem *doneButton = [[UIBarButtonItem alloc]
            initWithBarButtonSystemItem:UIBarButtonSystemItemDone
                    target:self action:)];
    self.navigationItem.rightBarButtonItem = doneButton;
    [doneButton release];

    UIBarButtonItem *cancelButton = [[UIBarButtonItem alloc]
            initWithBarButtonSystemItem:UIBarButtonSystemItemCancel
                    target:self action:)];
    self.navigationItem.leftBarButtonItem = cancelButton;
    [cancelButton release];
}
```

The code that's currently used in the viewWillDisappear: method can move to the savePerson: method. If the save is successful, the view controller can be popped off the navigation stack; if not, an error can be displayed, as shown in Listing 9.12. This listing also shows the cancelPerson: method, which just pops the view controller without modifying the currentPerson object.

LISTING 9.12   Saving the modified person object

```
- (IBAction)savePerson:(id)sender {
    // Make sure you remove the following from viewWillDisappear:
    currentPerson.firstName = firstNameTextField.text;
    currentPerson.lastName = lastNameTextField.text;
    currentPerson.dateOfBirth = dateOfBirthPicker.date;

    NSError *anyError = nil;
    BOOL success = [[currentPerson managedObjectContext]
                                        save:&anyError];
```

```
    if( !success ) {
        UIAlertView *errorAlert = [[UIAlertView alloc]
            initWithTitle:@"Couldn't save this person"
                  message:[anyError localizedDescription]
                  delegate:self cancelButtonTitle:@"OK"
          otherButtonTitles:nil];

        [errorAlert show];
    }
    else {
        [self.navigationController popViewControllerAnimated:YES];
    }
}


- (IBAction)cancelPerson:(id)sender {
    [self.navigationController popViewControllerAnimated:YES];
}
```

To test this, you'll need some validation tests set up for the AWPerson object. Chapter 6's "Data Validation" section includes information on validation tests for a managed object. If you don't already have any validation methods, add the code shown in Listing 9.13 to AWPerson.m.

LISTING 9.13   Validating that a person has a first name

```
- (BOOL)validateFirstName:(id *)ioValue error:(NSError **)outError {
    NSString *proposedName = *ioValue;

    if( !proposedName || [proposedName isEqualToString:@""] )
    {
        NSString *localizedDesc = NSLocalizedString(
                    @"You must supply a first name",
                    @"You must supply a first name");
        NSDictionary *errorUserInfo = [NSDictionary
                    dictionaryWithObject:localizedDesc
                            forKey:NSLocalizedDescriptionKey];
        if( outError ) {
            *outError = [NSError errorWithDomain:NSCocoaErrorDomain
                            code:NSValidationStringTooShortError
                        userInfo:errorUserInfo];
        }
        return NO;
    }
```

```
    return YES;
}
```

Rather than define its own error domain and code, the method shown in Listing 9.13 cheats slightly by using the relevant NSCocoaErrorDomain for an NSValidationStringTooShortError code. This is the code you would receive if you implemented validation in the data model file by specifying a minimum length for the firstName string, but for model-generated validation errors the localized string would just be Operation could not be completed. Listing 9.13 provides a localized description specifying that the first name must be provided.

Test this out by trying to remove a person's first name before pressing Done; you'll see the error shown in Figure 9.2. Note that if you press Cancel immediately after dismissing the error, the first name will be left blank. The context won't have saved, but it will appear as if the changes were made successfully. Next time you try to make a change to a different person and press Done, you'll get the old error displayed over the second (potentially valid) person. You'll see how to solve this problem later in the chapter, by using multiple managed object contexts.

FIGURE 9.2   Displaying a validation error

Working with Undo

iPhone OS 3.0 added support for Shake to Undo. This is implemented by default in controls like `UITextField`. The only undo support currently offered by the Random People application is while the first name or last name text fields are being edited. If you type some characters, then shake the phone or use the simulator's Hardware > Shake Gesture menu item (Control-⌘-Z), you have the option to undo your typing. Shake again and you'll be able to redo the typing.

The Core Data framework features automatic undo support for any changes within a managed object context. On iOS,[1] all you need to do is allocate a new `NSUndoManager` for a managed object context; any subsequent changes made within that context will trigger undo actions to be created for each change, automatically.

For a view controller to support undo and redo (outside of controls like `UITextField`) you need to provide access to an `undoManager` property on that view controller. The view controller also needs to be the first responder whenever you wish to be able to respond to a shake.

The first step is to enable the shake to edit feature, in the application delegate's `application:didFinishLaunchingWithOptions:` method, as shown in Listing 9.14.

LISTING 9.14   Enabling Shake to Edit in the Random_PeopleAppDelegate.m file

```
- (BOOL)application:(UIApplication *)application
             didFinishLaunchingWithOptions:(NSDictionary *)launchOptions {

    // Override point for customization after app launch
    application.applicationSupportsShakeToEdit = YES;

    [...]
}
```

Next, you need to ensure that the `AWPersonEditorViewController` can accept first responder status, set it to be the first responder when it first appears, and resign first responder status when it disappears. Implement the `canBecomeFirstResponder` method along with the `viewDidAppear:` and `viewWillDisappear:` methods, as shown in Listing 9.15. This listing also includes an `undoManager` method to return the undo manager for the current person's managed object context.

LISTING 9.15   Setting the view controller as first responder

```
- (BOOL)canBecomeFirstResponder {
    return YES;
}
```

---

[1] On the desktop, a managed object context is automatically configured with an undo manager, so there's no need to allocate one yourself.

```
- (void)viewDidAppear:(BOOL)animated {
    [super viewDidAppear:animated];

    [self becomeFirstResponder];
}

- (void)viewWillDisappear:(BOOL)animated {
    [super resignFirstResponder];

    [super viewWillDisappear:animated];
}

- (NSUndoManager *)undoManager
{
    return [[currentPerson managedObjectContext] undoManager];
}
```

At this point, the view controller is set to support undo, but the managed object context for the current object won't yet have an undo manager, as you haven't specifically assigned one.

Also, in order for the undo manager to track changes to the current person, you obviously need to modify the code for the view controller to set the properties of the managed object whenever the text fields or the date picker change. The only problem is that by setting the values of the object immediately, whenever they change, you lose the easy ability to cancel changes to an object. You wouldn't be able just to pop the view controller in the cancelPerson: method because the changes would already have been made to the object.

One way to avoid this problem is to use a second managed object context when editing the current person.

Multiple Managed Object Contexts

An instance of a managed object exists only within its managed object context. It's perfectly acceptable to have two different managed object contexts, each with a managed object instance tied to the same persistent object on disk. If you change the values on the object in one context, the values on the related object in the other context won't be affected. It's only when you tell one context to save: that the persistent object on disk is changed, and a notification is sent out, enabling the other context to merge the changes if required.

Multiple contexts offer the perfect solution to the problem of being able to edit a managed object while maintaining the ability to cancel changes. The AWPersonEditorViewController will need to maintain a second context. When the view controller is about to be pushed to edit a particular object, the controller will need to load a managed object instance for that object in its own managed object context. Any changes made in the secondary context won't affect the primary context until the user presses the Done button. At this point, you'll need to handle merging the changes from one context into another.[2] The first step is to enable the AWPersonEditorViewController to work with a secondary managed object context. It needs an instance variable for the secondary context, along with a method to set up the second context based on the main context; the easiest way is to write an init method for the view controller, taking a supplied primary managed object context from which it can create its secondary context. Listing 9.16 shows the method signature for this method, along with the new instance variable and property declaration.

LISTING 9.16   Adding support for the secondary managed object context

```
@interface AWPersonEditorViewController : UIViewController {
    [...]

    NSManagedObjectContext *editingContext;
}

[...]

@property (nonatomic, retain) NSManagedObjectContext *editingContext;

- (id)initWithPrimaryManagedObjectContext:
                            (NSManagedObjectContext *)primaryMOC;

@end
```

Remember to synthesize the editingContext property in AWPersonEditorViewController.m.

The new initWithPrimaryManagedObjectContext: method needs to start by initializing the view controller using UIViewController's designated initializer. Creating the secondary context is as easy as allocating and initializing a new managed object context, then setting its persistent store coordinator to that of the primary context, as shown in Listing 9.17.

LISTING 9.17   Initializing the view controller and creating a secondary managed object context

```
- (id)initWithPrimaryManagedObjectContext:
                        (NSManagedObjectContext *)primaryMOC {
    if( self = [super initWithNibName:@"AWPersonEditorViewController"
```

---

[2] The secondary context will load the instance from the persistent store, so if there are unsaved changes in the primary context, these won't appear in the second context. If you aren't saving after every change, make sure you save the primary context before loading into the secondary context.

```
                           bundle:nil] ) {

        editingContext = [[NSManagedObjectContext alloc] init];

        [editingContext setPersistentStoreCoordinator:
                          [primaryMOC persistentStoreCoordinator]];
    }

    return self;
}
```

When you work with multiple contexts, you need some way to be able to relate an object in one context with an object in another. At the moment, the currentPerson property will be set to an object outside of the current context.

Each managed object instance has an objectID, which can be used to retrieve a managed object instance in a context. Given a person object in one context, you can extract its objectID value and pass this to another context's objectWithID: method.

It's worth pointing out that if you are dealing with a newly-inserted and unsaved managed object, that object won't be accessible from any other managed object context. The value returned by objectID will be temporary, and will change once it's been saved. Since any object being edited in the Random People application will already have been saved (the RootViewController saves the context after every object is inserted), this won't be a problem here.

Let's implement the setCurrentPerson: method to check whether the provided person is in the editingContext. If it's not, you'll need instead to set the currentPerson instance variable to the person returned by using the objectID, as shown in Listing 9.18.

LISTING 9.18   Checking that a provided person is in the editing managed object context

```
- (void)setCurrentPerson:(AWPerson *)aPerson {
    if( [aPerson managedObjectContext] != self.editingContext )
        aPerson = (id)[self.editingContext
                              objectWithID:[aPerson objectID]];

    if( currentPerson != aPerson ) {
        [currentPerson release];
        currentPerson = [aPerson retain];
    }
}
```

Before testing whether this works, you'll also need to update the method that creates this view controller over in RootViewController.m, so that the new initWith... method is used, as shown in Listing 9.19.

LISTING 9.19 Creating the editing view controller using the new init method

```
- (AWPersonEditorViewController *)personEditorViewController {
    if( !personEditorViewController ) {
        personEditorViewController =
            [[AWPersonEditorViewController alloc]
          initWithPrimaryManagedObjectContext:self.managedObjectContext];
    }

    return personEditorViewController;
}
```

Build and run the application to test that you can still edit a person. You'll find that if you change the person in the editing view controller and click the Done button, the changes won't appear in the root view controller. If you edit the same person again, however, you'll find that the values you previously saved reappear in the editing view controller.

This shows how managed objects in separate managed object contexts can co-exist in separate states. In order to update the main context when the secondary context saves, you'll need to register for a notification sent out by a managed object context when it saves, NSManagedObjectContextDidSaveNotification.

Merging Changes from Other Managed Object Contexts

The userInfo dictionary provided with an NSManagedObjectContextDidSaveNotification notification object contains a list of the changes that have been saved to disk. The easiest way to deal with these changes is just to pass the whole notification object straight to NSManagedObjectContext's mergeChangesFromContextDidSaveNotification: method.

Let's register for this notification in the application's delegate object; you'll need a method to handle the notification and pass it through to the application's primary managed object context, but only if the context that sent the notification is *not* the primary context, as shown in Listing 9.20.

LISTING 9.20 Dealing with a notification that a managed object context was saved

```
- (void)application:(UIApplication *)application
          didFinishLaunchingWithOptions:(NSDictionary *)launchOptions {

    application.applicationSupportsShakeToEdit = YES;

    [[NSNotificationCenter defaultCenter] addObserver:self
              selector:@selector(contextSaved:)
                  name:NSManagedObjectContextDidSaveNotification
              object:nil];
```

```
    [...]
}

- (void)contextSaved:(NSNotification *)notification {
    if( [notification object] != self.managedObjectContext ) {
        [self.managedObjectContext
            mergeChangesFromContextDidSaveNotification:notification];
    }
}
```

If you build and run the application again, you'll find that any changes you save in the editor view controller now affect the information in the root view controller.

Changing Managed Object Values Whenever the Control Values Change

At this point, it's now possible to start implementing the undo strategy mentioned earlier in the chapter. Whenever the user finishes editing the contents of a UITextField, you'll need to set the relevant managed object value to the contents of the text field. You'll also need to add a method to be called if the value of the date picker is changed. Add the methods in Listing 9.21 into AWPersonEditorViewController.m.

LISTING 9.21   Changing the values of the managed object as soon as control values change

```
- (void)textFieldDidEndEditing:(UITextField *)textField {
    if( textField == self.firstNameTextField )
        [self.currentPerson setFirstName:textField.text];
    else if( textField == self.lastNameTextField )
        [self.currentPerson setLastName:textField.text];

    [self becomeFirstResponder];
}

- (IBAction)datePickerValueDidChange:(id)sender {
    if( sender == self.dateOfBirthPicker )
        [self.currentPerson setDateOfBirth:dateOfBirthPicker.date];
}
```

Remove the corresponding lines in the savePerson: method that set the values when the Done button is pressed.

Notice how the view controller makes itself the first responder once the text field has finished editing; this is so that the view controller is ready to accept any undo actions triggered by the user shaking the phone.

Add a method signature for the `datePickerValueDidChange:` method to `AWPersonEditorViewController.h` and connect this action to the date picker's Value Changed event in `AWPersonEditorViewController.xib`.

There are still a couple more changes that need to be made. Firstly, you'll need to allocate and initialize an undo manager when the editing context is created in the editor controller's `init` method, as shown in Listing 9.22.

LISTING 9.22   Setting the undo manager for the editing context

```
- (id)initWithPrimaryManagedObjectContext:
                        (NSManagedObjectContext *)primaryMOC {
    if( self = [super initWithNibName:@"AWPersonEditorViewController"
                         bundle:nil] ) {
        editingContext = [[NSManagedObjectContext alloc] init];
        [editingContext setPersistentStoreCoordinator:
                        [primaryMOC persistentStoreCoordinator]];
        NSUndoManager *undoManager = [[NSUndoManager alloc] init];
        [editingContext setUndoManager:undoManager];
        [undoManager release];
    }

    return self;
}
```

The undo manager is retained by its managed object context, so Listing 9.22 releases it once it's been set.

If you build and run to test this out, you'll find that you can now shake the phone to trigger the undo alert; if you click the Undo button, nothing will appear to have changed in the view controller, although whatever you changed will still be undone. Let's fix this now.

You'll need to register for a notification whenever an undo or a redo is triggered. Listing 9.23 registers for the notification in `viewDidLoad:` and adds a method that just updates the interface to match the values in the managed object whenever an action has been undone or redone.

LISTING 9.23   Registering for undo and redo change notifications

```
- (void)viewDidLoad {
    [...]

    [[NSNotificationCenter defaultCenter] addObserver:self
            selector:@selector(undoOrRedoAction:)
                name:NSUndoManagerDidUndoChangeNotification
              object:[self.editingContext undoManager]];
```

```
    [[NSNotificationCenter defaultCenter] addObserver:self
            selector:@selector(undoOrRedoAction:)
                name:NSUndoManagerDidRedoChangeNotification
              object:[self.editingContext undoManager]];
}

- (void)undoOrRedoAction:(NSNotification *)notification {
    [self updateInterfaceForCurrentPerson];
}
```

Build and run the application once again. You should now be able to undo and then redo any changes you make to a person.

There are two issues remaining; the Cancel button currently does nothing more than pop the view controller. If you make changes to a person, then click Cancel, then re-open the editor for the same person, you'll find that the changes you made previously are still there.

The second issue occurs if you make changes to one person, then save that person and go to edit another person. At this point, you can still shake the phone to undo the previous changes made to the other person. Let's address this issue first.

When the Done button is pressed, you'll need to tell the undo manager to removeAllActions before you pop the view controller. Obviously, you should only do this if the context saves successfully; if the save fails, the user might want to undo their actions. You could handle this at the end of the savePerson: method, but Listing 9.24 uses the viewWillDisappear: method, so that the undo actions will be cleared any time the view is about to disappear: either when a save is successful, or when the Cancel button is pressed.

LISTING 9.24   Removing all undo actions before popping the view controller

```
- (void)viewWillDisappear:(BOOL)animated {
    [super resignFirstResponder];
    [[self.editingContext undoManager] removeAllActions];
    [super viewWillDisappear:animated];
}
```

Now all you need to do is clear any changes to the managed object when the Cancel button is pressed.

Resetting a Managed Object Context

There are several ways to clear changes in a managed object context:

▶ You can do this on an individual object basis, using NSManagedObjectContext's refreshObject:mergeChanges: method.

This method will update the properties of the managed object based on the values currently in the persistent store. The mergeChanges flag indicates whether you want to reload the values into the managed object (YES), or just turn it into a fault (NO), leaving the values to be reloaded only when required.

▶ You can refresh all the objects in a managed object context at once, using either the reset method or the rollback method.

The reset method sets the managed object context to an empty state. All managed objects are forgotten, and will need to be reloaded before they can be used.

The rollback method takes the managed object context back to the state when it was last saved. It resets the undo manager and forgets any changes made to any managed objects in the context since the last save.

Since you're already clearing the undo manager in viewWillDisappear:, and want any managed objects edited in the future to be pulled straight from the persistent store, let's use the reset method on the managed object context. Change the cancelPerson: method as shown in Listing 9.25. Note that this method calls becomeFirstResponder, to trigger any active text fields to end editing *before* the context is reset. Otherwise, if the Cancel button were pressed with a text field still active, the app would crash when the text field delegate method (triggered when the view disappeared) tried to update the value on a managed object *after* it's been invalidated by this call to reset.

LISTING 9.25   Resetting the managed object context when the Cancel button is pressed

```
- (IBAction)cancelPerson:(id)sender {
    [self becomeFirstResponder];
    [self.editingContext reset];
    [self.navigationController popViewControllerAnimated:YES];
}
```

This time when you test the application, you'll find that any changes made to people are forgotten if you press the Cancel button.

Using the Editor Controller to Add New Objects

It would be great if the AWPersonEditorViewController could be used to add new objects as well as edit existing objects. This way, the user can change a person's information before they get saved into the persistent store.

Let's change the setCurrentPerson: method so that if the provided person is nil, a new person is created instead, as shown in Listing 9.26.

LISTING 9.26   Creating a new person if one isn't provided

```
- (void)setCurrentPerson:(AWPerson *)aPerson {
    if( !aPerson )
```

```
{
    self.title = @"Add person";
    aPerson = [AWPerson
        randomPersonInManagedObjectContext:self.editingContext];
}
else if( [aPerson managedObjectContext] != self.editingContext ) {
    self.title = @"Edit person";
    aPerson = (id)[self.editingContext
                            objectWithID:[aPerson objectID]];
}

if( currentPerson != aPerson ) {
    [currentPerson release];
    currentPerson = [aPerson retain];
}
}
```

Listing 9.26 also sets the title of the view controller to indicate whether the user is currently adding a person, or editing a person.

Change the addNewPerson method in RootViewController.m so it uses the editor view controller rather than just inserting an object immediately, as shown in Listing 9.27.

LISTING 9.27   Using the editor view controller to add a person

```
- (void)addNewPerson {
    [self.personEditorViewController setCurrentPerson:nil];
    [self.navigationController
            pushViewController:self.personEditorViewController
                    animated:YES];
}
```

Build and run the application to test this out. When you press the + button, a new person is created in the editing context and the editor view controller appears. If you press Cancel, the context is reset and the newly created person is destroyed. If you press Done, that person is saved into the editing context, a *managed object context did save* notification is posted, and the person is loaded into the primary context ready to be displayed when the root view controller reappears.

Summary

Although dealing with more than one managed object context can seem confusing, there are occasions when the possibility of having multiple "versions" of a managed object can be extremely useful. You've seen how to merge changes across contexts in response to the NSManagedObjectContextDidSaveNotification, and how to reset or rollback a context to forget any changes made to its objects.

If you were writing an application that needed to import large amounts of data, perhaps JSON or XML from a web service, you could use a secondary managed object context for the import. The import could then run on a background thread, leaving the main thread free for the user to interact with existing data in the primary context, with the import finishing when the background context saves, and the changes are merged into the primary context.

You've also seen how to enable an application and a specific view controller to support Shake to Undo. If you set an undo manager on a managed object context, it will provide automatic support for undoing and redoing actions on its managed object. All you need to do is listen for notifications about undo and respond accordingly.

PART III

Building a Simple Core Data Application

The third part of the book takes the reader through building a complete application using Core Data.

CHAPTER **10**

Sample Application: Note Collector

This chapter puts your Core Data knowledge into practice by walking through the creation of a more substantial application than you've worked with so far.

You'll see how to work with abstract entities and entity inheritance to save and fetch a hierarchy of related objects. You'll work with multiple view controllers to handle editing, and see how to re-use the primary view controller when navigating through the related items.

At the end of the chapter, you'll see how to supply a pre-populated data store inside your application's bundle, ready for use the first time the app is run on a user's device.

The Note Collector Application

The application you'll be building in this chapter is a relatively simple notebook application. It allows the user to create textual notes, storing these in collections, as shown in Figure 10.1.

Each collection can hold multiple notes, but it can also hold other collections. It would be possible, for example, to have a *Work* collection, containing a *Books* collection, which in turn contained a *Core Data for iOS* collection, which itself contained multiple notes made about that particular book.

FIGURE 10.1   The Note Collector application

Creating the Note Collector Project

The first step is to create a new project:

▶ Launch Xcode and choose File > New > New Project (Shift-⌘-N).

▶ Choose a Navigation-based iOS application.

▶ Call the project "Note Collector" and tick the Use Core Data checkbox.

The Application Data Model

As usual, let's start with the data model. The Note Collector application has two main types of data objects that will need to be persisted: notes and collections. A note contains textual note data and has a title; a collection has a title and can contain other notes and collections.

There is a complication that a Core Data fetch request can only be used to fetch one type of entity at a time, which is going to cause serious problems when writing the code to display the main table view containing *both* notes *and* collections, shown in Figure 10.1. Theoretically, it would be possible to perform two separate fetches and create a union of the results, but if you did do this you'd have to handle all the data source work yourself since a fetched results controller can only work with a single fetch request at a time.

In order to limit the amount of code you have to write, and use a fetched results controller, you'll need a way to be able to fetch both collections and notes using a single fetch request.

Back in Chapter 3, "Modeling Your Data," you saw that it's possible for Core Data entities to inherit from other entities, by specifying a Parent entity in the data model. The Note Collector application offers the perfect situation in which to make use of this functionality.

Modeling an Abstract Entity

A note object and a collection object have two things in common:

▶ They both have a name.

▶ Both can be contained within another collection.

These common features can be abstracted out into a separate entity, an AbstractItem entity. The Note and Collection entities can then be set to inherit from this AbstractItem entity, such that they both inherit a name attribute, and the reference to their containing collection.

This solves the problem for the fetched results controller mentioned above. The fetch request can now be set to fetch all instances of the AbstractItem entity, which means that it will also return all instances of both the Note and the Collection entities.

Open up Note_Collector.xcdatamodeld, and make the following changes:

▶ Rename the template Event entity to AbstractItem using the Data Model Inspector (Option-⌘-3)

▶ Set its Class to AWAbstractItem.

▶ Since you won't be creating any instances of the AbstractItem entity itself, only its sub-entities, mark AbstractItem as an Abstract Entity.

▶ Rename the existing timeStamp attribute to itemName, and set its type to String.

▶ Add a to-one relationship called superCollection that will be used to keep track of which collection an item belongs to, but don't set its Destination yet.

Modeling Sub-entities

Now that the abstract AbstractItem entity is created, you're ready to add the two concrete entities for notes and collections. Let's start with the collections:

▶ Create a new entity and call it Collection.

▶ Set its Class to AWCollection.

▶ Set its Parent Entity to AbstractItem.

▶ Add a relationship called subItems.

▶ Set the Destination of this relationship to be the AbstractItem entity, and its Inverse to be the superCollection relationship you created earlier.

10

▶ Since a collection can contain multiple items, mark the subItems relationship as To-Many.

▶ If a collection is deleted, you'll want its contents to be deleted as well, so set the Delete Rule for the subItems relationship to be Cascade.

NOTE

You don't need to model any additional attributes for the Collection entity; the only attribute needed is one for the name of the collection, and that will be inherited from the AbstractItem parent entity.

Next, let's model the notes:

▶ Create a new entity called Note.

▶ Set its Class to AWNote.

▶ Set its Parent to AbstractItem.

▶ Add a String attribute called textContent.

Figure 10.2 shows the three entities in the data model, displayed using the Graph editor style. Note the one-way arrows with hollow arrowheads, indicating the inheritance relationships; this inheritance hierarchy is also shown if you set the left Outline Style to Hierarchical.

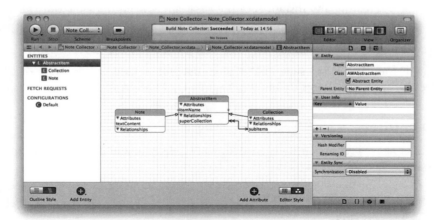

FIGURE 10.2   The Note Collector data model

Creating Managed Object Class Files

With the data model complete, it's time to create managed object class files for the three entities:

▶ Select all three entities in the data model and choose File > New > New File (⌘-N).

▶ Choose NSManagedObject subclass (under the Core Data group) and click Next.

▶ Select the Note_Collector data model, and create the files inside the Note Collector group (at the time of writing, you'll specifically need to select the group with the yellow icon in Xcode 4 before you can press Create).

Once the files have been created, open up `AWNote.h` and you'll see the interface shown in Listing 10.1.

LISTING 10.1   The AWNote.h file

```
#import <CoreData/CoreData.h>
#import "AWAbstractItem.h"

@interface AWNote :  AWAbstractItem {
@private
}

@property (nonatomic, retain) NSString * textContent;

@end
```

Notice how `AWNote` is set to inherit from `AWAbstractItem`? This obviously matches the inheritance set in the data model file, and means that an `AWNote` instance will also have the properties defined in `AWAbstractItem.h`, shown in Listing 10.2.

LISTING 10.2   The AWAbstractItem.h file

```
#import <CoreData/CoreData.h>

@class AWCollection;

@interface AWAbstractItem :  NSManagedObject {
@private
}

@property (nonatomic, retain) NSString * itemName;
@property (nonatomic, retain) AWCollection * superCollection;

@end
```

If you open `AWCollection.h`, you'll find that the `AWCollection` class also inherits from `AWAbstractItem`.

Most of the class files you'll be creating from now on will need to know about the AWCollection, AWNote and AWAbstractItem classes. As a time saver for this exercise, add the #import directives shown in Listing 10.3 into the Note_Collector_Prefix.pch precompiled header file (inside the project's Supporting Files group) so they are included for all the code in the project. If you don't do this, you'll need to add the #import lines where needed for the remaining steps.

LISTING 10.3   Importing the model class files in the precompiled header file

```
[...]

#ifdef __OBJC__
    #import <Foundation/Foundation.h>
    #import <UIKit/UIKit.h>
    #import <CoreData/CoreData.h>

    #import "AWAbstractItem.h"
    #import "AWNote.h"
    #import "AWCollection.h"
#endif
```

Configuring the RootViewController

With the data model and class files created, it's time to modify the existing RootViewController class to display collections and notes. Because of the inheritance you set up earlier, each collection or note has a superCollection relationship to keep track of its parent collection. The objects to be displayed by the RootViewController will be at the top of the tree of collections and notes, so their superCollection property will be nil.

Open the RootViewController.m file and change the method that creates the fetched results controller so that it's set to fetch instances of the AbstractItem entity. Set it to sort the items in ascending alphabetical order by their name, and set a predicate to fetch only the instances whose superCollection is nil, as shown in Listing 10.4.

LISTING 10.4   Creating the fetched results controller

```
- (NSFetchedResultsController *)fetchedResultsController {
    [...]

    NSFetchRequest *fetchRequest = [[NSFetchRequest alloc] init];
    NSEntityDescription *entity =
        [NSEntityDescription entityForName:@"AbstractItem"
                    inManagedObjectContext:managedObjectContext];
    [fetchRequest setEntity:entity];
```

```
    [fetchRequest setFetchBatchSize:20];

    NSPredicate *predicate = [NSPredicate
             predicateWithFormat:@"superCollection = %@", nil];
    [fetchRequest setPredicate:predicate];

    NSSortDescriptor *sortDescriptor =
        [[NSSortDescriptor alloc] initWithKey:@"itemName"
                                    ascending:YES];
    NSArray *sortDescriptors = [[NSArray alloc]
                        initWithObjects:sortDescriptor, nil];

    [fetchRequest setSortDescriptors:sortDescriptors];

    [...]
}
```

Next, you'll need to modify the method that configures the table view cells for display. The cell's text obviously needs to be set to the itemName property, but you'll also want to display a disclosure triangle on a collection item so that the user knows to click the collection to see its contents. Listing 10.5 checks the class of the current object to determine what kind of accessory to display and, if it's a collection, it displays a disclosure button. You'll write code later in this chapter to let the user change the name of the collection if they click on the button itself.

LISTING 10.5   Displaying the cell contents

```
- (void)configureCell:(UITableViewCell *)cell atIndexPath:(NSIndexPath *)indexPath {
    AWAbstractItem *currentItem = [self.fetchedResultsController
                                        objectAtIndexPath:indexPath];
    cell.textLabel.text = [currentItem itemName];

    if( [currentItem isKindOfClass:[AWCollection class]] )
        cell.accessoryType = UITableViewCellAccessoryDetailDisclosureButton;
    else
        cell.accessoryType = UITableViewCellAccessoryNone;
}
```

The last step before you can test the project is to rewrite the insertNewObject method to allow the user to insert either a new note item, or a new collection. Listing 10.6 uses a UIActionSheet to ask the user which type of item they want to create, creating the item in the sheet's delegate callback.

LISTING 10.6   Creating new items

```objc
- (void)insertNewObject {
    UIActionSheet *newItemSheet =
        [[UIActionSheet alloc] initWithTitle:nil
                                    delegate:self
                           cancelButtonTitle:@"Cancel"
                      destructiveButtonTitle:nil
                           otherButtonTitles:@"Add Note",
                                    @"Add Collection", nil];

    newItemSheet.actionSheetStyle = UIActionSheetStyleBlackOpaque;
    [newItemSheet showInView:self.view];
    [newItemSheet release];
}

- (void)actionSheet:(UIActionSheet *)actionSheet
        didDismissWithButtonIndex:(NSInteger)buttonIndex {
    switch (buttonIndex) {
        case 0: { // new note
            AWNote *newNote = [NSEntityDescription
          insertNewObjectForEntityForName:@"Note"
                inManagedObjectContext:self.managedObjectContext];
            newNote.itemName = @"New Note";
            break;}
        case 1: { // new collection
            AWCollection *newCollection = [NSEntityDescription
          insertNewObjectForEntityForName:@"Collection"
                inManagedObjectContext:self.managedObjectContext];
            newCollection.itemName = @"New Collection";
            break;}
        default:
            break;
    }

    NSError *anyError;
    if( ![self.managedObjectContext save:&anyError] )
        NSLog(@"Error saving: %@", anyError);
}

// Set the RootViewController class to adopt the
// UIActionSheetDelegate protocol to avoid compiler warnings:
@interface RootViewController : UITableViewController
    <NSFetchedResultsControllerDelegate, UIActionSheetDelegate> {
```

Build and run the application in the simulator and you'll find you can add and remove notes and collections, and that they are displayed correctly in the table view. They'll even reappear if you exit and re-launch the application. The names of new items are set by the code in Listing 10.6 and you can't navigate into collections yet. Let's add the navigation behavior next.

Displaying the Contents of a Collection

When the user taps on a collection, you're going to need to be able to push a new view controller to display the contents of that collection. This view controller should be a subclass of `UITableViewController`, and needs to fetch instances of the `AWAbstractItem` entity. It should also allow the user to add new items into the current collection.

It would be acceptable to write a dedicated view controller to handle all the above, but for the Note Collector app, it makes much more sense to modify the existing `RootViewController` class, which already has most of the necessary functionality.

Since this class will now be used for multiple view controller instances, let's use Xcode's refactoring tool to change its name:

▶ Open up the `RootViewController.h` file.

▶ Right-click (or control-click) on the `RootViewController` classname in the `@interface` text and choose Refactor > Rename.

▶ Change the refactor tool's settings to rename the class to `AWCollectionViewController`, and select the Rename related files checkbox.

▶ Click the Preview button to check what will be changed, as shown in Figure 10.3, then click Save.

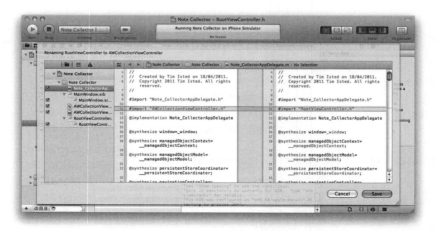

FIGURE 10.3   Using Xcode's Refactor tool to rename the RootViewController

Build and run the application before you do anything else to make sure it still works.

As of the time of writing, Xcode won't rename the xib file; it will still be called `RootViewController.xib`, so locate the file in the Project Navigator and change the name to `AWCollectionViewController.xib`. You'll also need to make a change to the `MainWindow.xib` file so that it knows which file to use to instantiate the application's root view controller:

▶ Open `MainWindow.xib`.

▶ Select the `Navigation Controller` item.

▶ Click the area that says `View Loaded from "RootViewController"` and use the Attributes Inspector (Option-⌘-4) to change the NIB Name to `AWCollectionViewController`.

Again, build and run to check that everything still works.

Keeping Track of the Collection to be Displayed

To use an `AWCollectionViewController` to display the contents of a particular collection, you're going to need to add an instance variable to keep track of the current collection; this variable can then be used to set the fetch predicate for the fetched results controller.

Start by adding the instance variable and a property declaration to `AWCollectionViewController.h`, as shown in Listing 10.7.

LISTING 10.7   Adding a property to keep track of the collection to be displayed

```
@interface AWCollectionViewController : UITableViewController
    <NSFetchedResultsControllerDelegate, UIActionSheetDelegate> {
    [...]

    AWCollection *currentCollection;
}

@property (nonatomic, retain) NSManagedObjectContext
                                    *managedObjectContext;
@property (nonatomic, retain) NSFetchedResultsController
                                    *fetchedResultsController;

@property (nonatomic, retain) AWCollection *currentCollection;

@end
```

Synthesize this property in `AWCollectionViewController.m`, add a line of code to the dealloc method to release the new instance variable, and change the method that creates the fetched results controller so that it sets the predicate based on this variable, as shown in Listing 10.8.

Because there will now be multiple instances of this class, each generating a fetched results controller, you'll either need to set the cacheName to nil, or only specify a cache if it's for the root view controller (i.e., if the currentCollection is nil). Since Note Collector doesn't make use of sections, it would be fine to disable caching altogether, but in case the future requirements of the app change, Listing 10.8 makes use of a ternary conditional to set a cacheName only if (self.currentCollection) is nil and evaluates as false.

LISTING 10.8   Synthesizing and using the property to set the fetch predicate

```
@implementation AWCollectionViewController

@synthesize currentCollection;

- (void)dealloc {
    [currentCollection release];
    [...]
    [super dealloc];
}


- (NSFetchedResultsController *)fetchedResultsController {

    [...]

    NSPredicate *predicate = [NSPredicate
            predicateWithFormat:@"superCollection = %@",
                                    self.currentCollection];
    [fetchRequest setPredicate:predicate];

    [...]

    NSString *cacheName = (self.currentCollection) ? nil : @"Root";
    NSFetchedResultsController *aFetchedResultsController =
            [[NSFetchedResultsController alloc]
                initWithFetchRequest:fetchRequest
                managedObjectContext:self.managedObjectContext
                  sectionNameKeyPath:nil cacheName:cacheName];

    [...]

}
```

Build and run the application again and you'll find that nothing appears to have changed. The instance variables on an object are automatically set to `nil` when the object is created. When the view controller is created at application launch, `currentCollection` will be `nil`, and the fetch predicate will be set exactly as it needs to be to display the items at the root level.

You'll need to create and push a new instance of this view controller whenever the user taps on a collection cell in the table view. Let's write an `init` method to initialize the view controller for a specific collection, as shown in Listing 10.9. Note that this method also sets the title of the view controller to match the name of the current collection, along with the managed object context. Remember to add a method signature for the `initWithCollection:` method into `AWCollectionView.h`.

LISTING 10.9   Initializing the view controller with a specific collection

```
- (id)initWithCollection:(AWCollection *)collection {
    if( self = [super initWithNibName:@"AWCollectionViewController"
                                              bundle:nil] ) {
        currentCollection = [collection retain];
        self.title = collection.itemName;
        self.managedObjectContext = collection.managedObjectContext;
    }

    return self;
}
```

NOTE

The root view controller instance of this class won't be initialized using this method, since it's instantiated from the `MainMenu.xib` file.

Take a look at the `awakeFromNib` method in `Note_CollectorAppDelegate.m` and you'll see that the managed object context is set by the delegate. Add a line to set the title of the root view controller to `Note Collector` as shown in Listing 10.10.

LISTING 10.10   Setting the title of the root view controller

```
- (void)awakeFromNib {
    AWCollectionViewController *rootViewController =
            (AWCollectionViewController *)[navigationController
                                                topViewController];
    rootViewController.managedObjectContext =
                                        self.managedObjectContext;
    rootViewController.title = @"Note Collector";
}
```

You're now ready to write code to open a new instance of this controller when the user taps on a collection. Open AWCollectionViewController.m and change the tableView:didSelectRowAtIndexPath: method as shown in Listing 10.11.

LISTING 10.11   Responding to taps on collection items

```
- (void)tableView:(UITableView *)tableView
               didSelectRowAtIndexPath:(NSIndexPath *)indexPath {
    id selectedItem = [self.fetchedResultsController
                                  objectAtIndexPath:indexPath];

    if( [selectedItem isKindOfClass:[AWCollection class]] ) {
        AWCollectionViewController *collectionVC =
                    [[AWCollectionViewController alloc]
                              initWithCollection:selectedItem];
        [self.navigationController
                    pushViewController:collectionVC animated:YES];
        [collectionVC release];
    }
}
```

There are a couple more changes to make before testing the application. You'll need to change the code that creates new items so that they are placed inside the current collection. And, in order for the navigation behavior to work, you'll need to comment out the existing line that sets the leftBarButtonItem in viewDidLoad, as shown in Listing 10.12.

LISTING 10.12   Placing new items inside the current collection

```
- (void)actionSheet:(UIActionSheet *)actionSheet
        didDismissWithButtonIndex:(NSInteger)buttonIndex {
    switch (buttonIndex) {
        case 0: { // new note
            AWNote *newNote = [NSEntityDescription
            insertNewObjectForEntityForName:@"Note"
                    inManagedObjectContext:self.managedObjectContext];
            newNote.itemName = @"New Note";
            newNote.superCollection = self.currentCollection;
            break;}
        case 1: { // new collection
            AWCollection *newCollection = [NSEntityDescription
            insertNewObjectForEntityForName:@"Collection"
                    inManagedObjectContext:self.managedObjectContext];
            newCollection.itemName = @"New Collection";
            newCollection.superCollection = self.currentCollection;
            break;}
```

```
        default:
            break;
    }

    NSError *anyError;
    if( ![self.managedObjectContext save:&anyError] )
        NSLog(@"Error saving: %@", anyError);
}

- (void)viewDidLoad {
    [super viewDidLoad];

    // Don't create an edit button, or it will take the place of a
    // 'back' button.
    // self.navigationItem.leftBarButtonItem = self.editButtonItem;

    [...]
}
```

Build and run the application to test it in the Simulator. Create a new collection in the root view controller, and then click on it to push a new view controller, which displays the contents of that new collection. Add several more collections inside collections to test that the navigation works for as many levels as you need.

Examining the Contents of a Raw Data File

When you created the data model for this application, you set a Delete Rule for the Collection entity's subItems relationship to Cascade. This should mean that if you delete a root-level collection with lots of sub-collections containing further sub-collections, all of those related items get deleted from the top down (hence the name "cascade").

It's not immediately clear how to check that this is happening; once you've deleted the collection at the top of the tree, there's no way to access any of its sub-items from within the application. It's certainly the case that the delete rule isn't having the same effect as Nullify (i.e., setting the superCollection property on sub-items to nil), because this would mean they would now appear at the root level of the navigation.

One way to check what's happening is to take a look inside the application's .sqlite data file using the sqlite3 command-line utility. If you're not comfortable using the Terminal, you might prefer to skip this section.

▶ With the application running in the iPhone Simulator (make sure you have a collection at the root level containing some notes and lots of other collections inside collections), use the Finder to locate the Note_Collector.sqlite data file for the application.

This will be in ~/Library/Application Support/iPhone Simulator/<Version Number>/Applications/<some UID>/Documents, as described in Chapter 8, "Migration and Versioning," in the section titled "Renaming Entities and Attributes."

▶ Open the Terminal and navigate to this folder.

An easy way to achieve this is to make sure both the Terminal window and the folder window in the Finder are visible on your screen, type cd<space> at the terminal prompt and then click-drag the little folder icon in the title bar of the Finder window, dropping it onto the terminal window so that the path is filled out for you, then press <enter>.

▶ Open the data file using the sqlite3 utility, by typing:

    sqlite3 Note_Collector.sqlite<enter>

You'll need to interact with the sqlite3 utility either by using its internal commands or by typing raw SQL queries, terminated with semi-colons.

▶ Start by typing .tables<enter> to get a list of database tables used by Core Data for the Note Collector application's data.

Notice that there's only one data model-related table, called ZABSTRACTITEM. You'll see why in a minute.

▶ Type .headers ON<enter> to display the table column headers in subsequent commands.

▶ Type SELECT * FROM ZABSTRACTITEM;<enter> (don't forget the semi-colon) and you'll see a list of the rows in the ZABSTRACTITEM table (this SQL command selects all the columns from all the rows in the ZABSTRACTITEM table). Your output will look like that shown in Figure 10.4.

Notice how all the items, whether they are notes or collections, are stored within this one database table.

Normally, Core Data uses one database table per modeled entity. The exception to this is when you have inherited entities—when you have one or more entities inheriting from a parent, Core Data creates a single table to hold all the instances of all those related entities.

The ZABSTRACTITEM table therefore contains columns both for its own ZITEMNAME and ZSUPERCOLLECTION, and also for the Note entity's ZTEXTCONTENT.

This behavior enables Core Data to translate a fetch request involving inherited entities into a single SQL SELECT statement from a single database table.

▶ Now check what happens when you delete a collection containing other collections and notes; you'll need to swipe across a collection row in the iPhone simulator to delete it, as you removed the Edit button earlier in this chapter.

▶ Once the collection is deleted, switch back to the Terminal and execute that same SELECT command again:

    SELECT * FROM ZABSTRACTITEM;<enter>

You'll find that all the related rows will also have been removed from the database, so the Cascade delete rule is functioning correctly.

▶ Exit the sqlite3 application by typing .quit<enter>, and then quit the Terminal application.

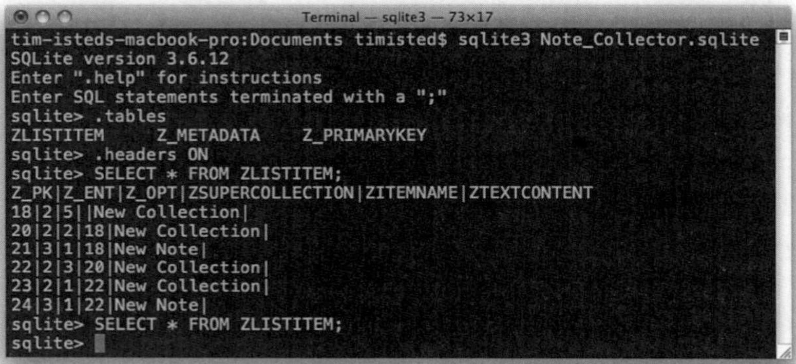

FIGURE 10.4   Examining the content of the application's data file

Setting and Editing an Item Name

So far, the underlying data functionality is pretty much complete—Core Data has taken care of most of the drudgery, so much of the code we've written up to now has related to view controllers and cell display rather than data persistence.

The navigational aspects of the application are working well, but there's no way to specify the name for new items, or change them once they've been created. You'll need to add functionality to do the following things:

▶ Set the name of a new collection item.

▶ Set the name of a new note item.

▶ Change the name of a collection item.

▶ Change the name and textual contents of a note item.

The first three of these points all relate to asking the user for a single string. The fourth point is going to need a dedicated view controller for viewing and editing notes.

Let's deal with the single string points first. It would be fine to create dedicated view controllers for each managed object class, using multiple managed object contexts and undo managers etc., like you did in Chapter 9, "Working with Multiple View Controllers and Undo." Since you're only dealing with one string, however, it would be much simpler just to write a single, generic string-editing view controller that can be displayed modally when required.

This new view controller needs to be able to request a string from the user, using a single UITextField with its contents optionally set to a pre-existing string. It also needs to be able to pass back enough information to whichever view controller is requesting the string such that new managed objects can be created, or existing objects changed.

Creating the New View Controller

Start by adding a new UIViewController subclass to your project, making sure to check the With XIB for user interface checkbox. Specify that you wish to subclass UIViewController, and call the class AWStringEditorViewController.

Open the resulting AWStringEditorViewController.h file. You'll need an IBOutlet for a text field, along with a property to hold an initial string, if any. In order to pass information back to another view controller, let's keep track of a delegate, and define an AWStringEditorVCDelegate protocol including methods to handle the user pressing either the Done or the Cancel button on the modal view controller. Listing 10.13 shows a protocol that makes use of a userInfo dictionary so that the delegate view controller can supply whatever it needs to know in order to respond correctly when the user closes the modal view controller.

LISTING 10.13   The interface for the AWStringEditorViewController class

```
#import <UIKit/UIKit.h>

@protocol AWStringEditorVCDelegate;

@interface AWStringEditorViewController : UIViewController {
    UITextField *editorTextField;
    NSString *initialString;
    id <AWStringEditorVCDelegate> delegate;
    NSDictionary *userInfo;
}

@property (nonatomic, retain) IBOutlet UITextField *editorTextField;
@property (nonatomic, retain) NSString *initialString;
@property (nonatomic, assign) id <AWStringEditorVCDelegate> delegate;
@property (nonatomic, retain) NSDictionary *userInfo;

- (id)initWithInitialString:(NSString *)string
               delegate:(id <AWStringEditorVCDelegate> )aDelegate
               userInfo:(NSDictionary *)dict;
```

@end

```
@protocol AWStringEditorVCDelegate <NSObject>

- (void)userDidSaveStringEditorVC:(AWStringEditorViewController *)vc
                       withString:(NSString *)string
                         userInfo:(NSDictionary *)dict;
- (void)userDidCancelStringEditorVC:(AWStringEditorViewController *)vc
                           userInfo:(NSDictionary *)dict;

@end
```

Open AWStringEditorViewController.m, synthesize the properties, set them in the init method, and release them in dealloc, as shown in Listing 10.14.

LISTING 10.14   @implementation AWStringEditorViewController

```
@synthesize editorTextField, initialString, delegate, userInfo;

- (id)initWithInitialString:(NSString *)string
                   delegate:(id <AWStringEditorVCDelegate>)aDelegate
                   userInfo:(NSDictionary *)dict {
    if( self = [super initWithNibName:@"AWStringEditorViewController"
                               bundle:nil] ) {
        initialString = [string retain];
        delegate = aDelegate;
        userInfo = [dict retain];
    }

    return self;
}

- (void)dealloc {
    [userInfo release];
    [initialString release];
    [editorTextField release];

    [super dealloc];
}
```

Open AWStringEditorViewController.xib and click the View object.

► Use the Attribute Inspector (Option-⌘-4) for the view to set its Background to groupTableViewBackgroundColor (which is in the iPhone SDK color palette if you need to find it by choosing Other...).

- ▶ Add a `UITextField` to the top of the view.

- ▶ Connect the File's Owner `editorTextField` outlet to the new text field.

- ▶ Set the `delegate` for the text field to be File's Owner.

- ▶ Use the inspector for the text field to set its Placeholder text to `Item Name`.

- ▶ Make sure the Clear When Editing Begins checkbox is unchecked.

- ▶ Set the text field to capitalize `Words`.

- ▶ Set the Return Key to `Done`.

Next, you'll need to set the Done and Cancel buttons in the
`AWStringEditorViewController`'s `viewDidLoad` method, along with two methods that call
the relevant protocol methods on the delegate when a button is pressed. Listing 10.15 also
implements the text field's `textFieldShouldReturn:` delegate method so that if the user
clicks the Done button on the keyboard after editing a string, it has the same effect as
pressing the Done button in the navigation bar.

LISTING 10.15   Setting up the Done and Cancel buttons and their corresponding methods

```
- (void)viewDidLoad {
    [super viewDidLoad];

    UIBarButtonItem *cancelButton = [[UIBarButtonItem alloc]
            initWithBarButtonSystemItem:UIBarButtonSystemItemCancel
                    target:self action:)];
    self.navigationItem.leftBarButtonItem = cancelButton;
    [cancelButton release];

    UIBarButtonItem *doneButton = [[UIBarButtonItem alloc]
            initWithBarButtonSystemItem:UIBarButtonSystemItemDone
                    target:self action:)];
    self.navigationItem.rightBarButtonItem = doneButton;
    [doneButton release];
}

- (IBAction)cancelAction:(id)sender {
    [self.delegate userDidCancelStringEditorVC:self
                                    userInfo:self.userInfo];
}

- (IBAction)saveAction:(id)sender {
    [self.delegate userDidSaveStringEditorVC:self
                        withString:[self.editorTextField text]
                            userInfo:self.userInfo];
}
```

10

```
- (BOOL)textFieldShouldReturn:(UITextField *)textField {
    [textField resignFirstResponder];

    [self saveAction:textField];

    return YES;
}
```

You also need to set the initial string for the text field, and make the text field the first responder when the view appears, as shown in Listing 10.16.

LISTING 10.16   Setting the string and first responder status

```
- (void)viewWillAppear:(BOOL)animated {
    [super viewWillAppear:animated];

    [self.editorTextField setText:self.initialString];
}

- (void)viewDidAppear:(BOOL)animated {
    [super viewDidAppear:animated];

    [self.editorTextField becomeFirstResponder];
}
```

That's it for the string editor; now all you need to do is write the code to make use of it.

Let's start with the ability to change the name of an existing collection. You'll need to implement the table view delegate method that gets called when the user presses a disclosure button. In order that the AWStringEditorVCDelegate methods you'll implement in a moment can work out what to do, you'll need to build a suitable userInfo dictionary containing a reference to the managed object being changed. Add the code shown in Listing 10.17 into AWCollectionViewController.m.

LISTING 10.17   Handling taps on accessory buttons

```
- (void)tableView:(UITableView *)tableView
 accessoryButtonTappedForRowWithIndexPath:(NSIndexPath *)indexPath {
    id tappedItem = [self.fetchedResultsController
                                objectAtIndexPath:indexPath];

    if( [tappedItem isKindOfClass:[AWAbstractItem class]] ) {
        NSDictionary *userInfo = [NSDictionary
                        dictionaryWithObject:tappedItem
                                forKey:@"kStringEditorAbstractItem"];
```

```
AWStringEditorViewController *stringVC =
  [[AWStringEditorViewController alloc]
    initWithInitialString:[(AWAbstractItem *)tappedItem itemName]
                  delegate:self userInfo:userInfo];

stringVC.title = @"Edit Item Name";

UINavigationController *navigationController =
        [[UINavigationController alloc]
                    initWithRootViewController:stringVC];

[self presentModalViewController:navigationController
                        animated:YES];
[navigationController release];
[stringVC release];
    }
}
```

Next, implement the AWStringEditorVCDelegate methods; the cancel method just needs to dismiss the modal view controller. The save method needs to change the name of an object, if there is one at the specified userInfo key, as shown in Listing 10.18.

LISTING 10.18   Cancelling and Saving edited strings

```
- (void)userDidCancelStringEditorVC:(AWStringEditorViewController *)vc
                           userInfo:(NSDictionary *)userInfo {
    [self dismissModalViewControllerAnimated:YES];
}


- (void)userDidSaveStringEditorVC:(AWStringEditorViewController *)vc
      withString:(NSString *)string userInfo:(NSDictionary *)userInfo {
    id objectToChange = [userInfo
                      valueForKey:@"kStringEditorAbstractItem"];

    if( objectToChange ) {
        [(AWAbstractItem *)objectToChange setItemName:string];
    }

    NSError *anyError;
    if( ![self.managedObjectContext save:&anyError] )
        NSLog(@"Error saving: %@", anyError);

    [self dismissModalViewControllerAnimated:YES];
}
```

10

```
// Set the AWCollectionViewController class to adopt the
// AWStringEditorVCDelegate protocol to avoid compiler warnings
// (in AWCollectionViewController.h):
#import "AWStringEditorViewController.h"

@interface AWCollectionViewController : UITableViewController
    <NSFetchedResultsControllerDelegate, UIActionSheetDelegate,
    AWStringEditorVCDelegate> {
```

Build and run the application to check that you can rename an existing collection by tapping its disclosure button.

Now let's change the code that creates new notes and collections so it asks the user for an item name. You'll need to change the UIActionSheetDelegate callback in AWCollectionViewController.m so that it creates a userInfo dictionary containing the name of the entity to be created, sets a suitable title for the view controller, before displaying the view controller, as shown in Listing 10.19.

LISTING 10.19   Asking the user to supply a name for new items

```
- (void)actionSheet:(UIActionSheet *)actionSheet
        didDismissWithButtonIndex:(NSInteger)buttonIndex {
    NSString *entityName = @"";
    NSString *vcTitle = @"";

    switch (buttonIndex) {
        case 0: // New note
            entityName = @"Note";
            vcTitle = @"New Note";
            break;
        case 1: // New collection
            entityName = @"Collection";
            vcTitle = @"New Collection";
            break;
        default:
            return; // User pressed Cancel so return early
    }

    NSDictionary *userInfo = [NSDictionary
            dictionaryWithObject:entityName
                        forKey:@"kStringEditorEntityName"];

    AWStringEditorViewController *stringVC =
        [[AWStringEditorViewController alloc]
                                    initWithInitialString:@""
            delegate:self userInfo:userInfo];
```

```
    stringVC.title = vcTitle;

    UINavigationController *navigationController =
        [[UINavigationController alloc]
                        initWithRootViewController:stringVC];

    [self presentModalViewController:navigationController
                        animated:YES];
    [navigationController release];
    [stringVC release];
}
```

Modify the userDidSaveStringEditorVC:... callback method so that if there is no existing object specified, it creates a new managed object using the relevant entity name from the userInfo dictionary, as shown in Listing 10.20.

LISTING 10.20   Creating new items with a user-specified name

```
- (void)userDidSaveStringEditorVC:(AWStringEditorViewController *)vc
    withString:(NSString *)string userInfo:(NSDictionary *)userInfo {
  id objectToChange = [userInfo
                    valueForKey:@"kStringEditorAbstractItem"];

  if( !objectToChange ) {
     NSString *entityName = [userInfo
                    valueForKey:@"kStringEditorEntityName"];

     if( !entityName ) return; // Don't know what to create

     objectToChange = [NSEntityDescription
        insertNewObjectForEntityForName:entityName
                inManagedObjectContext:self.managedObjectContext];

     [(AWAbstractItem *)objectToChange
                    setSuperCollection:self.currentCollection];
  }

  [(AWAbstractItem *)objectToChange setItemName:string];
  NSError *anyError;
  if( ![self.managedObjectContext save:&anyError] )
     NSLog(@"Error saving: %@", anyError);

  [self dismissModalViewControllerAnimated:YES];
}
```

Build and run to make sure that this works. When you ask to create a new note or collection, you'll be asked for the name before the item is created. If you Cancel the new item name view controller, no item will be created; if you type a name and press the Done button, the item will be created with the correct superCollection.

Displaying and Editing Notes

The last piece of functionality to add to the Note Collector application is the rather crucial ability to display and edit textual notes. Let's use a single view controller to handle both viewing and saving, and enable the user to edit both the note title and content on the same view.

Add another new UIViewController subclass to your project, making sure that the With XIB for user interface checkbox is still selected. Call it AWNoteEditorViewController.

When the user taps on a note in a list, this view controller should appear, displaying the text content in an uneditable UITextView taking up the entire view area. When the user asks to edit the text, the view will need to shrink to allow space for the keyboard to appear, as well as an additional text field to allow the user to edit the name of the note item, as shown in Figure 10.5.

FIGURE 10.5 Displaying and editing a note

Let's implement this using two separate text views on the view controller, one to display the text, one to edit it, along with a text field to edit the item name, shown only when the view controller is in Edit mode.

You'll need outlets in AWNoteEditorViewController.h for each of the text views and the text field, together with a property to keep track of the note being edited. Listing 10.21 also includes the method signature for a designated initializer to set up the view controller for a specified note.

LISTING 10.21   The interface for the note editor

```
@interface AWNoteEditorViewController : UIViewController {
    UITextView *noteDisplayTextView;
    UITextView *noteEditorTextView;
    UITextField *noteNameTextField;

    AWNote *currentNote;
}

@property (nonatomic, retain) IBOutlet UITextView *noteDisplayTextView;
@property (nonatomic, retain) IBOutlet UITextView *noteEditorTextView;
@property (nonatomic, retain) IBOutlet UITextField *noteNameTextField;

@property (nonatomic, retain) AWNote *currentNote;

- (id)initWithNote:(AWNote *)note;

@end
```

Open AWNoteEditorViewController.m, synthesize the properties, set the currentNote property in the init method, and release them in dealloc, as shown in Listing 10.22.

LISTING 10.22   @implementation AWNoteEditorViewController

```
@synthesize noteDisplayTextView, noteEditorTextView, noteNameTextField;
@synthesize currentNote;

- (id)initWithNote:(AWNote *)note {
    if( self = [super initWithNibName:@"AWNoteEditorViewController"
                               bundle:nil] ) {
        currentNote = [note retain];
    }

    return self;
}
```

10

```
- (void)dealloc {
    [currentNote release];
    [noteNameTextField release];
    [noteEditorTextView release];
    [noteDisplayTextView release];

    [super dealloc];
}
```

Open the AWNoteEditorViewController.xib file and click the View object to display it.

▶ Drag out a UITextView from the library palette, and hover it over the view until it expands to full size before dropping it.

▶ Check the Size Inspector (Option-⌘-5) for the text view and make sure the auto-resizing control has all the anchors and springs enabled.

▶ Use the Attributes Inspector (Option-⌘-4) to turn off the Editable checkbox.

▶ Select all of the Detection options.

▶ With the text view still selected, choose Edit > Format > Font > Show Fonts (Control-Shift-⌘-T) and reduce the font size to 14 pt.

▶ Connect the noteDisplayTextView outlet to this text view.

This text view will be used to display the note content when a note is first opened. Next, let's add the text field used to edit the note name:

▶ Drag out a UITextField and drop it at the top of the view. Resize it to fill the width of the view.

▶ Set the Placeholder text to Item Name and the Alignment to Center.

▶ Set the border style to a plain rectangular frame.

▶ Make sure the Clear When Editing Begins checkbox is unchecked.

▶ Change the font size to 18 pt.

▶ Set it to capitalize Words.

▶ Set the Return Key to Next.

▶ Set the delegate outlet on the text field to be File's Owner.

▶ Connect the noteNameTextField outlet to this text field.

Finally, add the second text view to edit the note contents:

▶ Drag out another UITextView and drop it just below the text field.

▶ Don't change the height, but resize just the width to fill the width of the view.

- ▶ Change the font size to 14 pt.

- ▶ Use the size inspector to enable all the auto-resizing springs and anchors (this shrinks the text view if necessary for the in-call status bar).

- ▶ Set the `delegate` outlet on the text view to be `File's Owner`.

- ▶ Connect the `noteEditorTextView` outlet to this text view.

The finished interface is shown in Figure 10.6.

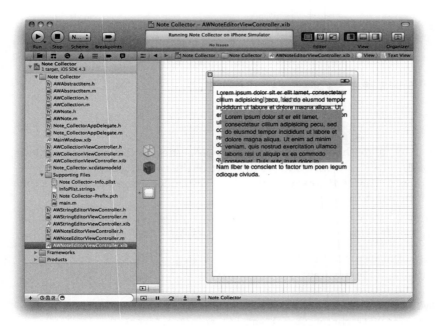

FIGURE 10.6   The note editor view in Interface Builder

You'll write code a little later in this chapter to push this view controller immediately when the user creates a new note, so the view would need to appear in editing mode; if so, the `noteEditorTextView` needs to be the first responder, ready for the user to start typing their note. The relevant controls also need to be shown or hidden when the view appears, and their text contents set. Add the code shown in Listing 10.23 into `AWNoteEditorViewController.m`.

LISTING 10.23   Configuring the controls when the view appears

```
- (void)viewWillAppear:(BOOL)animated {
    [super viewWillAppear:animated];

    self.title = [self.currentNote itemName];
```

```
    [self.noteNameTextField setText:[self.currentNote itemName]];
    [self.noteEditorTextView setText:[self.currentNote textContent]];
    [self.noteDisplayTextView setText:[self.currentNote textContent]];

    [self.noteNameTextField setHidden:!self.editing];
    [self.noteEditorTextView setHidden:!self.editing];
    [self.noteDisplayTextView setHidden:self.editing];
}

- (void)viewDidAppear:(BOOL)animated {
    [super viewDidAppear:animated];

    if( self.editing ) {
        [self.noteEditorTextView becomeFirstResponder];
    }
}
```

Next, implement delegate methods to set the relevant properties on the current note item, update the title of the view controller, and set the text of the noteDisplayTextView. Listing 10.24 also sets the noteEditTextView to be first responder when the user taps the Next button from the noteNameTextField.

LISTING 10.24   Implementing the text field and text view delegate methods

```
- (BOOL)textViewShouldEndEditing:(UITextView *)textView {
    [self.currentNote setTextContent:textView.text];

    NSError *anyError = nil;
    if( ![[self.currentNote managedObjectContext] save:&anyError] )
        NSLog(@"Error saving: %@", anyError);

    [self.noteDisplayTextView setText:textView.text];

    return YES;
}

- (BOOL)textFieldShouldEndEditing:(UITextField *)textField {
    [self.currentNote setItemName:textField.text];

    NSError *anyError = nil;
    if( ![[self.currentNote managedObjectContext] save:&anyError] )
        NSLog(@"Error saving: %@", anyError);

    self.title = [self.currentNote itemName];
```

```
    return YES;
}

- (BOOL)textFieldShouldReturn:(UITextField *)textField {
    [self.noteEditorTextView becomeFirstResponder];
    return YES;
}
```

You'll also need to configure the Edit button on the navigation bar when the view is loaded, and handle what happens when the controller changes between editing and display modes, as shown in Listing 10.25.

LISTING 10.25   Enabling editing mode on the view controller

```
- (void)viewDidLoad {
    [super viewDidLoad];

    self.navigationItem.rightBarButtonItem = self.editButtonItem;
}

- (void)setEditing:(BOOL)editing animated:(BOOL)animated {
    [super setEditing:editing animated:animated];

    [self.noteNameTextField setHidden:!editing];
    [self.noteEditorTextView setHidden:!editing];
    [self.noteDisplayTextView setHidden:editing];

    if( editing ) {
        [self.noteEditorTextView becomeFirstResponder];
    } else {
        [self.noteNameTextField resignFirstResponder];
        [self.noteEditorTextView resignFirstResponder];
    }
}
```

You're now ready to write the code to display the new view controller when the user taps on an existing note, or creates a new note.

Open AWCollectionViewController.m and make the changes shown in Listing 10.26.

LISTING 10.26   Displaying the note editor view controller

```
#import "AWNoteEditorViewController.h"

- (void)tableView:(UITableView *)tableView
```

10

```
                    didSelectRowAtIndexPath:(NSIndexPath *)indexPath {
    id selectedItem = [fetchedResultsController
                                objectAtIndexPath:indexPath];

    if( [selectedItem isKindOfClass:[AWCollection class]] ) {
        AWCollectionViewController *collectionVC =
                    [[AWCollectionViewController alloc]
                            initWithCollection:selectedItem];
        [self.navigationController
                    pushViewController:collectionVC animated:YES];
        [collectionVC release];
    } else if( [selectedItem isKindOfClass:[AWNote class]] ) {
        AWNoteEditorViewController *noteVC =
                    [[AWNoteEditorViewController alloc]
                            initWithNote:selectedItem];
        [self.navigationController
                    pushViewController:noteVC animated:YES];
        [noteVC release];
    }
}


- (void)userDidSaveStringEditorVC:(AWStringEditorViewController *)vc
        withString:(NSString *)string userInfo:(NSDictionary *)userInfo {
    id objectToChange = [userInfo
                                valueForKey:@"kStringEditorAbstractItem"];
    BOOL isNewObject = NO;

    if( !objectToChange ) {
        isNewObject = YES;
        NSString *entityName = [userInfo
                            valueForKey:@"kStringEditorEntityName"];

        if( !entityName ) return; // Don't know what to create

        objectToChange = [NSEntityDescription
            insertNewObjectForEntityForName:entityName
                    inManagedObjectContext:self.managedObjectContext];

        [(AWAbstractItem *)objectToChange
                        setSuperCollection:self.currentCollection];
    }

    [(AWAbstractItem *)objectToChange setItemName:string];
    NSError *anyError;
    if( ![self.managedObjectContext save:&anyError] )
        NSLog(@"Error saving: %@", anyError);
```

```
    if( isNewObject &&
                [objectToChange isKindOfClass:[AWNote class]] ){
        AWNoteEditorViewController *noteVC =
                    [[AWNoteEditorViewController alloc]
                                    initWithNote:objectToChange];
        [noteVC setEditing:YES animated:NO];
        [self.navigationController pushViewController:noteVC
                                            animated:NO];
        [noteVC release];
    }

    [self dismissModalViewControllerAnimated:YES];
}
```

Import the AWNoteEditorViewController.h file at the top of
AWCollectionViewController.m, then build and run the application. You'll find that you
can now open existing notes in the new view controller and click the Edit button to
change their title or content.

If you create a new note, you'll find that once you provide a name for the note, it will be
created and opened in the new view controller, ready to type the text content for that note.

Supplying a Pre-Populated Data Store

If you were going to sell this application, it might be a good idea to provide a few sample
notes and collections so that new users can see exactly what the app does the moment
they launch it.

Given the simplicity of the Note Collector application, it would be acceptable in performance terms to check at launch for an empty data store, and if necessary insert some
notes and collections programmatically. In a more advanced application, however, it
would be much better to supply a pre-populated data store *inside the app bundle*, which
can be copied to the application's Documents directory the first time the app is launched.

Before you continue, make sure you have some notes and collections stored in the existing Note Collector persistent store.

Working with a Data Store in the Application Bundle

The first step is to copy the existing Note_Collector.sqlite store into the application
bundle, so locate this file as you did earlier in the section *Examining the contents of a raw data
file* and copy it into the Note Collector project directory in the Finder. Switch to the Xcode
Project Navigator and right-click (or Ctrl-click) on the Supporting Files group and choose
Add > Files to "Note Collector" to add the Note_Collector.sqlite file to the project.

10

An iOS application cannot write to files stored in the application bundle, so for the Note Collector app, you can't just change the code that sets up the persistent store location to use this bundle resource. Instead, you'll need to check whether a persistent store file already exists in the Documents directory and, if not, copy the file from the bundle.

Since you might want to come back and change the default contents of this pre-populated store, let's use an #ifdef directive to make it easy to instruct the compiler to ignore the file-copying code—this would restore the standard behavior of generating an empty .sqlite store.

Open the Note_CollectorAppDelegate.m file, find the persistentStoreCoordinator method, and add the code shown in Listing 10.27.

LISTING 10.27   Copying the pre-populated data store if it doesn't already exist

```
- (NSPersistentStoreCoordinator *)persistentStoreCoordinator {
    if (__persistentStoreCoordinator != nil) {
        return __persistentStoreCoordinator;
    }

    NSURL *storeURL = [[self applicationDocumentsDirectory]
            URLByAppendingPathComponent:@"Note_Collector.sqlite"];

// Comment out this #define to create an empty store if necessary
#define NOTE_COLLECTOR_COPY_STORE_FROM_BUNDLE

#ifdef NOTE_COLLECTOR_COPY_STORE_FROM_BUNDLE
    if( ![[NSFileManager defaultManager]
                        fileExistsAtPath:[storeURL path]] ) {

        NSString *dataPath = [[NSBundle mainBundle]
                    pathForResource:@"Note_Collector" ofType:@"sqlite"
                                            inDirectory:nil];

        NSError *anyError = nil;
        BOOL success = [[NSFileManager defaultManager]
    copyItemAtPath:dataPath toPath:[storeURL path] error:&anyError];
        if( !success ) NSLog(@"Error copying file: %@", anyError);
    }
#endif

    NSError *error = nil;
    [...]
}
```

Before you run the app, delete the existing executable (and therefore its Documents) from the Simulator or the device. When you build and run the app, you'll find that it launches with the pre-populated store, showing the notes and collections you had previously added.

If you were writing an application that didn't allow the user to add data, such as a reference dictionary or recipe book, you obviously wouldn't be able to use the app to provide its own pre-populated information. Instead, you'd need to write a separate app to generate the data, and copy the .sqlite persistent store it creates over to the first application. As long as both apps use the exact same data model file (i.e. the Note_Collector.xcdatamodeld in the case of the Note Collector app), the persistent stores will be compatible. This will also work with Mac desktop applications—if you need to enter a large amount of information, and an iPhone or iPad isn't an appropriate input device, you can use a Mac app to generate the .sqlite file used by an iOS application.

Summary

This chapter should have given you a better idea of how Core Data fits into the development of a more "real world" application. Although there's been quite a lot of code in this chapter, very little of it has had anything to do with saving data to disk, since the Core Data framework handles so much of this for you.

You've seen how to work with abstract entities and inheritance, and even taken a look inside the internal .sqlite data files used by Core Data on iOS.

One of the benefits to the entity inheritance pattern is that it would be extremely easy to add different types of items to be stored, such as a picture note, or a voice recording. All you'd have to do would be to create a new entity inheriting from the AbstractItem entity, with any necessary additional attributes or perhaps a relationship to a separate entity to hold large data objects, and add a view controller to edit that item. Very few modifications would be needed to the existing classes, other than to add an extra item to the Add New Item sheet.

Over the course of the book, you've seen various different ways to edit managed objects. In this chapter, you used a view controller that allowed the user to edit a string, but handled all the managed object changes in delegate callbacks. You might like to try adding Undo capabilities to the AWNoteEditorViewController class, or implement the note editing functionality using a separate managed object context, as described in Chapter 9.

10

PART IV

Optimizing and Troubleshooting

The final part of the book looks at performance issues, optimization for the restricted memory requirements of iOS devices, and at debugging tools to aid in developing with Core Data on iOS.

CHAPTER 11

Optimizing for iOS Performance and Memory Requirements

The iOS runtime environment, as with all mobile devices, offers much less in raw hardware capabilities than laptop or desktop systems. Mobile CPUs are generally much slower and much less memory is available. To ensure that your software runs reasonably fast and does not run out of memory, you'll need to work within these restrictions and pay close attention to resource usage. Also, since people frequently use iOS software while out and about, they are less likely to tolerate slow performance than if they were sitting at home or in an office.

The restrictions can seem difficult at first but if you can view them as a challenge—as an opportunity to make your software the best it can be—then the restrictions of the environment can spur you on to writing much better software than you might if you had more resources available. The runtime environment won't tolerate bloated or slow software nearly as well as a desktop, so your software will need to be correspondingly better.

This chapter covers a variety of techniques for optimizing speed and limiting memory usage while balancing the conflicting demands of these two goals. This includes methods for optimizing your Core Data fetch requests and analyzing Core Data performance at run time. The chapter also covers the question of whether Core Data is right for your situation or whether you'll get better performance with other data management techniques.

Performance, Optimization, and Speed

Performance optimization involves two conflicting techniques. Improving speed generally means keeping more of your data in memory, which makes it more likely that you'll run out of space. Reducing memory usage implies keeping less data in memory, reading it in only when needed, but that imposes speed penalties since the data is not immediately available. Which techniques you'll need to apply will depend on your application's behavior and requirements. There's no single approach to optimizing both speed and memory usage, so you'll need to understand which methods can be combined in your application for the best result.

Optimizing memory usage involves limiting the amount of data you read into memory, and then freeing up that memory when the data is no longer needed. With Core Data, the faulting process can cause data to load without explicitly allocating memory space for it, and releasing that memory requires talking to Core Data. We'll explore both methods.

It's also important to remember that while Core Data can and does allocate memory on your behalf, this does not imply that you're exempt from the usual Cocoa memory management techniques. This chapter assumes you already understand about retain counts and when objects are deallocated, which affects your memory usage but which are not directly related to Core Data.

Speed improvements lean more toward reading data into memory in advance of actually needing it, and minimizing the number of round trips to the data store. Even if you have plenty of memory available, it's not always as simple as just reading in a bunch of data in one shot and keeping it around. In many cases, the real test of speed is not the total time taken for a task, but rather how responsive the app seems to the user. One long read from the data store could result in a perceived slowdown even if it minimizes the total data store access time. It's often better to spread out store access even if it means you'll spend more total time reading data.

Data Store Types

Core Data supports three types of data stores on iOS:

- ▶ A SQLite-based store
- ▶ An atomic binary store
- ▶ An in-memory store

Which store you choose will affect speed and memory usage of your app. In most cases you'll probably want the SQLite data store, but not always. Core Data abstracts the details of the data store completely, so that any code using one store type will work with a different one. This means you can experiment with both if you're not sure which would be best for your situation.

NOTE

You may have read about an XML-based Core Data store; while you may use an XML-based data store in a Core Data app for the desktop, this option is currently not available on iOS.

Binary and Memory Data Stores

Two of the store types are essentially equivalent, at least from a performance perspective. The *binary* and *in-memory* data stores are entirely memory-resident at runtime. Although the binary data store is written to a file, Core Data will read the entire file into memory and keep it there while the application is running. The in-memory store, as the name implies, only exists in memory and is never written to a file.

The memory-resident status of these stores puts them at one extreme in the speed versus memory trade-off. By keeping everything in memory you'll get the best performance possible, but at the expense of potentially needing a lot of memory to manage that data. There's not a lot of room to optimize a memory-resident data store since there are no unexpected file accesses slowing things down and likewise not much room to reduce the memory footprint without simply deleting unnecessary data.

SQLite Data Store

When using a SQLite data store, memory usage and performance are more flexible, and the overall results will depend on how you handle your objects. Objects in a SQLite store aren't read into memory until they're needed, and even then they may be read in only as placeholders with no property data. This can dramatically reduce memory usage compared to a binary store, since you could have millions of objects in the store but only a handful in memory at any given time.

Speed can be slower, since it's necessary to make round-trips to the SQLite store to retrieve objects when they're requested. Performance is generally very good, though, especially since iOS devices save files to solid-state disks instead of rotating media. Since the app doesn't have to search the drive for data, the app will be more responsive.

There are numerous techniques available to tune how Core Data loads objects from the store, and these will in turn affect both speed and memory usage with SQLite-based stores. Since the stores are abstracted through Core Data, the same code applies across the different store types, but the effects will be most noticeable when using SQLite.

In most cases you'll find that a SQLite store is the best choice, unless speed is critical or your data set is very small.

Monitoring SQLite Stores

Many of the techniques that follow relate to managing round-trips to the data store. Every time Core Data needs to go to the store for data, there's an extra delay that would not occur if the data were already in memory. But what if you're not sure whether Core Data is talking to the data store? Fortunately the SQLite store has a debug option that allows you to see *exactly* what's happening at the database level, right down to the actual SQL.

NOTE

You shouldn't rely on the SQL table format, since it's undocumented and could change without warning (and has in the past). But seeing what's happening at this level can be a useful way to understand how Core Data uses SQLite, and provide clues to the changes you might need to make to improve performance.

To enable the debug option, you pass in an argument to the application when it starts up. This is just like what you'd do if you were using a Unix command-line, even though you won't be doing that on iOS. For Unix systems, arguments are just parameters passed to an application when it starts, and the presence or absence of a command line isn't really important. For an iOS app, however, you can arrange for Xcode to pass the argument for you.

To configure this argument in Xcode 4, choose Product > Edit Scheme (Shift-⌘-<). Make sure the Run Note Collector scheme is selected, and click the Arguments tab to select it, as shown in Figure 11.1.

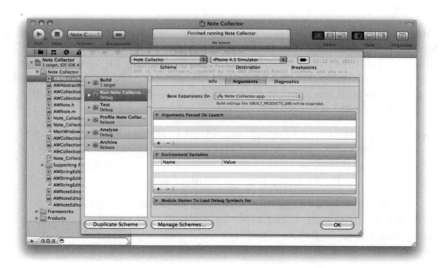

FIGURE 11.1   The Edit Scheme window for arguments and environment variables

This tab lets you set arguments and environment variables for the application. Arguments set here will be available to the application as if you had run the application from the command-line and typed in the argument there.

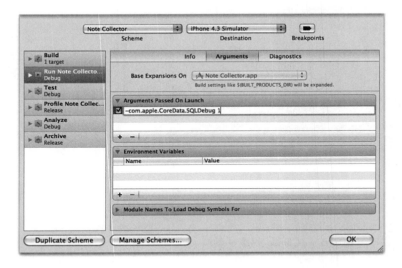

FIGURE 11.2   Adding the Core Data SQLDebug argument

Click the add button (+) under the Arguments Passed On Launch section. The argument you need to add is `-com.apple.CoreData.SQLDebug`, which should be set to an integer value. Type the argument and the integer value all in the one area, as shown in Figure 11.2. Any value greater than zero will turn on Core Data SQLite debugging, and higher numbers will make the output more verbose.

Arguments Under Xcode 3

If you're using Xcode 3, the procedure to set an executable argument is a little different. You'll need to start by finding the executable in the Xcode project window. Make sure you've selected the application name in the Executables section (and not in Products or Targets); the one in Executables is the compiled executable file.

Double-click the executable to bring up the info window, and click the Arguments tab, then click the + button and type the argument as shown in Figure 11.3.

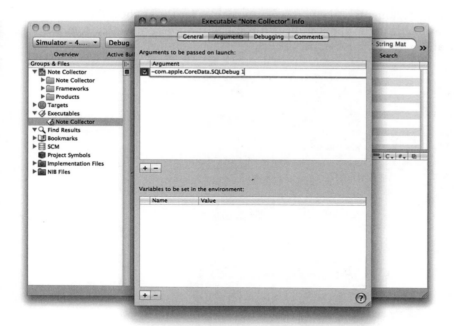

FIGURE 11.3   Setting the Core Data SQLDebug argument in Xcode 3

Use the checkbox next to an argument to control whether Xcode uses it when running the app, or select the argument and click the remove button (–) to completely remove the argument.

Build and run the application, and you'll find that debug messages appear in Xcode's console window. If you start up the Note Collector app with no pre-existing data (i.e., creating a blank store and not copying the pre-populated data file), the output will resemble Listing 11.1.

LISTING 11.1   Running Note Collector with SQLite debug level 1

```
CoreData: annotation: Connecting to sqlite database file at
    "/Users/timisted/Library/Application Support/iPhone Simulator/4.3.2/
        Applications/A1D4F6F6-B479-478F-86DF-A0B6F925DAF3/
            Documents/Note_Collector.sqlite"
CoreData: annotation: creating schema.
CoreData: sql: pragma page_size=4096
CoreData: sql: pragma auto_vacuum=2

CoreData: sql: BEGIN EXCLUSIVE

CoreData: sql: CREATE TABLE ZABSTRACTITEM
```

```
    ( Z_PK INTEGER PRIMARY KEY, Z_ENT INTEGER, Z_OPT INTEGER,
      ZSUPERCOLLECTION INTEGER, ZITEMNAME VARCHAR, ZTEXTCONTENT VARCHAR )

CoreData: sql: CREATE INDEX ZABSTRACTITEM_ZSUPERCOLLECTION_INDEX
                      ON ZABSTRACTITEM (ZSUPERCOLLECTION)

CoreData: sql: CREATE INDEX ZABSTRACTITEM_Z_ENT_INDEX ON ZABSTRACTITEM (Z_ENT)

CoreData: annotation: Creating primary key table.

CoreData: sql: CREATE TABLE Z_PRIMARYKEY
    (Z_ENT INTEGER PRIMARY KEY, Z_NAME VARCHAR, Z_SUPER INTEGER, Z_MAX INTEGER)

CoreData: sql: INSERT INTO Z_PRIMARYKEY(Z_ENT, Z_NAME, Z_SUPER, Z_MAX)
                         VALUES(1, 'AbstractItem', 0, 0)

CoreData: sql: INSERT INTO Z_PRIMARYKEY(Z_ENT, Z_NAME, Z_SUPER, Z_MAX)
                         VALUES(2, 'Collection', 1, 0)

CoreData: sql: INSERT INTO Z_PRIMARYKEY(Z_ENT, Z_NAME, Z_SUPER, Z_MAX)
                         VALUES(3, 'Note', 1, 0)

CoreData: sql: CREATE TABLE Z_METADATA
    (Z_VERSION INTEGER PRIMARY KEY, Z_UUID VARCHAR(255), Z_PLIST BLOB)

CoreData: sql: SELECT TBL_NAME FROM SQLITE_MASTER WHERE TBL_NAME = 'Z_METADATA'

CoreData: sql: DELETE FROM Z_METADATA WHERE Z_VERSION = ?

CoreData: sql: INSERT INTO Z_METADATA (Z_VERSION, Z_UUID, Z_PLIST)
                         VALUES (?, ?, ?)

CoreData: sql: COMMIT

CoreData: sql: pragma cache_size=200

CoreData: sql: SELECT t0.Z_ENT, t0.Z_PK FROM ZABSTRACTITEM t0
             WHERE t0.ZSUPERCOLLECTION IS NULL ORDER BY t0.ZITEMNAME
CoreData: annotation: sql connection fetch time: 0.0013s
CoreData: annotation: total fetch execution time: 0.0019s for 0 rows.
```

A number of things happen in this listing. First, since the app was not previously installed in the Simulator, Core Data issues a series of SQLite statements to create the tables it needs. Some of these tables have names that resemble the entities in the managed object model, while others are created for Core Data's own undocumented use.

If you increase the debug level you can get more debug information. Experiment a little and see what you find. At level 3 you'll find that the debug output includes values for SQL prepared statements, so you'll see what SQLite will fill in for the question marks in the INSERT statements. That can help if you have a lot of SQL statements and need to know which SQL corresponds to which object. In general, though, this kind of debugging is most useful simply to help clarify how often your code causes Core Data to make round trips to the store.

Optimizing Fetching

When fetching objects from Core Data, it's easy to make general requests that ask for more items than you really need, or to format predicates in a manner that makes Core Data do more work than necessary to satisfy the request. This section looks at several techniques that will help optimize your fetch requests so you don't fall into these traps.

Setting Fetch Limits

The simplest optimization is to consider how many objects you actually need before fetching. If there might be hundreds or thousands of matching objects, but you can only display 10 at a time, don't fetch all of the objects in one shot. Instead, fetch enough to show the user the first 10 items, and do further fetches when necessary. This will reduce the memory needed as well as improve the perceived performance by getting results to the user as quickly as possible. It's usually better to set a predicate on the fetch and retrieve only relevant objects, but even then there can be cases where the total number of matching objects is more than you can actually use at the same time.

NSFetchRequest has a fetchLimit property, which tells it how many items it should return. For subsequent fetches, it also has a fetchOffset property, which tells it how many objects to skip before completing the request. With these two properties you can make repeated requests to step through a large number of objects a few at a time.

These properties are comparable to SQL's LIMIT parameter for the size of the result, and to SQL cursors for stepping through the results. Note that these properties only affect SQLite stores; the properties are ignored in binary stores and the entire result is returned.

To use these parameters, set the fetchLimit on the request before executing it. Set the fetchOffset to 0 the first time, and on later calls increment it by the number of objects returned so it skips previously found objects. Listing 11.2 shows how you might do this in a controller class managing data from the Note Collector app. The method fetchMoreNotes: gets the next 10 notes from the data store each time it is called. Note that fetchOffset needs to maintain its value from one call to the next, so it has been added as an instance variable.

LISTING 11.2   Using fetch limits to limit fetch size

```
@interface MyController : NSObject {
    NSUInteger fetchOffset;
}
- (NSArray *)fetchMoreNotes;
@end

@implementation MyController
- (NSArray *)fetchMoreNotes
{
    NSFetchRequest *fetchRequest = [[NSFetchRequest alloc] init];
    NSEntityDescription *entity = [NSEntityDescription
                    entityForName:@"Note"
          inManagedObjectContext:managedObjectContext];
    [fetchRequest setEntity:entity];

    fetchRequest.fetchLimit = 10;
    fetchRequest.fetchOffset = fetchOffset;

    NSError *anyError = nil;
    NSArray *nextTen = [managedObjectContext
        executeFetchRequest:fetchRequest error:&anyError];
    fetchOffset += [nextTen count];
    return nextTen;
}
@end
```

If you're using `NSFetchedResultsController` to display Core Data objects in a table view, it will handle this for you automatically if you specify a `fetchBatchSize`.

Optimizing Predicates

If you're using an `NSPredicate` to select objects from a data store, and the predicate has more than one test, the order in which they appear in the predicate can make a big difference to fetch performance. Multiple conditions will be checked in the same order as they appear in the predicate, and if the first test fails, the rest are short-circuited and are not evaluated. You can take advantage of this in a couple of ways:

▶ If you expect one condition to be much more restrictive than the others, put that one first. Consider each condition on its own, and what fraction of the objects in the store they would match. If one likely matches only 1 percent of the objects while the others match much higher percentages, put the 1 percent match first. Then you'll completely skip the other conditions 99 percent of the time.

It may not always be possible to know which conditions are the most restrictive. If they're very close it may not matter. Testing the application should give you a better idea of how restrictive the various conditions will be, and you can optimize performance based on the results.

▶ Put text conditions at the end of the predicate, since they will take longer to evaluate than numeric tests. Core Data permits full text searching via NSCondition tests such as LIKE and CONTAINS, and these can be extremely useful; however, they're also much slower to evaluate than simply comparing numbers. The difference is significant enough that numeric tests should go first, even if the text condition is likely to be more restrictive.

As an example of this, suppose we expand the Note Collector app by adding a creation date to the AbstractItem entity. With this field, you could record the date when each item was created. The managed object model would look like Figure 11.4.

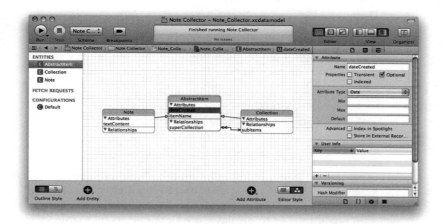

FIGURE 11.4   Note Collector model with creation date added to the AbstractItem entity

Now suppose you wanted to find all notes created within the past 24 hours that contain a specific string in the itemName field. That gives you two conditions you'll want to check. Start by setting up the fetch request and the target date:

```
NSFetchRequest *fetchRequest = [[NSFetchRequest alloc] init];
NSEntityDescription *entity = [NSEntityDescription
                   entityForName:@"Note"
         inManagedObjectContext:managedObjectContext];
[fetchRequest setEntity:entity];

NSDateComponents *oneDayAgoComponents =
    [[NSDateComponents alloc] init];
oneDayAgoComponents.day = -1;
```

```
NSDate *referenceDate = [[NSCalendar currentCalendar]
        dateByAddingComponents:oneDayAgoComponents
                        toDate:[NSDate date]
                       options:0];
```

You could put the predicate conditions in either order and get the same results:

```
NSPredicate *predicate = [NSPredicate
    predicateWithFormat:@"(itemName CONTAINS '%@') AND
    (dateCreated > %@)", searchString, referenceDate];
[fetchRequest setPredicate:predicate];
```

Or equivalently:

```
NSPredicate *predicate = [NSPredicate
    predicateWithFormat:@"(dateCreated > %@) AND
    (itemName CONTAINS '%@')", referenceDate, searchString];
[fetchRequest setPredicate:predicate];
```

These are logically equivalent, but the second will run faster in most cases because dateCreated is a date field, which implies a numeric comparison when evaluating the predicate. Putting it first means that whenever that condition is false, the slower text search is skipped.

Pre-Fetching Relationships

An object is normally loaded by Core Data as a fault, and its property values are filled in automatically when requested. If the object has relationships to other objects, the relationships will still be faults even after the properties are available. That's good for keeping memory use under control, since automatically following and firing faults on relationships could potentially load the entire data store into memory.

In the Note Collector app this means that when a Collection is loaded, displaying its itemName does not automatically cause the contained AbstractItems to load. They get loaded on demand, when you use the relationship. For example, a Collection object in this state would appear like this in the console:

```
(gdb) po managedObject
<AWCollection: 0x3a29830> (entity: Collection; id: 0x3a28060
    <x-coredata://786ECA6E-8799-4F80-9873-34140D1E0BE2/Collection/p1> ;
data: {
 itemName = "My Collection";
 subItems = "<relationship fault: 0x3a29080 'subItems'>";
 superCollection = nil;
})
```

Although the itemName has been loaded to display to the user, subItems still appears as a relationship fault.

If you know you're going to need the objects in a relationship, you can arrange to pre-fetch them as part of the initial fetch request. This allows you to extend the fetch request to include related objects that aren't matched by the fetch predicate, or that aren't even the same entity as the one used by the fetch request. You do this with NSFetchRequest's setRelationshipKeyPathsForPrefetching: method. For example:

```
NSEntityDescription *entity = [NSEntityDescription
                entityForName:@"Collection"
        inManagedObjectContext:managedObjectContext];
[fetchRequest setEntity:entity];
[fetchRequest setRelationshipKeyPathsForPrefetching:
                [NSArray arrayWithObject:@"subItems"]];
```

By specifying that the subItems relationship key path should be preloaded, all of the collection's note objects will be loaded from the data store when the fetch executes. Going back to the debugger console, we see that the subItems have been loaded:

```
(gdb) po managedObject
<AWCollection: 0x3a47fa0> (entity: Collection; id: 0x3a47650
    <x-coredata://786ECA6E-8799-4F80-9873-34140D1E0BE2/Collection/p1> ;
data: {
 itemName = "My Collection";
 subItems =     (
 0x3c02090 <x-coredata://786ECA6E-8799-4F80-9873-34140D1E0BE2/Note/p2>,
 0x3c01a60 <x-coredata://786ECA6E-8799-4F80-9873-34140D1E0BE2/Note/p3>
 );
 superCollection = nil;
})
```

The setRelationshipKeyPathsForPrefetching: method operates on key paths, so it's possible to traverse multiple levels of relationship in a single call. Also, since it accepts an array of key paths, you can include multiple relationships. This gives you fine-grained control over which relationships are pre-fetched.

Pre-Fetching Any Object

Core Data maintains a cache of data read from the data store. If an object is in the cache, fetching it will be fast because no round trip to the data store is necessary. So how can you force an object into the cache if you expect to need it?

It turns out that you don't need to fetch the entire object to cache it; just getting its managed object ID will do. You can ask the fetch request to retrieve only object IDs, but behind the scenes the objects are cached and made ready for quick fetching later on. You enable this by telling the fetch request that you want the object IDs, as shown here:

```
[fetchRequest setResultType:NSManagedObjectIDResultType];
```

When you execute the fetch, you won't receive your model objects as you might expect. Instead you'll receive a collection of NSManagedObjectID instances. While the managed object context is getting those IDs, it caches the objects corresponding to those IDs, and makes them available for fast fetching with no round trip to the store. This can be useful on a background thread, running a fetch for IDs of a list of objects that will be needed later on the main thread. The main thread can then fetch them more quickly.

You can also use the NSManagedObjectID instances to retrieve the full object from the managed object context directly by using the objectWithID: method, again with the speed benefit from the cache:

```
NSArray *results = [managedObjectContext
            executeFetchRequest:fetchRequest error:&anyError];
NSManagedObject *last = [managedObjectContext
                        objectWithID:[results lastObject]];
```

Pre-Loading Property Values

Normally objects are returned from the data store as fault objects, and their property values are filled in on demand. If you know you'll be wanting to make use of property values immediately, you can tell the fetch request to return complete, non-fault objects with all property data available. This is a simple flag on the fetch request:

```
[fetchRequest setReturnsObjectsAsFaults:NO];
```

This does not affect whether relationships are pre-fetched. If you need that as well, use the setRelationshipKeyPathsForPrefetching: method, described earlier.

NSFetchedResultsController and Sections

One convenient feature of NSFetchedResultsController is that it can work seamlessly with a table view to display data in different sections, by using its sectionNameKeyPath property.

In order to group objects by section, Core Data needs to compute all sections and their names. If you have a data store with preloaded data, all of it will be scanned on the first run of the app in order to compute the sections. Section information will be cached, so this isn't an ongoing issue, but if you have a very large preloaded data set then you might have a slow startup on the application's first run. Batching doesn't affect this, since it's still necessary to find the section names. If you expect to preload a large data set then you might want to consider either not using sections or not using NSFetchedResultsController.

Managing Faulting

In addition to optimizing your fetch requests, it helps to understand when Core Data will fire faults to load property data or relationships. If data has not yet been loaded from the store, firing a fault can cause a database round trip and a corresponding performance hit. Also, firing faults increases the amount of memory in use, so if you're concerned about memory use then you need to understand when faulting will happen.

"Safe" Fault-Free Methods

Many useful methods will work on a fault object without causing it to fire. Mostly, these relate to memory management and introspection of the object. The complete list is:

▶ isEqual:

▶ hash

▶ superclass

▶ class

▶ self

▶ zone

▶ isProxy

▶ isKindOfClass:

▶ isMemberOfClass:

▶ conformsToProtocol:

▶ respondsToSelector:

▶ retain

▶ release

▶ autorelease

▶ retainCount

▶ description

▶ managedObjectContext

▶ entity

▶ objectID

▶ isInserted

▶ isUpdated

▶ isDeleted

▶ isFault

If you implement any of these methods in an NSManagedObject subclass, be careful about whether your version might cause a fault to fire. For example, the default implementation of description doesn't cause a fault to fire, but if your version looks up some of the object's properties, it might require looking up data from the store.

With these methods you can do a lot while keeping objects as faults. Collection classes like NSArray rely on the isEqual and hash methods, for example, so you can add objects to collections or check whether an object is in a collection without firing faults.

Preventing Property Loading

If you're only going to be using the "safe" fault-free methods on all of the objects returned from a fetch, you can reduce memory use by ensuring that the property values aren't loaded at all, not even into the row cache. Using setIncludesPropertyValues:, you can tell the fetch request not to include property values; you'll receive fault objects as usual, only with less memory used by the row cache.

```
[fetchRequest setIncludesPropertyValues:NO];
```

If you end up needing property values on one of the returned objects, they're still loaded automatically, but it will take longer since it will be necessary to go to the data store to find them.

Batch Faulting

If you've read a bunch of objects and kept them as faults, you may later have a need to load a collection of them into complete objects. You could fire the faults individually, but there's a better way which makes it possible to fire all of the faults in a single shot. Do this by collecting the objects in an array and creating a predicate using the "self IN <array>" syntax. The self part of the predicate corresponds to the objects being evaluated, and the array contains the fault objects you want to fire; for example:

```
NSPredicate *predicate = [NSPredicate predicateWithFormat:
                          @"self IN %@", faultObjectArray];
```

Use this predicate on a fetch request with its entity matching that of the fault objects, and the result will be complete, non-fault versions of the original objects. Relationships will still be subject to the same faulting behavior described earlier, and can be pre-fetched if you need them.

Re-faulting Objects

If you know you won't be using a managed object for a while, but you still need to keep it around for later use, it's possible to convert it back into a fault object to reduce the memory it uses. You can do this using the managed object context's refreshObject:mergeChanges: method.

This method takes two arguments: the first is the target object, and the second is a Boolean flag that indicates whether you want to reload the object's values from the data store. You could pass YES for this argument if you had multiple managed object contexts and wanted one context to load changes that had been saved by another. If you pass NO for this argument, the managed object context converts the target object back into a fault:

```
[managedObjectContext refreshObject:myObject mergeChanges:NO];
```

A crucial detail when doing this is that since you're telling the managed object context not to merge any changes from the data store, any pending updates on the target object will be lost. If there are no unsaved changes, that won't be a problem. But if you have made changes you don't want to lose, then you must save them before calling this method.

Re-faulting objects also implies that any objects connected via relationships will be released. Managed objects retain their relationships, which can lead to keeping related objects in memory even if you're not explicitly retaining them. These related objects may use more memory than is immediately apparent by examining the code, but re-faulting the object that retains them will allow them to be removed from memory.

Once you have re-faulted an object, firing its faults continues to work normally. Property values and relationships will load on demand, just as they do when the object is first read from the data store.

Managing BLOBs

How you manage BLOBs (Binary Large OBjects) can have a major impact on memory usage. In Core Data, a BLOB is any binary data not representable with the standard numeric or string types. Common uses include images, sounds, or other media associated with your data. As these can be very large compared to other properties, some care is needed when dealing with them to avoid severe memory problems.

Core Data represents BLOBs with the Binary Data type and for relatively small data sizes it's reasonable to keep BLOBs in the data store, while larger ones should probably be kept separate. There's no hard rule about how big a binary object must be before it's considered "large" for these purposes—a more important question is how many BLOBs you're likely to have in memory at any given time, what the total combined size of those BLOBs is, and whether you have enough memory available to hold them.

If you're using a binary data store the answer is simple. Since the entire data store is read into memory, all BLOBs will be in memory at all times. For all but the smallest BLOBs, this quickly leads to an untenable situation.

For SQLite the answer is more nuanced. You'll need to consider faulting behavior to be sure about which BLOBs are in memory at any given time. Putting BLOBs in the data store is much more convenient than putting the data in separate files. Also, SQLite is actually faster than using external files for BLOBs up to about 50 kB, so if you're careful about faulting then this convenience can improve speed as well. Since SQLite can scale to databases in the terabyte range, you won't run into problems with total store size on an iOS device anytime soon.

This section looks at three strategies for managing BLOBs, by expanding the Note Collector application to include an image for each note.

Putting BLOBs in the Entity That Uses Them

The simplest method is just to put the binary data right in the associated entity. In the case of Note Collector, just add a new `imageData` property to the `Note` entity with its type set to Binary data, as shown in Figure 11.5.

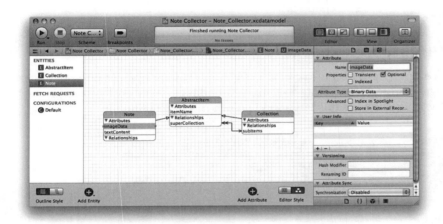

FIGURE 11.5   Adding a BLOB property to the Note entity

The user will choose images via a `UIImagePickerController`; the picker will give the app a `UIImage` containing the user's selection. You'll need to convert this to `NSData` to save it in the note, since that's the Cocoa class corresponding to the Core Data binary data type. Listing 11.3 shows how it's done.

LISTING 11.3   Putting image data in the Note entity

```
- (void)imagePickerController:(UIImagePickerController *)picker
                    didFinishPickingMediaWithInfo:(NSDictionary *)info {
    UIImage *image = [info
            objectForKey:UIImagePickerControllerOriginalImage];
    NSData *imageData = UIImagePNGRepresentation(image);

    // Put the image right in the note entity
    self.currentNote.imageData = imageData;

    [self dismissModalViewControllerAnimated:YES];
}
```

Once the image data is stored in the Note, getting a displayable UIImage from it is a single line of code:

```
UIImage *image = [UIImage imageWithData:currentNote.imageData];
```

Adding a BLOB to the entity that will use it is convenient, but it requires the most care with regard to memory use and faulting. As soon as any object properties are loaded into memory, the full BLOB will be loaded as well, and the BLOB will remain in memory so long as the object using it is not deallocated or re-faulted. So, although it requires the least work and is the easiest to understand, it also requires the greatest care of these three methods in managing memory.

Putting BLOBs in a Separate Entity

A slightly more complex approach is to create a separate entity for the sole purpose of holding the image data, and then create a relationship from the Note entity to this new image data entity. This results in the data model shown in Figure 11.6.

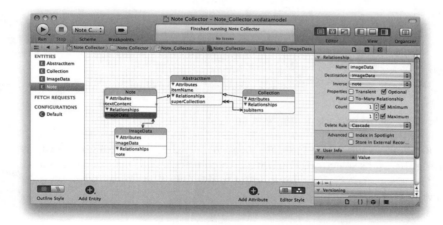

FIGURE 11.6   Creating a separate entity to hold the image data

There's a new entity called ImageData, and a one-to-one relationship between Note and ImageData. The ImageData entity has one attribute, a Binary Data attribute called imageData. There's no need for a custom NSManagedObject subclass for ImageData, since it's just a container with no code of its own.

The advantage of this approach is that it allows you to read, inspect, and modify instances of Note without automatically loading the image BLOB. The BLOB will be loaded only when you traverse the relationship from Note to ImageData. You could also re-fault instances of ImageData without doing the same to the corresponding Note. This could even provide the flexibility of having more than one image per Note if desired, simply by changing the relationship from one-to-one to one-to-many.

In this case the code to save a new image is slightly longer, since you now need to create a new managed object to hold the image. Listing 11.4 shows how it works.

LISTING 11.4   Putting image data in its own entity

```
- (void)imagePickerController:(UIImagePickerController *)picker
                    didFinishPickingMediaWithInfo:(NSDictionary *)info {
    UIImage *image = [info
                objectForKey:UIImagePickerControllerOriginalImage];
    NSData *imageData = UIImagePNGRepresentation(image);

    // Create an instance of the ImageData entity to hold the data
    NSManagedObject *imageDataContainer = [NSEntityDescription
     insertNewObjectForEntityForName:@"ImageData"
            inManagedObjectContext:currentNote.managedObjectContext];
    [imageDataContainer setValue:imageData forKey:@"imageData"];

    if (self.currentNote.imageData != nil) {
        [currentNote.managedObjectContext
                    deleteObject:self.currentNote.imageData];
    }
    // Create the relationship from the note to the
    // image data container
    self.currentNote.imageData = imageDataContainer;

    [self dismissModalViewControllerAnimated:YES];
}
```

Besides creating a new object to hold the image, the code makes sure to remove any previously existing image on the current note. Without this step, changing the image on a note would leave an orphaned image data BLOB in the data store.

Once the image data has been stored in this way, getting a displayable image is one somewhat-longer line of code:

```
UIImage *image = [UIImage imageWithData:
            [currentNote.imageData valueForKey:@"imageData"]];
```

Although this approach makes it easier to keep memory use under control than putting the image data in the note entity, it's still necessary to be careful about managing the image containers. Once an image has been loaded, the related note will retain the image data even when you're not showing the image any more. You'll need to make sure and re-fault container objects to avoid keeping the image data in memory.

This general pattern can also be useful in cases where you're not using BLOBs but where some of a managed object's properties won't be used very often. For example, you might have an entity representing a person that included address information, where the person objects would be used frequently but the address only once in a while. In that case, creating a separate entity to hold the address information would give the same memory usage benefits as with BLOBs, though on a smaller scale.

Putting BLOBs in External Files

You can bypass managing faulting of BLOB data by the obvious approach of not putting BLOBs in the data store. Although Core Data and SQLite are up to the task, putting BLOB data in separate files has the advantage of completely bypassing any questions about whether the data has been loaded. If it's in a separate file, it's only loaded when you explicitly load it, and you can manage the memory by following the usual Cocoa memory management rules. This approach amounts to optimizing Core Data performance by knowing when and how to keep certain data out of the data store.

In this case you'd need to add a new attribute to the Note entity, but this time use a String attribute that holds the name of the external file. This gives you the data model shown in Figure 11.7.

As in previous examples, you'll need to convert the UIImage to NSData, but this time you'd write the data to a file and save the filename in the Note's imageFilename property. The code for this is shown in Listing 11.5.

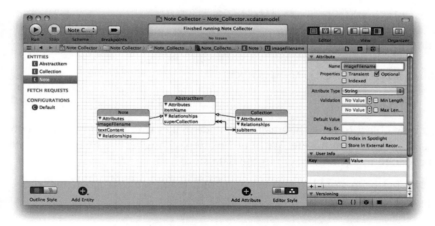

FIGURE 11.7   Adding an imageFilename property to the Note entity

LISTING 11.5   Writing image data to an external file, and saving the filename

```
- (NSString *)applicationSupportDirectoryPath {
    NSString *applicationSupportPath =
        [NSSearchPathForDirectoriesInDomains(
            NSApplicationSupportDirectory, NSUserDomainMask, YES)
        lastObject];
```

```objc
    [[NSFileManager defaultManager]
            createDirectoryAtPath:applicationSupportPath
        withIntermediateDirectories:YES
                       attributes:nil
                            error:nil];
    return applicationSupportPath;
}


- (void)imagePickerController:(UIImagePickerController *)picker
            didFinishPickingMediaWithInfo:(NSDictionary *)info {
    UIImage *image = [info
                objectForKey:UIImagePickerControllerOriginalImage];
    NSData *imageData = UIImagePNGRepresentation(image);

    // Create a unique filename for the image
    CFUUIDRef uuid = CFUUIDCreate(kCFAllocatorDefault);
    CFStringRef uuidString = CFUUIDCreateString(kCFAllocatorDefault,
                                                uuid);
    NSString *filename = [NSString stringWithFormat:@"%@.png",
                                                uuidString];
    NSString *path = [[self applicationSupportDirectoryPath]
                        stringByAppendingPathComponent:filename];
    CFRelease(uuid);
    CFRelease(uuidString);

    // Write the image to a file
    [imageData writeToFile:path atomically:YES];

    // Remove the previous file, if any
    if (self.currentNote.imageFilename != nil) {
        NSString *previousPath =
            [[self applicationSupportDirectoryPath]
                stringByAppendingPathComponent:
                        self.currentNote.imageFilename];
        [[NSFileManager defaultManager
                removeItemAtPath:previousPath error:nil];
    }

    // Save the file name in the note
    self.currentNote.imageFilename = filename;

    [self dismissModalViewControllerAnimated:YES];
}
```

Listing 11.5 creates a unique filename using Core Foundation functions to create a UUID. It then saves the image data into that filename, in a directory returned from a utility method called applicationSupportDirectory.

NOTE

Listing 11.5 doesn't save the full path in the Note entity because when you're working in the Simulator, the path changes every time Xcode installs a new copy of the app. If the Note had the full path, the next run of the app would be unable to find the images.

Instead, it's best just to save the filename and generate the full path at runtime. As with the previous example, make sure to clean up any previously-existing images so as not to leave orphaned files behind.

Getting an image from the data takes a little more code than in previous examples:

```
NSString *path = [[self applicationSupportDirectoryPath]
          stringByAppendingPathComponent:currentNote.imageFilename];
NSData *imageData = [NSData dataWithContentsOfFile:path];
UIImage *image = [UIImage imageWithData:imageData];
```

Putting BLOBs in external files involves more code but using this approach is the easiest way to monitor and control memory use. Questions of faulting don't apply to the BLOB because it's not in the data store. The only extra memory used by managed objects is a short filename string. The BLOB data doesn't load until you explicitly load it, and only remains in memory until it's deallocated.

A Cautionary Note About BLOBs and Migration

If you're keeping BLOBs in your data store, there's an extra memory usage issue to consider if you later need to migrate your data to a new version of the data model. Migration using a mapping model requires loading managed objects into memory in order to recreate them in the migrated data store. The migration process tracks associations of managed objects in the old store to their successors in the new store, and the objects can remain in memory throughout the migration process. With BLOBs in the store this can quickly lead to an impossible memory situation. In this case you may need to do custom data migration, if only to keep memory use under control.

It's not always a problem, though. If your model changes can be done using automatic lightweight migration, and if you're using a SQLite data store, then the entire migration will be done directly in SQLite. That means the managed objects don't need to be loaded into memory, so BLOBs in the data store don't lead to high memory use during migration. (If you're putting BLOBs in the data store you should be using a SQLite store anyway, because in-memory and atomic stores could easily run into memory problems even when not migrating.)

Monitoring Core Data with Instruments

The iOS SDK includes a performance-monitoring tool called Instruments, which can help diagnose performance issues. Instruments includes various virtual performance monitoring "instruments" for monitoring an application's execution as it runs, graphing the results and helping you to find the exact line of code where your application is slowing down or using excessive memory.

Instruments can analyze applications running on the device or in the iPhone and iPad Simulators, but not all instruments are available in all situations. If you run Instruments, you'll notice that although there are Core Data instruments, they're only listed as being available for Mac OS X and not for iOS at all.

However, the iPhone/iPad Simulator, as the name implies, *simulates* the iOS environment, but does not actually *emulate* the iOS hardware. The distinction is important for many reasons but in this case because it implies that a Simulator build of an app actually runs on Mac OS X as an Intel binary. As a result, you can treat it as a Mac OS X application when using Instruments.

> **NOTE**
>
> Not all instruments will work with an iPhone/iPad Simulator app since Mac OS X has features not found on iOS, but Core Data instruments work on both.

Start off by running Instruments and looking in its instrument browser under Mac OS X. The available instruments include Core Data monitoring, as shown in Figure 11.8.

If you choose the Core Data template you'll be able to monitor your app's Core Data performance. There are four Core Data instruments:

- ▶ **Core Data Fetches**, which monitors fetch activity.
- ▶ **Core Data Cache Misses**, which monitors filesystem access resulting from row cache misses in the managed object context.
- ▶ **Core Data Saves**, which monitors saving of managed objects.
- ▶ **Core Data Faults**, which monitors firing of managed object faults.

If selecting Core Data as shown in Figure 11.8 doesn't add all of these instruments, you can find them in the Instruments Library window.

FIGURE 11.8   Core Data instrument selection

To start monitoring your app, start by running it in the Simulator; note that it doesn't matter whether you do this from Xcode or directly in the simulator. Once the app is running, go to Instruments and attach it to the running process as shown in Figure 11.9.

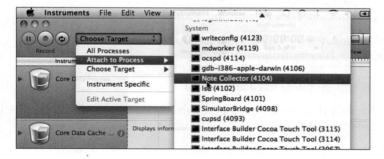

FIGURE 11.9   Attaching Instruments to a running iPhone Simulator process

Once Instruments attaches to the running process, click Record then go back to the simulator and use your application. As you do so, Instruments will monitor and display Core Data performance. When you've finished with the actions you need to test, either quit the application in the simulator or go to Instruments and click the Stop button to stop Instruments without quitting the app.

Instruments shows its results as a timeline for each instrument in the session, as shown in Figure 11.10. Periods of heavy Core Data activity will show up as denser grouping of lines on the timeline or as higher peak values.

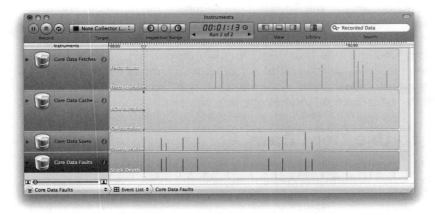

FIGURE 11.10   Core Data Instruments in action

Drag the time indicator above the timeline to zero in on areas of interest. Instruments will overlay information about the performance at that time and automatically select the event that triggered a particular event in the lower part of its window. It can also display the corresponding stack trace in your app on the right side of its window, right down to the specific line number where the event occurred. Figure 11.11 shows what this might look like.

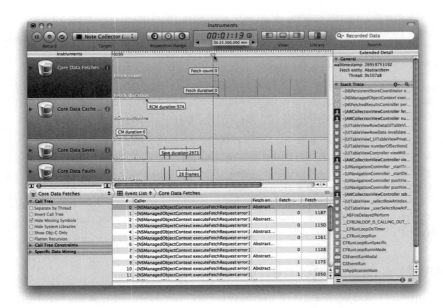

FIGURE 11.11   Examining a Core Data fetch request in Instruments

Keep in mind that performance in the Simulator can be misleading in comparison to device performance. Applications will run much faster in the Simulator since they'll have a laptop or desktop CPU available instead of one designed for a mobile device. Using Instruments with an iOS app can be a great way to find areas of heavy or unexpected Core Data usage, but don't make the mistake of thinking that it's an accurate indicator of device performance. A slowdown found in the Simulator will correspond to a slowdown on the device but the actual performance may be very different.

When Not to Use Core Data

This might seem like a strange topic to include in a chapter on performance and optimization, but it's an important performance concern. In some situations, Core Data can have performance problems simply because it's not well-suited for the task at hand. Improving the performance won't be possible because while Core Data may be capable of a task, that doesn't necessarily mean it's the best tool available.

The key concept to remember is that *Core Data is not a database*. It's easy to mistake it for one, especially since it so often uses SQLite as its back end data store.

Core Data is designed as an object store, a way to manage your model objects while leaving file management to the framework. It's not suited to cases where your data more closely resembles a traditional relational database, and while it can frequently be made to work in those cases, there are better ways. You can use SQLite directly for more database-like situations. Open-source frameworks like FMDB and PLDatabase provide convenient Objective-C-based wrappers for SQLite database files.[1] If you're not sure whether Core Data is right for your needs, a key point to consider is that Core Data must read objects into memory individually before you can work on them, while SQLite is capable of updating records in the database file without reading each row and without using extra memory for each row.

If you need to update 1000 items with Core Data, you'll have to read all 1000 into memory to make the update. With direct SQLite use, however, you could make the same update with a single SQL call. A similar calculation applies if you needed to delete 1000 items.

In these cases it's more or less impossible for Core Data to accomplish the task without taking a long time and requiring very careful memory management on your part. That doesn't imply anything being wrong with Core Data, but it's not always the best choice. It's often said that if your only tool is a hammer then every problem starts to look like a nail. When considering whether to use Core Data, look at all the tools in your toolbox, and don't pull out the hammer for cases where a screwdriver is more appropriate, even if you think you can bash screws pretty well with the hammer.

Other Memory Management Tips

This final section provides you with a list of useful memory management tips for getting the most from your Core Data-based app.

---

[1] *FMDB is available at **http://code.google.com/p/flycode/**, and PLDatabase is available from **http://code.google.com/p/pldatabase/**.*

11

Don't Use an Undo Manager If You Don't Need It

The managed object context can work with an NSUndoManager to provide automatic undo/redo capabilities in your application. That's incredibly useful when you need it, but it also increases memory use, since objects potentially subject to undo actions will be kept in memory just in case. On iOS, no undo manager is created by default, so none will exist unless you create one.

You may have apps where undo would be useful, but where certain memory-intensive operations would not require undo capability. This might happen if you have large batch import operations, for example. A large import might deal with a large number of objects, but is unlikely to be something you'd want to undo one step at a time.

If you're using an undo manager, be aware that there are situations where you may want to avoid the capability. One way to manage this would be to create a secondary managed object context accessing the same data store, to be used solely for the undo-free operations.

Resetting the Managed Object Context

Re-faulting individual objects is useful in reducing memory use, but what if you have a bunch of managed objects you won't be needing anymore? It turns out that you can have the managed object context forget about everything loaded from the data store and clear out all of its managed objects as well as the row cache. The reset method tells the managed object context to act as if it has just been initialized, based on the currently saved state of the data store. This invalidates all managed object instances and can drastically reduce memory use in a single shot.

Using reset requires some care, though. If you have any current references to managed objects loaded from the context, they're invalid and can't be used. They're not simply re-faulted; rather, the managed object context will effectively deny any knowledge of their existence. If you reset the context, make sure you also discard any managed object references you may have.

Summary

Core Data is extremely useful for managing your data model. If you're dealing with a lot of data, or data with large binary objects, it can take special considerations to keep performance acceptably fast and to avoid running out of memory. Issues like inter-object relationships can complicate the usual Cocoa memory management techniques since you may have objects retained without realizing it. In this chapter you've seen several approaches to optimizing your Core Data code, including knowing when to use other methods for your data model.

The next chapter looks at how things can go wrong when using Core Data, and how to find and fix the causes of these problems.

CHAPTER 12

Troubleshooting Core Data

When things go amiss with Core Data, the symptoms and error messages can seem obscure, even if you've been using it for a while. You can't very well fix your code if you don't understand what's wrong. This chapter will help you diagnose and fix some of the most common Core Data problems.

Keep in mind that Core Data can be affected by problems that are not specific to Core Data. For example, memory management errors can affect any Cocoa object, and managed objects are no exception. This chapter focuses on problems specifically related to Core Data.

Your First Core Data Error

The first Core Data problem you're likely to run into will probably come up very soon, and while it's easy to deal with, it's also worth understanding why it occurs and the different ways of dealing with it. The initial symptom is simply that your app crashes on launch. If the Xcode console isn't open, you may not even be sure why, but the common trick of deleting the app from the device will get things working again. Why?

TIP: USING XCODE'S CONSOLE

Always keep Xcode's console open when debugging Core Data. It's the best source of information about what's happening, and what may be going wrong. When an app crashes, the console is where you'll find error messages that help explain what went wrong. Under Xcode 4, the console is part of the Debug Area, which you can show using View > Show Debug Area (Shift-⌘-Y), or by using the View segmented control in the main toolbar (it's the bottom bar option). Under Xcode 3, the console is a separate window: choose Run > Console (Shift-⌘-R).

If you have the console open, you'll see something like this:

```
2011-05-04 16:03:41.579 Note Collector[81557:207] Unresolved error Error
 Domain=NSCocoaErrorDomain Code=134100 UserInfo=0x3d0da80 "Operation could not be
 completed. (Cocoa error 134100.)", {
    metadata =     {
        NSPersistenceFrameworkVersion = 248;
        NSStoreModelVersionHashes =         {
            Collection = <1df78ca5 f1c330fc 40070cca 7868a6fc c7473231 a40cb891
0b1723ea 34b105b6>;
            ListItem = <43437d50 6096468b 6ad0e976 3b85c49f e97d4053 41f573fd
77890cf5 51179ae9>;
            Note = <f3da8089 c5920d86 5fb7d1e1 1778e82b 5c87372e 0945c267 83550977
578d5034>;
        };
        NSStoreModelVersionHashesVersion = 3;
        NSStoreModelVersionIdentifiers =          (
        );
        NSStoreType = SQLite;
        NSStoreUUID = "80DE6808-EC54-4ACD-8888-A20F5F4367BA";
        "_NSAutoVacuumLevel" = 2;
    };
    reason = "The model used to open the store is incompatible with the one used to
create the store";
}
```

This error happens because you've changed the data model but still have a data store from a previous version of the model in the Simulator or on your device. This is a common occurrence during development. Regardless of how much planning you've done it's almost inevitable that you'll make changes to the model diagram as you go along.

The code to initialize the persistent store coordinator part of an app's Core Data stack typically starts off looking something like Listing 12.1, which is how Xcode's project templates set it up.

LISTING 12.1   Initializing a Core Data stack

```
- (NSPersistentStoreCoordinator *)persistentStoreCoordinator {
    if (__persistentStoreCoordinator != nil) {
        return __persistentStoreCoordinator;
    }

    NSURL *storeUrl = [[self applicationDocumentsDirectory]
            URLByAppendingPathComponent:@"Note_Collector.sqlite"];

    NSError *error = nil;
    __persistentStoreCoordinator =
            [[NSPersistentStoreCoordinator alloc]
                    initWithManagedObjectModel:[self managedObjectModel]];
    if (![__persistentStoreCoordinator
        addPersistentStoreWithType:NSSQLiteStoreType
                    configuration:nil
                              URL:storeUrl
                          options:nil
                            error:&error]) {
            NSLog(@"Unresolved error %@, %@", error,
                                    [error userInfo]);
        abort();
    }

    return __persistentStoreCoordinator;
}
```

This method creates the persistent store, then adds the data store file found at storeURL, creating the file if necessary.

If a data store exists, the model file tells the persistent store coordinator how to use it. The model file defines the structure that the existing store contains, but if you've just changed the model but left a data store in place, it doesn't actually do that any more. Instead, the data store contains data structured by the old data model, which is no longer available. That makes it impossible to add the store file, and the project template code just calls abort(). Your app crashes. If you delete the existing copy of the app from the device, you also delete the old data store file, so the problem disappears.

During app development this is usually a reasonable solution. After removing the old copy of the app, you create new testing data and continue working. But in some cases you may have a large test data store or one that's just harder to recreate on the fly.

If that's the case, you'll need to set up model migration as described in Chapter 8, "Migration and Versioning," even though you haven't yet released your app. Each time you update your data model you'll also arrange to migrate existing data. This might mean you end up with several versions of your model before you've even finished the app. Once you're finished though, you can delete any existing development versions and just ship the finished version with the application.

The Missing Model

Another problem that can come up early in app development also involves an unexpected crash when the app starts, this time with an error such as:

```
entityForName: could not locate an NSManagedObjectModel for entity name 'Song'
```

This seems pretty puzzling at first, because you've probably just been editing the model, so why is the app complaining it's not available?

More than likely the model file is available but you're attempting to use it before the Core Data stack has been initialized. This might happen because you're trying to make Core Data calls in a view controller's viewDidLoad method, and this method is running earlier in the app's startup process than you expected.

Listing 12.2 shows how an application delegate object might load the app's main view controller.

LISTING 12.2   Application delegate loading the main view controller

```
- (BOOL)application:(UIApplication *)application
                didFinishLaunchingWithOptions:(NSDictionary *)launchOptions {
    MainViewController *aController = [[MainViewController alloc]
                            initWithNibName:@"MainView" bundle:nil];
    self.mainViewController = aController;
    [aController release];

    mainViewController.view.frame =
            [UIScreen mainScreen].applicationFrame;
    mainViewController.managedObjectContext =
            self.managedObjectContext;

    [window addSubview:[mainViewController view]];
    [window makeKeyAndVisible];

    return YES;
}
```

It looks fairly innocuous, and in fact it usually is. What might not be obvious, though, is that assigning a value to a main view controller's frame will trigger a call to viewDidLoad. The view controller's managed object context isn't assigned until the following line. If viewDidLoad attempts to fetch managed objects, it will be doing so with a nil value for managedObjectContext. No context means no model, and no model means no data store access. Creating an NSEntityDescription is often the first thing you'll do when setting up a fetch, but it will fail since the model is unavailable.

The fix in this case is simple: just reverse the order of assignments in Listing 12.2 so the managed object is assigned before doing anything that would load the view, like this:

```
mainViewController.managedObjectContext =
                            self.managedObjectContext;
mainViewController.view.frame =
                [UIScreen mainScreen].applicationFrame;
```

Or, if you prefer, defer any Core Data code until viewDidAppear: is called later.

Classes Not Found?

When you create a new project, Xcode's project templates will take care of setting up a number of Core Data-related details for you, so that your project compiles and links. If you're adding Core Data to an existing project it can be easy to miss important steps that will prevent your app from building.

One possibility is Xcode complaining about every Core Data class you have used, but not providing any line numbers where errors have occurred. This would be similar to Figure 12.1.

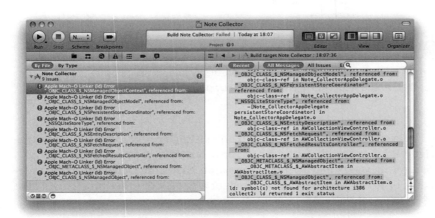

FIGURE 12.1   Core Data link errors

These are linker errors, as indicated by the line near the bottom that reads:

```
ld returned 1 exit status
```

This means that you forgot to add the Core Data framework to the project, so the linker can't find any definitions of Core Data classes. Start by selecting the project icon itself in the Xcode 4 Project Navigator, select the Note Collector target in the Editor that appears, and click the Build Phases tab. Expand the Link Binary with Libraries section and click the + button. Find the Core Data framework in the list and add it to your project, as shown in Figure 12.2.

FIGURE 12.2   Adding the Core Data framework in Xcode 4

NOTE

To add a framework under Xcode 3, just right click on the Frameworks group in the Groups and Files list, and select Add > Existing Framework.

Another potential error when adding Core Data to an existing project looks similar to the linker errors in Figure 12.1 except that now Xcode provides links to source code lines it can't process. The error messages may include complaints that Core Data classes are undeclared, that instances of these classes are undeclared, or a variety of other problems. There may be dozens of error messages.

These are compiler errors rather than linker errors and simply mean that you forgot to include the Core Data header file in your project:

```
#import <CoreData/CoreData.h>
```

Without this line, Xcode can't find declarations for any Core Data classes, and the compiler fails. If you're using Core Data throughout the application then you can include the line in the precompiled header file, a *.pch* file, which is implicitly included in every source file. If you will be using Core Data only in a few specific places, add the #import to those files as needed.

Core Data Threading Issues

The Core Data stack is not thread-safe, but it is possible to use Core Data in multi-threaded applications provided you follow some simple rules. Multithreading with Core Data is useful for tasks like warming up the row cache or importing data in the background. This section deals with how to make use of Core Data in a multithreaded application; the trouble you may encounter if you don't handle threading correctly falls into two major areas:

> ▶ **Errors saving data.** If you make conflicting changes on different threads, the managed object context will fail when saving changes and will return an error status.

> ▶ **Lost data.** When you make conflicting changes on different threads you can merge the changes to resolve save errors, but some data will be discarded. If you don't handle merging properly, you might lose changes you wanted to keep.

These problems can occur even if you're not using multiple threads in your application, but they're more likely if you are. The same issues apply regardless of how the separate thread is created—whether via NSThread, NSOperationQueue, or by convenience methods such as performSelectorInBackground:withObject:.

This section covers both of these areas so you can safely manage threads with Core Data.

Basics of Core Data Multithreading

The lack of thread safety in Core Data means that you cannot safely use managed objects in multiple threads without providing your own locking around critical code sections. This extends to the rest of the Core Data stack as well, so managed object contexts and persistent store coordinators also require locking before they can be used on multiple threads. The NSManagedObjectContext and NSPersistentStoreCoordinator classes do conform to the NSLocking protocol, so instances of these objects can be locked and unlocked directly rather than using a separate lock.

However, there is an easier way—threading is already hard enough without adding extra locking just for Core Data. The key is that, while NSManagedObjectContext is not thread-safe, you can create more than one context using the same persistent store coordinator and ultimately the same data store. With different contexts in different threads you don't share objects between threads, so no locking is needed. The NSManagedObjectContext will automatically handle locking the persistent store coordinator, so the context is the only part of the Core Data stack that needs to be duplicated.

The persistent store coordinator is normally created and maintained by the application delegate, so you create a second managed object context by getting the existing coordinator and simply creating a new context referencing it, as shown in Listing 12.3.

LISTING 12.3   Creating a secondary managed object context from an existing persistent store coordinator

```
- (NSManagedObjectContext *) managedObjectContext {
    if (managedObjectContext != nil) {
```

```
        return managedObjectContext;
    }


    Note_CollectorAppDelegate *appDelegate =
            [[UIApplication sharedApplication] delegate];
    NSPersistentStoreCoordinator *coordinator =
                [appDelegate persistentStoreCoordinator];
    if (coordinator != nil) {
        managedObjectContext = [[NSManagedObjectContext alloc] init];
        [managedObjectContext
            setPersistentStoreCoordinator:coordinator];
    }
    return managedObjectContext;
}
```

But, I hear you say, "What about the managed objects themselves?" Didn't I just say they were not thread safe? So how can different threads pass changed data to each other? Managed objects aren't thread safe. Not only that, managed objects are tied to the context that loaded them, so you can't fetch an object on a background thread and safely use it on the main thread with that thread's context. Any faulting or changes on the object would use the context that loaded it, which would lead to using the same context across threads.

NSManagedObjectID is the loophole that makes it possible for threads to share managed object data. The ID object uniquely identifies a managed object regardless of which context loaded it. And since it's immutable, sharing one between threads doesn't raise any special threading concerns. Get a unique ID for the managed object on one thread:

```
NSManagedObjectID *uniqueID = [managedObject objectID];
```

Then pass this to another thread and retrieve the same object from Core Data by looking up the object for the ID:

```
NSManagedObject *object = [managedObjectContext objectWithID:uniqueID];
```

This gives you a separate managed object loaded from a different managed object context but which refers to the same underlying data store object.

Coordinating Data Between Threads

Getting managed objects on both threads that represent the same data store object is a step in the right direction, but you'll probably also want changes made on one thread to be visible on others. You'll also have to consider that loading the same data into managed objects on different threads raises the potential for conflicting versions of the same object. Changing a managed object and saving changes on one context doesn't automatically update other managed objects loaded from different contexts, even if they correspond to the same underlying object in the data store. Fortunately the managed object contexts provide notifications and data to help deal with this.

When you tell a managed object context to save changes, it posts two notifications, the aptly named NSManagedObjectContextWillSaveNotification and NSManagedObjectContextDidSaveNotification, which are posted before and after the save occurs. If you are using the same objects on multiple threads and at least one of the threads might make changes to the objects, you can listen for one of these notifications as an indication that currently-loaded managed objects may have changed.

LISTING 12.4   Observing context-save notifications

```
[[NSNotificationCenter defaultCenter]
    addObserver:self
        selector:@selector(changesSaved:)
            name:NSManagedObjectContextDidSaveNotification
          object:nil];
```

When adding an object as an observer to one of these notifications, be sure to pass nil as the object argument. You won't have references to managed object contexts created on other threads, and passing nil ensures that you get the notification regardless of which context posted it.

A key detail that's easy to overlook is that NSNotifications are received on the same thread that posts them. If one thread saves changes to a managed object context, the corresponding notifications will be received on that thread even if the observing object normally works only on a different thread. Since the point of observing the notification here is to update objects on a different thread, it's necessary to redirect the notification to the appropriate thread. If the above code were run on the main thread, then the implementation of changesSaved: might look like Listing 12.5.

LISTING 12.5   Receiving a context-save notification and passing it to the main thread

```
- (void)changesSaved:(NSNotification *)notification {
    [self performSelectorOnMainThread:@selector(changesSavedOnMainThread:)
                           withObject:notification
                        waitUntilDone:YES];
}
```

Listing 12.5 simply takes the existing notification and passes it to the main thread, ensuring that the main thread's managed object context is not used on a different thread.

The notification's userInfo dictionary tells you what changes have been made to which objects. It contains three keys, NSInsertedObjectsKey, NSUpdatedObjectsKey, and NSDeletedObjectsKey. Your code can look through these collections and update the current thread's managed objects as needed. Or if your changes are relatively simple you can ask the managed object context to process them automatically by calling mergeChangesFromContextDidSaveNotification: as shown in Listing 12.6.

LISTING 12.6   Handling a context save notification on the main thread

```
- (void)changesSavedMainThread:(NSNotification *)notification {
    if ([notification object] != managedObjectContext) {
        [managedObjectContext
                mergeChangesFromContextDidSaveNotification:notification];
    }
}
```

This method refreshes any managed objects that have been changed, faults in any newly inserted objects, and invokes deleteObject: on any that have been removed. The code in Listing 12.6 looks to see which object posted the notification and only attempts to merge changes if the notification came from some other thread's managed object context. If it was the current thread's context, the changes are already available, so there's no need to merge on this thread.

If you may be deleting objects on one thread that could have been loaded from another thread, you should check the NSDeletedObjectsKey as well to avoid continued use of a deleted object. In this case you might still have an instance of a managed object that's no longer in the store. You can also check individual managed objects using the isDeleted method.

Of course these steps are only necessary if you plan on changing managed objects on one thread where another thread needs to know about those changes. Using a secondary thread to load objects into the row cache, without making changes, doesn't raise any threading issues since the objects are not changed.

When Threads Collide, or Handling Data Conflicts

If you're planning on updating objects on more than one thread, you'll need to give some thought to how you want to manage conflicting changes to the same underlying object. By default *you cannot save changes in a managed object context if the data store has conflicting data* for objects, such as those from a different managed object context. One way or another you'll have to deal with it.

Merging changes automatically as described earlier is often the best way, but it can discard some property changes, so it's important to understand how it works so you'll know whether it's appropriate for your situation. When merging in this manner, any updated objects from the data store are first refreshed as if you had called refreshObject:mergeChanges: with the mergeChanges argument set to YES. Then, any property changes made in the current context are reapplied to the objects. If you've changed the same property on the same object in more than one context, changes made in other contexts are not available.

To illustrate this, consider an application with a simple single-entity data model representing a song, as shown in Figure 12.3.

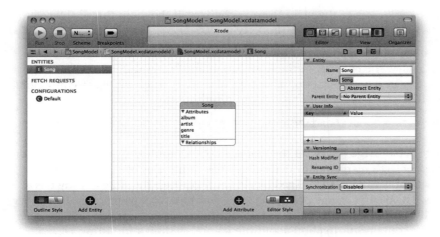

FIGURE 12.3   Single-entity data model representing a song

Suppose we have a Song object, which initially holds the values shown in the Original Values column in Table 12.1, which is then modified on two different threads (main and background threads).

TABLE 12.1   Conflicting changes on multiple threads

Property	Original Value	Main Thread Changes	Background Thread Changes
title	Metal on Metal	**Europe Endless**	Metal on Metal
artist	Kraftwerk	Kraftwerk	**Bacalao**
album	Minimum-Maximum	**Trans-Europe Express**	**8-Bit Operators**
genre	Electronica	Electronica	Electronica

The two different threads fetched their managed objects corresponding to this Song from their respective contexts, and have made conflicting changes to their attributes.

If the background thread saves its changes and the main thread has its managed object context auto-merge the changes, the main thread's copy will be refreshed and its local changes will be reapplied. The main thread didn't change the artist, so after the merge it will acquire the new value set by the background thread. Since the main thread did change the title and album properties, those values won't change after the merge. The background thread's value for album won't be loaded into the main thread's object as doing so would overwrite one of the main thread's changes. If the main thread then saves the object, the background thread's album property is lost.

If that's appropriate for your app, that's great, but it's not always correct. If it's not, your code will need to review the changes in the notification and merge differently. Look up NSUpdatedObjectsKey in the notification's userInfo dictionary to get an NSSet containing updated versions objects:

```
NSSet *changedObjects = [[notification userInfo] objectForKey:NSUpdatedObjectsKey];
```

It's also possible to set a merge policy on the managed object context that will apply when saving. A managed object's merge policy determines how it handles conflicting property values if an app attempts to save a managed object context when the store already has conflicting values. The default merge policy is NSErrorMergePolicy, which prevents saving conflicting data. If there's a conflict, calling save: on the merge context will fail, and the error parameter will contain information about the failure, as shown in Listing 12.7.

LISTING 12.7   Saving a managed object context and receiving an error

```
NSError *error = nil;
BOOL success = [self.managedObjectContext save:&error];
if( !success ) {
    NSLog(@"Save error: %@", [error userInfo]);
}
```

In this case [error userInfo] is a dictionary that contains a conflictList key, which in turn contains details about the conflicting data values.

Other merge policies are available which deal with conflicts automatically in various ways. They are:

▶ NSMergeByPropertyStoreTrumpMergePolicy

Conflicts are merged on a property-by-property basis. Values from the data store overwrite in-memory property values wherever a conflict exists. In-memory changes remain where conflicts don't exist.

▶ NSMergeByPropertyObjectTrumpMergePolicy

Conflicts are merged on a property-by-property basis. Values in memory change to match values from the data store only where there is no conflicting in-memory change.

▶ NSOverwriteMergePolicy

Changes in memory overwrite changes in the data store, and the in-memory object is not changed.

► NSRollbackMergePolicy

Changes in the data store overwrite changes in memory, and any in-memory changes are discarded. Data store values are not changed.

If the changes from Table 12.1 were made and the main thread then saved its in-memory changes, the conflicts would be resolved as shown in Table 12.2, based on the merge policy in use.

TABLE 12.2   Resolving conflicts with different automatic merge policies

Property	NSMergeByPropertyStore TrumpMergePolicy	NSMergeByProperty ObjectTrumpPolicy	NSOverwrite MergePolicy	NSRollback MergePolicy
title	Europe Endless	Europe Endless	Europe Endless	Metal on Metal
artist	Bacalao	Bacalao	Kraftwerk	Bacalao
album	8-Bit Operators	Trans-Europe Express	Trans-Europe Express	8-Bit Operators
genre	Electronica	Electronica	Electronica	Electronica

NOTE

NSMergeByPropertyObjectTrumpPolicy produces the same result as the auto-merging described earlier.

If none of the merge policies are appropriate for your app, but you still need to make changes on multiple threads, you'll need to resolve the conflicts yourself. To do this, you can compare values on the current thread with those saved to the store from a different thread for each conflicting object and decide which values to keep. Resolve the conflict state by telling the managed object context to refresh the object, and save changes again. Listing 12.8 demonstrates one possible approach to this with Song objects. In this example, the code keeps the main thread's changes to the Song's title property, but accepts the background thread's changes to the artist and album properties. After resolving the conflict it saves this version of the data to the store.

LISTING 12.8   Resolving conflicting data from a managed object context save

```
- (void)changesSavedMainThread:(NSNotification *)notification {
    // Merge the changes from the other background context
    if ([notification object] != self.managedObjectContext) {
        NSError *error = nil;
        [self.managedObjectContext save:&error];
        if (error != nil) {
            NSArray *conflictList =
```

```
                    [[error userInfo] objectForKey:@"conflictList"];
          for (NSDictionary *conflictInfo in conflictList) {
              Song *conflictSong =
                              [conflictInfo objectForKey:@"object"];
              NSDictionary *mainThreadChanges =
                              [conflictSong changedValues];
              // Re-fault the object
              [self.managedObjectContext
                  refreshObject:conflictSong mergeChanges:NO];

              // Reapply the change to the title property
              conflictSong.title =
                      [mainThreadChanges objectForKey:@"title"];
          }
          error = nil;
          [self.managedObjectContext save:&error];
          if (error != nil) {
              NSLog(@"Main thread repeated save error: %@",
                                              [error userInfo]);
          }
      }
   }
}
```

In your app you will, of course, need to decide which conflict resolution approach makes sense for your data. In extreme cases it may be necessary to ask the user which data is correct. The conflictList key contains detailed information about both versions of the data, which can be useful when deciding what to keep and what to discard.

Danger! Temporary ID!

There's an exception to the rule that managed object IDs can be passed between threads and used on different managed object contexts, and it has to do with the one situation where a managed object's ID changes.

When a managed object is first created, it has a temporary objectID. The managed object keeps this ID until you save it in a managed object context, at which point the context replaces it with a permanent ID. Temporary IDs can only be used to look up the object from the same managed object context they're inserted in, and as a result are not useful if you pass them to a different thread with a different context. This makes sense because until the object has been saved, managed object contexts on other threads have no way of fetching them. Different contexts are linked by the underlying data store and persistent store coordinator, and don't exchange data directly. One context doesn't know what another is doing until a save succeeds.

The danger of passing a temporary ID to a different context is that data values can't be loaded, so any object loaded from the ID will appear to have `nil` values for its properties. If for some reason you're not sure about the `objectID`, you can query it to find out whether it's temporary or permanent, as shown in Listing 12.9.

LISTING 12.9   Testing for a temporary object ID

```
if (![objectID isTemporaryID]) {
    Song *song = (Song *)[self.managedObjectContext
                                objectWithID:objectID];
    NSLog(@"Song info: %@", [song description]);
} else {
    NSLog(@"Can't load object info for a temporary ID");
}
```

In Listing 12.9, it would be possible to get a `Song` object from the temporary ID using `objectWithID:`, but it would not be useful since we couldn't access any property data.

Problems Using Managed Objects

This section provides some solutions to the problems you may encounter while using managed objects.

Crashing When Setting Property Values

If you don't initialize your managed objects correctly, your app might crash when attempting to set a property value with a message like this:

```
2010-05-06 17:32:42.499 Conflicter[88621:207] *** Terminating app due to uncaught
 exception 'NSUnknownKeyException', reason: '[<Song 0x3b1b910>
setValue:forUndefinedKey:]: the entity (null) is not key value coding-compliant for
the key "title".'
```

But when you find the line where the app crashed, it seems to be fine, since it uses a property that exists in the Song entity:

```
[song setValue:@"Crash" forKey:@"title"];
```

A different crash message with a related cause might look like this:

```
2010-05-06 17:38:53.106 Conflicter[88669:207] *** Terminating app due to uncaught
 exception 'NSInvalidArgumentException', reason: '*** -[Song setTitle:]: unrecognized
 selector sent to instance 0x3d10d10'
```

In this case the crashing line in the app used a custom setter method, thanks to a @property declaration, but it still looks correct:

```
[song setTitle:@"Crash"];
```

So what could be wrong with these lines? The Song entity has a title property, and the @property declaration means it should be possible to use a synthesized setter method. If you look closely at the console output, in both cases there's probably a line that reads:

```
2010-05-06 17:38:53.095 Conflicter[88669:207] Failed to call designated initializer
 on NSManagedObject class 'Song'
```

This is the key. These errors occur when you allocate and initialize a managed object without using NSManagedObject's designated initializer. You probably created the object like this:

```
Song *song2 = [[Song alloc] init];
```

You can create an instance that way, but by not using the designated initializer you'll miss critical initialization that NSManagedObject needs to work properly. Without that the instance won't know anything about the attributes declared in the data model, and both key-value coding and synthesized accessor use will fail badly.

The fix is to use one of the two documented ways to create a managed object. The first is to call the designated initializer explicitly:

```
NSEntityDescription *songEntity =
    [NSEntityDescription entityForName:@"Song"
                inManagedObjectContext:self.managedObjectContext];
song = [[Song alloc] initWithEntity:songEntity
        insertIntoManagedObjectContext:self.managedObjectContext];
```

The other is to use NSEntityDescription, which calls the designated initializer for you:

```
song = [[NSEntityDescription insertNewObjectForEntityForName:@"Song"
                inManagedObjectContext:self.managedObjectContext] retain];
```

If Custom Accessor Methods Aren't Called

Managed objects provide dynamically generated accessor methods for each attribute declared in the corresponding entity in the data model. If you're implementing your own accessors in an NSManagedObject subclass, you might encounter a situation where your custom accessors are not being called, even though they're named correctly.

This almost certainly indicates that you've forgotten to assign your custom subclass to the corresponding entity in the model diagram. For example, suppose that the Song entity had been set up as shown in Figure 12.4 instead of as in Figure 12.3.

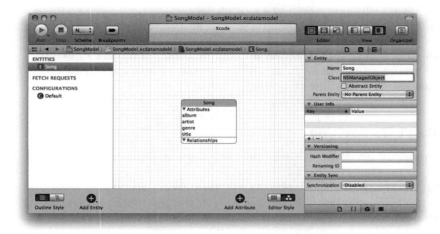

FIGURE 12.4   Song entity without custom subclass

Core Data doesn't assume that a class should be used for an entity even if it has the same name. With the Song entity set up as in Figure 12.4, we could still create instances with all the attributes shown in the diagram; however, they would be NSManagedObject instances, and not instances of Song. It would still be possible to assign values to the title, even via dot syntax. But if Song had a custom setter setTitle: for the title property, that accessor would not be called.

If your custom subclass declared other methods that were not accessors, your app would crash when attempting to use those methods—since the managed object would be an NSManagedObject it wouldn't implement your custom methods. Calling these methods would result in an "unrecognized selector" error and an app crash.

Managed Object Invalidated

Dealing with memory usage by resetting the managed object context requires some care, or else your app may crash with an error indicating that a managed object has been invalidated:

```
2010-05-07 11:22:53.134 Conflicter[90108:4703] *** Terminating app due to uncaught
 exception 'NSObjectInaccessibleException', reason: 'The NSManagedObject with
 ID:0x3d076a0 <x-coredata://D9129330-D542-4C65-B2B1-533CA5E29D6F/Song/p149> has been
 invalidated.'
```

This indicates that you reset the context but still kept references to managed objects loaded from the context in memory. Since resetting the context makes the context "forget" about any managed objects, any existing objects become faults. They can't be automatically removed from memory without violating Cocoa memory management rules, but no data is available either. It's not possible to fire the faults on these objects since the context no longer knows anything about them.

You can watch for the transition to a fault in a custom NSManagedObject subclass by implementing willTurnIntoFault or didTurnInfoFault. Be aware, though, that this method can be called at other times as well; for example, when intentionally re-faulting an object by calling refreshObject:mergeChanges: on the managed object context. It's much better to be careful about when you decide to reset the context and dispose of objects loaded from the context at the same time.

Faults That Can't Be Fulfilled

Since faulting is normally automatic, it can be puzzling to get an error that looks like:

```
2010-05-07 17:36:39.417 Conflicter[91506:207] *** Terminating app due to uncaught
 exception 'NSObjectInaccessibleException', reason: 'CoreData could not fulfill a
 fault for '0x3d1ab40 <x-coredata://D9129330-D542-4C65-B2B1-533CA5E29D6F/Song/p177>''
```

Fault can't be fulfilled? Why not?

As with an invalidated object, this stems from a case where the managed object context no longer has any information about a managed object. The cause is different, though. This time the problem is that you've told the managed object to delete the object and then saved changes, but you kept the object around and later attempted to use it. A simple example that would cause this is shown in Listing 12.10.

LISTING 12.10   Improperly using a managed object after deleting it

```
Song *song = [NSEntityDescription
    insertNewObjectForEntityForName:@"Song"
            inManagedObjectContext:self.managedObjectContext];
song.title = @"Fault line";

[self.managedObjectContext save:nil];

NSLog( %@", song);

[self.managedObjectContext deleteObject:song];
[self.managedObjectContext save:nil];

// This will crash since we're using a reference to a deleted object.
NSLog( %@", song);
```

The reason this isn't possible is the same as with invalidated objects caused by calling reset. Changes made by the managed object context can't destroy references you might have to objects loaded from the context without violating Cocoa memory management rules.[1] If you take an action that causes a managed object to be unusable, you need to make sure you don't attempt to use that object. In this case, when you delete an object from the context you should be sure to clean up any references you have to that object.

This situation can also arise if you delete an object that has incoming relationships from other managed objects, where there's no corresponding inverse relationship with an appropriate delete rule. Delete rules apply starting from the object being deleted, so when an object is deleted, only its outgoing delete rules are activated. If the incoming relationship is one-way with no inverse, then you would need to clean up that relationship yourself instead of relying on Core Data. Otherwise the relationship might need to fault at some point, but since the relationship leads to a deleted object, it would be impossible to fulfill.

One indication that this object is not usable is that its `managedObjectContext` property will be `nil` after it has been deleted. Checking that can prevent problems, but it's better to take a more active role and be sure to delete object references when the object itself has been deleted.

Problems Fetching Objects

Even when everything seems to be going well, sometimes you might find that your fetches are not working as expected. Your model looks good and is loaded, you're handling threads correctly, but for some reason fetching fails or gives you managed objects with unexpected properties. This section will help you resolve some common fetch problems.

Trouble Sorting Data During Fetches

When fetching objects from a managed object context, not all sort descriptors can be used with fetch requests. If you see an error complaining about an unsupported sort descriptor, you're encountering this situation.

```
2010-05-07 14:08:23.902 Conflicter[90694:207] *** Terminating app due to uncaught
  exception 'NSInvalidArgumentException', reason: 'unsupported NSSortDescriptor
  selector: myCustomCompare:'
```

This doesn't mean the sort descriptor is bad per se, and it might be just fine if you were sorting an `NSArray` with a method like `sortedArrayUsingDescriptors:`, but not all sort descriptors work with Core Data, at least not with SQLite data stores.

When you're using a SQLite data store, a fetch request is translated into an SQL statement. SQLite performs the fetch and returns sorted results to your app. Core Data can translate common comparison methods into equivalent SQL, but not arbitrary Cocoa code. Handling sorting in this way can dramatically improve performance but at the expense of being somewhat less flexible. When doing a fetch with sort descriptors you'll need to restrict yourself to the following selectors on iOS:

---

[1] See: http://bit.ly/b8IbFG

- ▶ `compare:`

- ▶ `caseInsensitiveCompare:`

- ▶ `localizedCompare:`

- ▶ `localizedCaseInsensitiveCompare:`

If you need some other custom sort comparison you'll have to fetch the objects into an array and then sort the array in memory. Or, if appropriate, use a binary data store instead of SQLite since sort operations for a binary store are run in memory instead of in a database.

This problem can only occur if you specify a selector on the sort descriptor and if the selector is not on the supported list. If you initialize a sort descriptor with `initWithKey:ascending:` then you won't have this problem.

Fetch Results Not Showing Recent Changes

Normally a fetch request should include all changes known by the target managed object context, regardless of whether the changes have been saved. This means that your fetch results will include your unsaved changes.

There's one possible exception, though. If you make changes to some managed objects and then immediately do a fetch, the results might not reflect those changes. This is most likely if the fetch is on the same pass in the application's event loop. It sounds like a race condition, but there's a simple solution. Just make sure to call `processPendingChanges` on the managed object context before the fetch. This won't save the changes, but it will ensure that the context's picture of the data includes all changes to its managed objects.

Summary

With a little bit of care you can avoid most Core Data problems completely. The most common issues are easily solved. More complex issues generally relate to threading problems, which often occur regardless of whether you're using Core Data. With an eye on the console window and a little debugging skill you'll be able to track down and eliminate Core Data bugs quickly and effectively.

Index

 **FREE Online Edition**

Your purchase of *Core Data for iOS* includes access to a free online edition for 45 days through the Safari Books Online subscription service. Nearly every Addison-Wesley Professional book is available online through Safari Books Online, along with more than 5,000 other technical books and videos from publishers such as Cisco Press, Exam Cram, IBM Press, O'Reilly, Prentice Hall, Que, and Sams.

SAFARI BOOKS ONLINE allows you to search for a specific answer, cut and paste code, download chapters, and stay current with emerging technologies.

Activate your FREE Online Edition at
www.informit.com/safarifree

> **STEP 1:** Enter the coupon code: EVZFQGA.

> **STEP 2:** New Safari users, complete the brief registration form. Safari subscribers, just log in.

If you have difficulty registering on Safari or accessing the online edition, please e-mail customer-service@safaribooksonline.com